Glassroom Learning

Glassroom Learning

Virtual Culture and Online Pastoral Education

JASON MILLS

Foreword by Doug Blomberg

PICKWICK *Publications* · Eugene, Oregon

GLASSROOM LEARNING
Virtual Culture and Online Pastoral Education

Pickwick Publications
An Imprint of Wipf and Stock Publishers
199 W. 8th Ave., Suite 3
Eugene, OR 97401

www.wipfandstock.com

PAPERBACK ISBN: 978-1-6667-5849-8
HARDCOVER ISBN: 978-1-6667-5850-4
EBOOK ISBN: 978-1-6667-5851-1

Cataloguing-in-Publication data:

Names: Mills, Jason, author. | Blomberg, Doug, foreword.

Title: Glassroom learning : virtual culture and online pastoral education / Jason Mills ; foreword by Doug Blomberg.

Description: Eugene, OR : Pickwick Publications, 2023 | Includes bibliographical references.

Identifiers: ISBN 978-1-6667-5849-8 (paperback) | ISBN 978-1-6667-5850-4 (hardcover) | ISBN 978-1-6667-5851-1 (ebook)

Subjects: LCSH: Chaplains—Training of. | Education, Higher—Effect of technological innovations on Internet in higher education. | Technology—Philosophy.

Classification: BV4375 .M56 2023 (print) | BV4375 .M56 (ebook)

07/27/23

For Dad
1942–2019

Contents

Foreword

DR. JASON MILLS WROTE a timely and well-crafted dissertation that he researched comprehensively and wrote articulately, challenging the suggestion that online education is second best when compared to face-to-face pastoral formation. The title of this book is different than his dissertation in which the first phrase was, "In Vitro Education" and left me somewhat mystified. However, I came to realize how evocative this term is: The glass screen is a barrier to person-to-person embodiment, which Jason investigated throughout . . . similar to a "test tube" (i.e., grounded in empirical evidence) and examined the effects of Web-based education on students and programs of pastoral formation. In August 2022, he and his wife Erika moved from the University of Toronto where he was studying for his doctorate and appointed as Dean of the Seminary and Assistant Professor to serve in Briercrest College and Seminary in Saskatchewan.

In September 2017, Jason enrolled in my Wisdom and Schooling course at the Institute for Christian Studies, Toronto and I agreed to be his supervisor in June 2018. He subsequently asked me to oversee his Reading and Research unit, Curriculum and Pedagogy, and both courses were in distance mode. This bears significantly on his dissertation and its completed title, "In Vitro Education: Examining the Virtual Culture of Online Pastoral Education." The "distance education" of the 90s relied on printed study guides, which later morphed into online teaching and learning, namely, cyber education, with a cell phone, laptop, or a computer on the desk. He understands there has to be a major change, as most courses in the Association of Theological Schools are now online, rather than learning through field placements or internships. He is well aware of the necessity of online learning in a high-tech age, even more so in the social isolation borne by the ongoing Covid pandemic, and requiring open and flexible dialogues with others.

Working closely with Jason, I learnt a great deal from his project that expanded my horizons. He struck me as astute, articulate, enthusiastic, and committed to his project and we had an immediate rapport, sharing educational, philosophical and theological concerns. I thoroughly enjoyed and valued the opportunity to work closely with him. His reflections incorporate interaction between practical experience and theoretical understanding. Inquisitive across various fields of study and eager to explore their value professionally and personally, he has the special ability to convey the meaning of a text, ensuring his communication is apt. I have no doubt he will make a significant contribution to both research and teaching. He is energetic, conscientious and creative, bringing passion, experience, and fundamentally, his faith in Christ. Rather than leaving behind his practice as a pastor of more than twenty years, his goal is to continue building a platform for himself and many others.

Dissertations and books often end with a tidy conclusion, whereas leaving open a number of unfinished questions can be quite productive for the exploration of one's future. Jason stresses the importance of the latter, which some would call "messy conclusions," and how he and his readers could proceed fruitfully from these. He offers two questions: "What effects do shifts toward online courses have on those enrolled in programs of pastoral formation? Are students preparing for ordained ministry via online education being adequately trained?" He agrees intellectual virtues can be strengthened by Web-based learning, yet is quite concerned about the inhibition of "student character, virtue formation and self-differentiation" in which social isolation, anxiety, and depression in students abounds. Such behaviour foments distraction, leading to lack of empathy, focus and reflection, which should not rely on the Web alone but go hand in hand with "embodied learning opportunities."

If the Association of Theological Schools (ATS) recognizes the value of embodied learning for pastoral formation programs, how has Jason developed a standard to meet this requirement? Whereas MA programs rest on academic theology, field placements for MDiv programs enable students to gain practical experience. These contexts help to develop embodied relationships with supervisors/mentors and compensate for two main types of field placements, neither of which is guaranteed. Jason suggests online learning has only exacerbated a turn toward academic virtues without nurturing student character. He also addresses the need for ATS to formulate clearer standards for "formation," specifically character formation and self-differentiation in pastoral students.

Jason's research is informed by the real-life problems identified in his vocation. In the field of education, down-to-earth learning is compulsory. He has a love of teaching in undergraduate and graduate teaching in a range of courses, with a rich experience based on his erudition, certainly not only in abstract, academic theorising. His extensive bibliography and the extracts drawn from his reading further emphasise his commitment to research, a demanding yet rewarding task essential in an academic vocation. The quality of his research is convincing and he has made a stellar contribution unravelling the problems he has encountered. He writes carefully and self-critically, with creative, logical steps. This steady if not plodding journey is essential for an academic vocation.

Jason completed his Final Oral Examination on September 8, 2021, graduating as Dr. Mills on November 13 at the University of St. Michael's College, Toronto. In this context, he was awarded the Governor General's Gold Medal for his academic achievements, with a PhD in Theological Studies at St. Michael's College in the University of Toronto. His book provides solid foundations for his ongoing calling. May the Lord continue to bless him in his vocation!

Doug Blomberg
BA (Hons), PhD (Sydney), MEdSt, EdD (Monash),
Emeritus President and Professor of Philosophy of Education,
Institute for Christian Studies, Toronto

Acknowledgments

I AM GRATEFUL FOR my brilliant yet humble PhD supervisor, Dr. Doug Blomberg. His knowledge and vocabulary know no bounds as does his faith in my ability to write. He returned whole chapters to me in days with insightful comments and sage advice. I am grateful for his willingness to serve as my supervisor even as he wrapped up his work at the Institute for Christian Studies and headed to Australia. I could not have done this without him.

The unwavering support, encouragement, and grace of my wife and children, Erika, Shawna, and Elijah, carried me to this project's completion. Their patience and kindness, as I struggled through the dark days of writing with little time for anything else, were amazing gifts. Thank you for loving me.

Thanks to my dad and mom. Dad's unexpected death meant having to say goodbye shortly before I started writing. While the subject of this book would have meant very little to him, the author meant the world. Dad and mom have always believed in me, and mom's cheerleading continues. I am grateful for her support and care.

Lastly, thank you to my God who redeems, calls, and patiently accompanies me through all of life's rivers and fires (Isa 43:1–2).

Introduction

CHRISTIAN HIGHER EDUCATION INSTITUTIONS across Canada are experimenting with radical shifts in educational content and delivery. Cyber education is becoming an increasingly popular supplement or replacement for embodied learning, especially during the global coronavirus pandemic. While keen to start my research on web-based theological education for years, the pandemic happened to coincide with this project's timely beginnings. Merely days after gathering a backseat full of books from the University of Toronto libraries, the whole world started shutting down, including those libraries. As students and teachers vacated classrooms, schools quickly shifted courses to the Web.[1] Today, there are more online courses being offered than ever before. Now that the pandemic rush is over, Web-based courses and theological programs have been integrated into most school curriculums.

This book was originally written as my PhD dissertation. The title of that project was "In Vitro Education." In vitro is a Latin term meaning "within the glass" or "in glass." The title was an attempt to describe online education as akin to processes performed in glass test tubes, such as fertilization. That process is well known; if a couple is unable to conceive, a medical laboratory assists by providing In Vitro Fertilization (IVF). In vitro can be a helpful procedure in extenuating circumstances. In vivo, on the other hand, is Latin for "within the living" or "in a living thing." Most babies are born in vivo rather than via in vitro fertilization. Online education is in vitro learning. In vivo education, that which has been traditionally delivered through social, residential education experiences, is giving way to educational processes that are taking place within or behind or in front of glass

1. See Gallagher and Palmer, "Pandemic."

1

computer screens. I am calling these learning spaces "glassrooms." Whereas students traditionally encountered other learners and teachers in a shared, face-to-face, physical context, Web-based education has students looking at their classmates and assignments on screens using peer-to-peer software programs like Zoom and learning management systems (LMS) like Canvas. The educational content is similar, but the context differs significantly.

Just like IVF, glassroom learning can be helpful in some situations. Geographic distance may prevent someone from attending a residential seminary classroom, but online learning allows that person to participate from a distance. Likewise, the pandemic, where people may risk illness by gathering in the same physical space, made Internet learning a good option. Yet, students being taught via learning management systems and interacting with teachers and peers in small boxes that are digitally mediated using systems like Zoom or MS Teams, strikes me as somehow removed from embodied life, almost artificial. While the learning outcomes appeal the same in online and embodied contexts, the process of getting there differs significantly. This book grapples with the online/in-person tension guided by the following questions: what effect do shifts toward online courses have on those enrolled in programs of pastoral formation? Are *online* learners studying for ordained ministry being adequately prepared? At the start of this project, I hypothesized that online programs subtly shift the focus and purpose of ministerial education, from shaping the whole person for ministry toward shaping the intellect alone, resulting in pastors being educated with deficiencies in character virtue and self-differentiated leadership. While this hypothesis turned out to be sound, it did not go far enough. The Internet itself, a technological instrument, plays a far greater role in human formation than simply providing a medium for enhancing cognitive capacities and increasing opportunities for learning through dialogue. This book provides an overview of online education with a view of technology as a formational instrument. Two aspects of pastoral formation are examined in detail: self-differentiation and character formation. I investigate each through the lens of Internet education and the role technology plays in developing or inhibiting those aspects of pastoral maturity. Pastoral formation programs like the Master of Divinity (MDiv), unlike their academic counterparts such as the theological Master of Arts (MA), require field placements so students may gain practical experience in ministry. Therefore, the final chapter explores these field placements as possible contexts where embodied relationships with supervisors/mentors make up for the deficiencies of remote, technologically-mediated forms of education and create the environment for self-differentiation and character virtues. In the conclusion, I consolidate my research and make recommendations for change as well as areas of further exploration.

A BRIEF HISTORY OF THEOLOGICAL EDUCATION

In the first chapter I review the history of theological education. I begin by describing how nurturing virtue in students used to be the goal of the early university. However, that ideal is now largely absent in secular as well as theological schools. David H. Kelsey's work describes this turn as a shift from *Paideia*,[2] an education focused on developing a culture of learning through community focused on the Good or divine, to *Wissenschaft*, an education focused on dialectics and dialogue about theories and ideals as a way of thinking differently.[3] Paideia appears in the early church, through the monastic and cathedral schools, with a shift toward *Wissenschaft* dialectics when universities started to emerge. Friedrich Schleiermacher's work carved out a place for pastoral programs in the university, but they were designed with what Gavin D'Costa calls the "science of research" and professional training in mind rather than creating a learning culture promoting character formation.[4] Pastoral apprenticeships and academic research were governed by denominations and their established universities, with no standardized ways of training from school to school and denomination to denomination. In 1918, a handful of theological school presidents formed the Association of Theological Schools (ATS) to fill that gap. The ATS created academic standards, yet questions of formation remain today.

The second half of the chapter addresses online theological education, providing an overview of the strengths of online education generally and online *theological* education specifically, plus the deficiencies of online education generally and online *theological* education specifically. Internet education's rapid rise has proven to be a boon for institutions of higher education, including theological schools.[5] The ATS has recognized the

---

2. The terms *Paideia* and *Wissenschaft* will be used at various times throughout this book. *Wissenschaft* will be capitalized and italicized throughout while paideia will be capitalized and italicized only when introduced.

3. Kelsey, *Between Athens and Berlin*.

4. D'Costa, "Missiology."

5. Cannell, "Review"; Tanner, "Online Learning at ATS Schools: Part 2."

value of online education and has been quick to help theological schools move online. In 1999, two schools gained approval to deliver courses remotely. Three years later, the first mainly online MDiv was approved. By 2017, two thirds of ATS member schools offered online courses.[6] The reasons for this speedy uptake are clear: Online education provides flexibility for schools and students, higher student enrolment, and opportunities to connect with students and faculty around the world. Research affirms the benefits of online theological learning, including the low cost of delivery, the expansion of the school's reach, and increasing student engagement with materials, peers, and teachers. There has been excellent research into finding ways to maximize cognitive and social learning elements, such as the Community of Inquiry (COI) model developed by educators Randy Garrison, Terry Anderson, and Walter Archer.[7] Their work has gone a long way to help online educators make the most of the shift online. However, not everyone sees the shift online with positivity. Some cite the difficulty engaging students, social isolation, and technological glitches that inhibit learning, as barriers to online learning.[8] Additionally, theological schools have struggled with faculty buy-in, questions of how to promote spiritual formation online, and whether practical pastoral skills can be formed via online contexts.[9] These last two aspects are raised as questions with very few answers, as very little research exists. The final section of this chapter looks at the ATS and their decision to allow institutions to define student "formation" without a standard, a problematic issue as Web-based learning continues to grow.[10] The lack of definition about "formation" surfaces again in chapter 5 in the context of theological field education.

TECHNOLOGY AND ITS EFFECTS ON LEARNING

I begin chapter 2 by trying to uncover theological educators' research about the impact of Internet technology on learning. There is very little research to be found. Instead, theological educators have focused on discovering creative ways to leverage technologies to teach more effectively online.

6. Tanner, "Online Learning at ATS Schools: Part 1."

7. Garrison, *E-Learning in the 21st Century.*

8. Kibby, "Hybrid Teaching and Learning"; Pike and Gore, "The Challenges."

9. Miller and Scharen, "(Not) Being There."

10. Smith Brown, "Accessible, Effective"; The Association of Theological Schools, *Educational Models and Practices.*

Rather than looking more deeply at how technologies may be used more effectively for theological education, the heart of this book centres on the understudied aspect of how technology forms students. I begin with the question, "how might technology itself affect student formation?" My answer asserts that the interaction of a person with technology, as in online education, shifts social behavior and brain development. Therefore, online learning programs and courses are not ideal for those seeking to develop character virtues and skills.

My argument begins by outlining three views of technology described by Heather Kanuka.[11] I take up the "Technological Determinism" position, which becomes the backbone of the chapter. I recount a surprising human-computer relationship described by MIT professor Joseph Weizenbaum in the mid-1960's.[12] Weizenbaum's observation of the connections between a machine and those who interacted with it convinced him of the shaping power of technology on human beings. Philosopher Martin Heidegger also argues that technology changes the natural order of creation, including human behavior.[13] He sees this unnatural re-ordering at the hands of technology as changing human beings and human societies in ways that make them more machine-like. Media theorist and educator, Neil Postman, argues along the same lines as Heidegger, suggesting humans are now perceived as "thinking machines."[14] This, says Postman, impacts all of humanity, including spirituality. The findings uncovered by these authors contribute significantly to my understanding of humanness and technology's influence on human "being."

Online educational technologies shape humans generally, but they also limit the ways educators educate. How computers store and use data restricts what educators can and cannot do. Computers and Web platforms, rather than a teacher, become the focal point for students, as described by a faculty mentor of mine who suggested, ". . . the student's attention is not on the instructor but [the online learning platform]." This increasing dependency on technology has its pros and cons. One downside is the potential erosion of skill development and capacity for human judgement. I cite an example raised by Postman about the way the invention of the stethoscope

---

11. Kanuka, "Understanding E-Learning."

12. Weizenbaum, *Computer Power and Human Reason.*

13. Heidegger, *The Question Concerning Technology.*

14. Postman, *Technopoly.*

changed the practice of medicine.[15] I also briefly reference technology's impact on pastoral skill development in this chapter, taking it up more fully in chapter 4.

Part of this chapter focuses on the rise of generating data and numbers as offering greater legitimacy than direct human experience. It appears this shift has downplayed certain educational aspects, such as the humanities. According to McMaster University Professor of Religious Studies Travis Kroeker, the value of embodied human presence and such things as "love, justice, beauty, and goodness" are ignored when data collection is the goal.[16] Family therapist Edwin Friedman also has concerns with the modern reliance on data and its impact on human "being."[17] He sees leaders, including those serving congregations, turn to data as "a form of substance abuse" to cope with chronic anxiety in the communal systems of which they are a part. Friedman sees this "appeal to data" phenomenon in congregations, families and societies as a whole. Friedman points his finger at academic institutions, in which the societal "cortex" is detached from the emotional processes driving it. Friedman's idea about academic institutional anxiety is briefly covered here and further taken up in chapter 3 when I look at the possible role of chronic anxiety in theological school administrations. As a counterpoint to institutional anxiety, I suggest the use of Paulo Freire's pedagogy.[18] Freire focuses on setting students free to learn based on "the generative theme." This is "the investigation of people's . . . praxis" and this investigation works against the potentially oppressive methods of education that could be tied to "a banking model" of online education focusing on content and data.

In the second half of this chapter, I narrow my focus on technology by looking specifically at media, the Internet and their effects on human beings. Drawing significantly on Marshall McLuhan, I suggest the shift from print culture to digital mediums of communication has altered the focus of educators and students. This shift appears to be largely unnoticed by theological educators, due to the absence of research on this subject. McLuhan posits media can be separated into what is noticed ("figure") and what remains unnoticed ("ground").[19] I explore the figure/ground relation-

15. Postman, *Technopoly*.

16. Kroeker, "Technology as Principality."

17. Friedman, *A Failure of Nerve*.

18. Freire, *Pedagogy of the Oppressed*.

19. Coupland, *Mashall McLuhan*; Gordon, *McLuhan*.

ship in detail and demonstrate its relevance for online education. McLuhan goes on to suggest that people become numb to the figure and the ground becomes obscured. I offer McLuhan's description of Narcissus as a way of showing how the online medium can affect the ability to perceive reality. As I have demonstrated, interacting with technology *changes* human beings, making us more machine-like and affecting our ability to perceive reality. These shifts have major implications for Christology and the doctrine of the incarnation. They also have implications for teaching theology. For example, how do theologians instill the value of the incarnation in students through a disembodying medium? Regent College Professor Craig Gay suggests there is an urgent need to remember the significance of human embodiment in the face of the growing influence of modern technology.[20] He argues Protestant believers have been quicker to adopt technology in worship and learning because their experience is already desacramentalized, making it difficult to perceive the life of God in embodied life. Likewise, James K. A. Smith invites Christians into a renewed sacramental embrace of "ashes and dust, blood and bodies, fish and bread" as a way of experiencing God's grace.[21]

I wrap up this chapter by looking at two aspects of human formation affected by technology and the Internet: social well-being and the brain. The Internet promotes helpful connections with others, but research shows it can leave people feeling isolated and depressed.[22] Large quantities of time online have been shown to lead to increases in depression. Technostress, a term used by researchers Sharon Horwood and Jeromy Anglim to describe stress arising from smartphone usage, arises from "cognitive-emotional preoccupation with . . . the smartphone."[23] Furthermore, Leonard Reinecke et al., found "everyday Internet use" has been linked to "procrastination and its psychological effects."[24] These aspects of social well-being affect ways of interacting. There are also changes to the brain that affect thinking. According to Joseph Firth et al., smartphones promote habitual "checking" behaviors reinforced by "information rewards."[25] As a result, Firth et al., conclude those who practise these behaviors "perform worse in

20. Gay, *Modern Technology*.
21. Smith, *Desiring the Kingdom*.
22. Kraut et al., "Internet Paradox."
23. Horwood and Anglim, "Problematic Smartphone Usage."
24. Reinecke et al., "Permanently Online."
25. Firth et al., "Online Brain."

various cognitive tasks" than others. Similarly, Mark Ellingsen concludes "concentration and memory (and intelligence)" suffer because of brain changes due to sustained Internet usage.[26] He stands with Nicholas Carr, author of *The Shallows*, drawing on Carr's conclusions to state: "heavier online use is making us more shallow . . . [and] less transcendent in our thinking and behaviors."[27]

BOWEN FAMILY SYSTEMS THEORY AND PASTORAL SKILL DEVELOPMENT

Building on chapter 2, in this chapter I suggest that the online learning interface acts as a third-party entity in the teacher-student relationship. I suggest the Web application or device serves as a member of an emotional system and I apply three Bowen Family Systems Theory concepts to that system. Very little has been studied about web-based education's effect on the emotional system of teachers and students and that system's impact on learning and ministerial formation. I define triangulation, differentiation of self, and societal emotional process and apply those concepts to aspects of learning, relationships with devices, theological schools and the accrediting associations' decision-making.

I begin by defining anxiety and its role in traditional emotional systems. Drawing on theorists and therapists Peter Steinke and Edwin Friedman, I describe the chronic and systemic form of unhelpful anxiety as different from the acute and temporary stress that can be a motivator.[28] After clarifying how anxiety is understood in Bowen Family Systems Theory, I describe how it manifests in relationships, including relationships with technology using Bowen's three concepts.

The first concept, the Triangle, describes the dynamic Bowen observed in a three-person emotional system. Triangulating a person into a two-person relationship serves to stabilize the emotional system when chronic anxiety rises. Most research on triangles focuses on human emotional systems but some authors, such as Michael Kerr and Monica McGoldrick, describe triangles that include technological devices.[29] I provide an example of how technology gets triangled into a two-person relationship

---

26. Ellingsen, "Neurobiological Data."

27. Carr, *The Shallows*.

28. Friedman, *A Failure of Nerve*.

29. Kerr and Bowen, *Family Evaluation*, McGoldrick et al., *Genograms*.

through a personal experience Psychologist Sherry Turkle recounts in her book, *Alone Together*.[30] This serves to demonstrate how technology can be triangled into a relationship.

The second Bowenian concept I address is Differentiation of Self (DoS). DoS, according to Peter Titelman, is ". . . an individual's capacity to be an individual while functioning as part of a group."[31] This is an important trait for pastors, ministering as servant-leaders in complex congregations that have the potential to be chronically anxious emotional systems. I suggest there are two challenges to self-differentiated learning in online contexts: students' home contexts may be poorly differentiated emotional systems, thereby inhibiting a student's development toward higher levels of differentiation; and students may become increasingly "emotionally fused" with technology, thereby inhibiting their ability to develop healthy relationships with others. In both cases, I review dynamics unique to web-based students who may not have the opportunity to interact with their peers and teachers in an embodied context. My examination of students in potentially poorly differentiated systems looks at James Fowler's Individuative-Reflective stage of faith and the importance of learning differentiation through distance during this stage.[32] My look at student "emotional fusion" with devices draws on Monica McGoldrick's definition of the term; I apply her concept to research showing lower levels of self-differentiation along online students.[33] These findings are important for online theological educators seeking to nurture non-anxious, self-differentiated pastoral leaders.

The third Bowen Family Systems Theory concept I apply to online education is Societal Emotional Process. Bowen defines this concept as a "societal fusion" that results from chronic anxiety in society as a whole.[34] He describes the inability of individuals to take a stand different from those of society as indicating a lack of self-differentiation within an emotionally regressive society. I apply this concept to theological schools and the relative haste with which they have taken up online learning for pastoral formation to suggest there may be "societal fusion" at play. I cite examples of how thinking is being offloaded to search engines like Google and software

---

30. Turkle, *Alone Together*.

31. Titelman, "The Concept of Differentiation."

32. Fowler, *Stages of Faith*.

33. McGoldrick et al., *Genograms*.

34. Bowen, *Family Therapy*.

programs requiring less creative and deep thinking.[35] These are examples of the societal emotional process at work, wherein theological schools appear to be shifting the delivery of courses and programs online, without careful consideration of what is being lost.

In the final section of this chapter, I describe discipleship for pastoral formation and the importance of taking difficult and costly decisions for the sake of faith. I draw on the work of Dietrich Bonhoeffer,[36] Dallas Willard,[37] and Richard Foster[38] to describe the radical act of following Jesus and the way of Christian discipleship. This aspect of enduring and overcoming challenge and difficulty is important for learning skills. I draw on the work of Hubert Dreyfus to show how Internet learning can only support learning to the point of competency in skill development and that embodied learning allows the student to gain proficiency and mastery of the subject.[39] I conclude this section by reviewing the role of pastor and arguing that this is to serve as a reminder to God's people how to be human and that this happens best through embodied teacher-mentors.

CHARACTER VIRTUES AND ONLINE THEOLOGICAL EDUCATION

I pick up where chapter 3 left off by arguing that character virtue, similar to self-differentiation, is taught and developed as a skill. I begin by defining what virtue is and how it can be nurtured. I draw on Olli-Pekka Vainio's understanding of Aristotelian excellence as it relates to virtues and Shannon Vallor's work on practical wisdom's dependence on contextual application, concluding with an appeal to Doug Blomberg's exploration of wisdom as "a way of being."[40]

I address the question, "How are virtues acquired?" beginning with Aristotle's position: virtues are developed in the same way as a trade or a skill.[41] Practice is essential. Practice is one part of the equation; relationships are another part. Virtues are first learned, according to Ross A.

35. Tenner, *The Efficiency Paradox.*

36. Bonhoeffer, *Life Together*, Bonhoeffer, *The Cost of Discipleship.*

37. Willard, *The Great Omission.*

38. Foster, *Celebration of Discipline.*

39. Dreyfus, *On the Internet.*

40. Blomberg, *Wisdom and Curriculum*, Vainio, *Virtue*, Vallor, *Virtue Ethics.*

41. Aristotle, *Aristotle.*

Thompson, through "intuitive . . . sensibility" in parent-child encounters.[42] Primary caregivers provide the first experience of character virtues such as love, empathy, and generosity and as one grows, developing those virtues and others requires something more. According to David James, "other-directed emotional insights" and "shared activities" are two important factors.[43] Therefore, understanding one's own emotions and those of others are important for the growth of virtue.

After describing and defining virtue and virtue acquisition, I examine the place of virtue formation in theological education. After searching for articles written about virtue in the journal *Theological Education*, Marvin Oxenham found only one written between 1964 and 2017.[44] This, I argue, is due to the focus on *Wissenschaft* as a way of educating rather than the character formation goal of paideia education. I trace this particular shift by showing how the training of 1840's Anglican clergy in Upper Canada offered more of an enculturing apprenticeship program, becoming more focused on academic learning after the program moved to Trinity College in Toronto.[45] This tension between a focus on *Wissenschaft* academics or paideia enculturation of character continues in theological schools today. I cite examples of both perspectives in recent literature before turning to the question of whether character virtues can be learned online. First, I look at this question through the lens of those who educate with a *Wissenschaft* perspective. As Oxenham observed above, "virtue" is not broadly used in theological education literature. Thus, broadening my search to include "formation," I discovered a number of *Wissenschaft* educators who concluded that healthy Christian formation may indeed take place online. Their concepts of formation centre on intellectual virtues, (i.e., thinking rightly, healthy dialogue, etc.) and professional practice and skills rather than dealing with the character of the student.[46] When I examined those who appealed to paideia (i.e., developing wisdom and empathy in students), there were very few examples. In one instance, Thomas Esselman describes a "spirit of mutuality and openness . . ." among his students.[47]

---

42. Thompson, "A Perspective."

43. James, "The Acquisition of Virtue."

44. Oxenham, *Character and Virtue.*

45. Westfall, "Some Practical Acquaintance."

46. Hess, *Engaging Technology*, Mercer and Simpson, "What Would Kant Tweet," Nichols, "The Formational Experiences."

47. Esselman, "The Pedagogy."

An article entitled "Virtual Empathy?" provides another example of paideia where the authors describe a context in which anxieties can be turned to empathy.[48] While a small number of articles described how virtue could be manifested online, not a single article showed how character virtues were taught and learned online.

After concluding that Learning Management Systems and learning paideia virtues do not mix particularly well, I consider two theological education vices that could be promoted by online education. The first, technological consumption, argues that technology can become the focus for students and educators. This consumption of technology leads toward *using* technology as an end in itself and away from the *giving* required in embodied relationships and interaction with others. The second vice is distraction. I draw on the writing of David I. Smith and Nicholas Carr to show how Internet usage, in general, can work against traditional aspects of spiritual formation, such as empathy, patience, and contemplation.[49]

I conclude chapter 4 with an appeal to consider the value of "on the job training" in character formation. I reference Bob Gidney's insights about the role of work sites and the way "hanging around," a feature of paideia enculturation, plays out in apprenticeship and skill development.[50] Since character virtues are developed like skills, I appeal to Arthur Zajonc's "epistemology of love" to show that a higher education built on relational learning that results in the formation of character virtues is possible, but certainly not through online learning alone.[51] Charles Ess argues embodied teachers and learners "who incarnate the skills and wisdom that mark the highest levels of human accomplishment" are necessary.[52]

THEOLOGICAL FIELD EDUCATION FOR ONLINE STUDENTS

So far, I have argued that the Internet is not an ideal context for teaching and learning self-differentiation and character virtues. In my final chapter I show how theological school pastoral programs rely on theological field education placements for practical skill development and character virtue

---

48. McGarrah Sharp and Morris, "Virtual Empathy."

49. Carr, *The Shallows*, Smith et al., *Digital Life Together*.

50. Gidney, "Madame How."

51. Palmer and Zajonc, *The Heart*.

52. Ess, "Liberal Arts."

formation. I begin with an introduction to field education and describe what it is according to the Association of Theological Schools Standards. I explore my assumption that the pandemic-induced rush to move courses online should have resulted in greater need to attend to embodied learning, with more attention given to field education as a growingly important aspect of pastoral education. However, my assumptions were incorrect, as I found very little written about field education just before or during the current pandemic.

After describing the current state of the ATS' view of field education and embodied contexts of formation, I provide a brief history of theological field education. I outline three field education models as defined by Richard J. Leyda, showing there is no standardized way of organizing field education from school to school or program to program.[53] I then outline the purposes of field education and summarize those in two broad categories: a vocational purpose focused on developing pastoral skills and a meaning-making purpose emphasizing reflection on praxis. Various programs focus on both, leaning one way or the other, and can be situated within these categories. It appears all field placements provide opportunities for students to work alongside embodied mentors in congregational and clinical settings. I focus on two specific types of field education experiences: placements directed by the Canadian Association for Spiritual Care (CASC/ACSS) predominantly situated in hospital settings; and seminary directed placements predominantly situated in congregational or para-church settings. CASC/ACSS offers Supervised Psychospiritual Education (SPE) units delivered by highly trained specialist-supervisors, whereas seminary-directed programs vary widely from school to school. I provide an overview of the history and development of Clinical Pastoral Education (CPE), originating in the United States and evolving in terminology to become Supervised Psychospiritual Education (SPE) in Canada.[54] In Canada, Supervised Psychospiritual Education (SPE) is the umbrella term for Clinical Psychospiritual Education (CPE) and Psychospiritual Therapy Education (PTE).[55] Both programs are

53. Leyda, "Models of Ministry."

54. Jernigan, "Clinical Pastoral Education."

55. In June 2022 members of CASC/ACSS voted to change the names of the following programs: Supervised Pastoral Education (SPE) was changed to Supervised Psychospiritual Education (SPE); Clinical Pastoral Education (CPE) was changed to Clinical Psychospiritual Education (CPE); and Pastoral Counselling Education (PCE) was changed to Psychospiritual Therapy Education (PTE). Wherever possible the latest terms will be used. Citations from works before 2022 and references by American authors or the American system will not be changed.

accredited by CASC/ACSS. I focus on whether SPE can be a way to develop character virtues in ministerial students by highlighting articles by three SPE educators. These educators describe the need to prioritize the assessment of virtues in SPE students and educators.[56] This shows the program is capable of being used for those purposes, but because they are arguing for virtue assessment, it appears virtue assessment is not currently part of the expectations for students or educators.

After reviewing SPE and its capacity to nurture character virtues in students and educators, I focus on seminary-directed theological field education. I begin by describing these placements and suggesting there is no clear way to determine how character virtues are nurtured because expectations for students and supervisors vary significantly from school to school. I highlight two educational factors found to play large roles in theological field education and student formation: the quality of the community and the quality of supervision.[57] One of the challenges determining the health of the community for online students is that distance may not allow a seminary director to determine the quality of the community where the student will be placed. Additionally, many students already function as leaders and pastors in those communities.[58] This is a change from the historical norm, where a student would gradually gain pastoral expertise under the direction of a seasoned guide. Nonetheless, the outcome of theological field education's effectiveness is unknown.

I dive deeper into the role of the supervisor in seminary-directed field education because this appears to be a larger factor than the quality of the community in student formation (this based on recent studies published in *Reflective Practice*).[59] The results show the importance of the supervisor-student relationship, but they also show inconsistencies in the types of role and the quality of supervision students receive in their placements. This makes it nearly impossible to determine whether character virtues and self-differentiation are part of learning outcomes for students in their placements. Additionally, a survey by the Association of Theological Field Education (ATFE) schools unearthed obstacles to training field-based

---

56. Hilsman, "Tandem Roles," Jones, "I Walk," Lasair, "What's the Point."

57. Jin Lee, "The Art of Supervision," Oxenham, *Character and Virtue*.

58. Singer, "Supervisory Practice."

59. Floding et al., "Excellence in Supervision: Listening," Zaker et al., "Excellence in Supervision: Training."

supervisors.[60] Seminaries had inconsistent guidelines for identifying and preparing supervisors; expectations for supervisors varied. This makes it next to impossible to determine if the supervisors prioritized nurturing character virtues and self-differentiation in students.

I explore the broad challenges for seminary-directed field education and SPE placements. One of the obstacles of seminary-directed field education is being on the margins of the theological seminary. I gather insights from Steven Studebaker and Lee Beach,[61] as well as Bruce P. Powers,[62] who describe the disconnect between academic programs and practicums. Academic courses are perceived as more important and valuable, garnering more attention.

Like seminary-directed placements, SPE also has challenges. I suggest SPE has three areas of concern for pastoral students: First, Homer L. Jernigan describes a growing disconnect between SPE programs and theological education.[63] In the same way seminary field education is on the margins, SPE may experience similar struggles when it comes to theological school formation program integration. This seems more pronounced in the United States than in Canada. Second, SPE's system of supervision does not necessarily provide supervised reflection on the Christian Story, something Regina Coll and Thomas Groome deem crucial for student formation.[64] Third, SPE seems oriented toward chaplaincy and the context of paideia is generally clinical.[65] While these are excellent programs, it is not clear how they influence congregational ministry in parish settings. If anything, they may be shifting the role of pastor to become more of a chaplain to their congregation.

I finish this chapter by looking at an emerging model of pastoral education called Competency-Based Theological Education (CBTE). It focuses on nurturing expected competencies or outcomes in theological students. Once they gain mastery of a subject or skill, they are assessed (often by a team of mentors) to have completed that aspect of their education.[66] ATS has cautiously approved some CBTE degree programs, and they are offering

---

60. Zaker et al., "Excellence in Supervision: Training."

61. Studebaker and Beach, "Friend or Foe."

62. Powers, "Developing a Curriculum."

63. Jernigan, "Clinical Pastoral Education."

64. Coll, *Supervision of Ministry*, Groome, *Sharing Faith.*

65. Sullender, "New Forms."

66. Stiller, "Enthusiasts."

support for schools looking to shift their learning models.[67] Rather than a program with practical experiences on the periphery, CBTE may provide a way to use web-based learning in conjunction with embodied mentors as an integrated whole.

67. "Guidelines on Competency-Based."

1

Theological Education Today
Tracing the Path to the Online MDiv

THE ONLINE MDIV APPEARED as part of technological evolution in education rather than theological reasons. In this chapter I examine the history of theological education and trace its development until the emergence of the first accredited online theological courses. As part of my review of online education, I offer an overview of the strengths and deficiencies of Internet based courses generally as well as looking at the pros and cons of theological education specially when delivered online. The chapter concludes with the present state of online theological education in institutions that are accredited by the Association of Theological Schools (ATS).

A BRIEF HISTORY OF THEOLOGICAL EDUCATION: FROM A HABIT OF KNOWING GOD TOWARD PROFESSIONALIZATION OF CHURCH MINISTRY

Beginnings: Paideia and Nurturing the Whole Person

The original impetus of theological education appears to be lost. Today a student can be granted a Master of Divinity degree, the most widely accepted academic credential for admittance into pastoral ministry, without exhibiting a definitive standard of virtues. This is a significant deviation from ancient practice of teaching and learning where paideia was paramount.

David Kelsey, Professor Emeritus of Theology at Yale Divinity School, describes the concept of paideia used by the Greeks during Plato's time. He explains, "In ancient Athens, 'paideia' simply named an unself-conscious educational process through which young free males were 'formed' by those virtues they would need in order to function as responsible adult citizens. The process involved the whole person."[1] Kelsey describes four aspects of paideia that are significant for understanding the manner in which students were educated. He describes:

1. The goal of paideia, which is the cultivation of the excellence or *arete* of the soul, consists not in acquiring a clutch of virtues but in knowledge of the Good itself.

2. The Good is not only the underlying essence of the moral and intellectual virtues; it is the highest principle of the universe. It is the divine.

3. The goal of paideia cannot be taught directly—for example, by simply conveying information about various philosophers' doctrines regarding virtue. Knowledge of the Good only comes through contemplation, the ultimate fruit of which is an intuitive insight, a *gnosis* of the Good.

4. Insightful knowledge of the Good requires a conversion, a turning around of the soul from preoccupation with appearances to focus on reality, on the Good . . . Education as paideia is inherently communal and not solitary.[2]

According to Kelsey's description of paideia, students were educated to know and practise the Good. This is echoed by Edward Farley of Vanderbilt Divinity School as he describes the long history of theological education. Farley states, ". . . a salvifically oriented knowledge of divine being was part of the Christian community and tradition long before it was named theology."[3] He describes that salvifically oriented knowledge manifesting in learners as "habitus." The focus was on nurturing a habit of knowing God characterized by wisdom. This form of educating the whole person in community is not only a Greek concept adopted by the early church, it appears in ancient Jewish culture as well. Judaism required students to be formed in knowing God by living life in close proximity to their teachers.[4]

1. Kelsey, *Between Athens and Berlin*, 7.
2. Kelsey, *Between Athens and Berlin*, 9.
3. Farley, *Theologia*, 33.
4. Brad Young describes how Jewish disciples in Second Temple Judaism would care

Formed out of both Greek and Jewish influences, the early church focused on neither theology as an academic discipline nor education as a formal pursuit but on knowing God and knowledge of God's ways in the world.

In this context theological education took place in two settings—the Service of the Word and the catechumenate.[5] By the second century, a pattern of formation emerged. Catechumens would spend two or more years in preparation for baptism. This system operated to ensure the baptized were sufficiently prepared for life under persecution. Things changed after the conversion of Constantine. The church began to produce some of the greatest theologians including Athanasius, Eusebius, Basil the Great, John Chrysostom, Jerome, Ambrose, and Augustine while at the same time the commitment to the catechumenate declined. With large portions of the population becoming Christians and societal forces contrary to the Christian faith no longer an issue the need for rigorous instruction, leading to a virtuous life in a hostile world, lost relevance. By the time of Pope Gregory the Great (590–604 AD) the catechumenate lasted a mere forty days.[6] As described by Queensland Theological College's Andrew Bain, up until this time, the priority of pastoral development in the early days was rooted in the individual's qualities rather than their knowledge or skills:

> Besides mirroring the approach of the Pastoral Epistles in this regard, these authors [e.g. Chrysostom, Ambrose, and Gregory the Great] believed that the most critical factors relating to "success" in ministry, and those most clearly providing reasons for failure, were questions of character rather than deficiencies in biblical or practical training, and therefore they attended above all to the former.[7]

Bain further drives home the importance of the individual's traits and character for pastoral witness, not skills or performance, when he writes, "In considering the literature explicitly on the pastorate in late antiquity, a striking and fundamental feature of it, is its near-total concern with matters of personal character and godliness."[8] During the early centuries of the Church the focus of education was on nurturing a virtuous life and community.

---

and perform menial tasks for their Rabbi. "The disciple is expected to serve his master teacher in caring for personal needs. By serving the master the disciple learns how to conduct his affairs in everyday life situations. He listens to his master's teaching while doing menial chores to assist his mentor." Young, *Meet the Rabbis*, 30.

5. González, *The History*, 9.

6. González, *The History*, 15.

7. Bain, "Theological Education," 50.

8. Bain, "Theological Education," 50.

The Emergence of Monastic and Cathedral Schools

From the eighth to the eleventh centuries, education became more formalized through the establishment of two institutions: the monastic schools and the cathedral schools. In Monastic schools, the rigorous instruction in character formation, formally taught to all Christians, was being taught to a smaller group of devout Christians, the monastics.[9] According to Bain, the monastery offered a whole life formation through training:

> The monasteries offered two particular benefits in terms of training in late antiquity. The first was *community*, the opportunity for those eager to progress in the Christian faith to spend substantial time with likeminded Christians, enabling keen and often able Christians to sharpen one another thoroughly . . . The second benefit concerned the *Scriptures*: at least in this period, the monasteries provided a context in which participants could spend several months or years being saturated with the Bible, more than would be possible at other times in their lives.[10]

The monastery brought together Scripture and community for students to be trained to think and live Christianly. The newly enrolled and long-time faithful were guided in their individual formation through meditation on sacred texts as well as contributing to one another's formation in community. They shared their learning, eating, worshipping, and living with each other in order to be mutually formed. Their time with the text was not for the purpose of intellectual mastery over its contents but to embrace it and be nourished by it. French Benedictine Monk, Jean Leclercq describes their approach:

> For the ancients, to meditate is to read a text and to learn it "by heart" in the fullest sense of this expression, that is, with one's whole being: with the body, since the mouth pronounced it, with the memory which fixes it, with the intelligence which understands its meaning, and with the will which desires to put it into practice.[11]

The cathedral schools, on the other hand, functioned separately from the monastic communities. Students did not take vows or live in community in the same way as those in the monastic schools. However, the goal was similar in that the learner would be educated to become a well-rounded

9. González, *The History*, 30.

10. Bain, "Theological Education," 56.

11. Leclercq, *The Love*, 17.

and wise person. Educators Parker Palmer and Arthur Zajonc write, "In the cathedral schools of twelfth-century Europe, the Seven Liberal Arts were, in the words of Alain de Lille, intended to produce 'the good and perfect man,' all of whose parts were so refined and in harmony with one another that he could make the spiritual journey to God."[12] Those seven liberal arts were meant for a common goal. They were chosen to teach about God and all that God created. Professor of Catholic Theology at the University of Bristol, Gavin D'Costa provides an overview of the liberal arts and their purposes:

> The Faculties were structured into the "inferior": arts (made up of the *trivium*, where three roads meet, grammar, rhetoric, and logic; and the *quadrivium*, made up of arithmetic, music, geometry and astronomy), followed by the "superior": canon law, medicine, and theology. The benefit of such division was the assumption that all the disciplines were founded on a common unifying principle: that creation was from God, ordered, for the good of man, and to be used as such.[13]

The University and the Fragmentation of Theology

Theological education moved out of the monastery and cathedral schools and into the university in the twelfth century.[14] That transition created a shift in how students learned. While the seven liberal arts continued to be used, their common focus on God shifted toward a focus on the distinct and segregated disciplines. D'Costa describes the changes by drawing on Leclercq's writings:

> Leclercq goes so far as to say that scholastic university theology, being wedded to the form of disputation and dialectics, eventually "lost contact with the life of prayer." This loss would eventually lead to the slow divorce between "knowledge and love, science and contemplation, intellectual life and spiritual life" and it would then become necessary to construct categories of mystical and spiritual theology, the worse for their separation from dogmatic theology.[15]

12. Palmer and Zajonc, *The Heart*, 7.

13. D'Costa, "Missiology," 214.

14. D'Costa, "Missiology," 213.

15. D'Costa, "Missiology," 212–13.

In the thirteenth century people went to study in universities, not to serve as ministers, but for their own spiritual and intellectual development.[16] During this time, education maintained a confidence in God as its foundation. God was understood to have ordered all things and it was toward the things of God that learning was focused. Describing theology during this time, González writes, "The end of theology is knowledge of God so as to do God's will: to honour God . . . in all our acts. Thus the course and conduct of the Christian life is that to which theology is ordered."[17]

At the beginning of the nineteenth century the method and approach to theology underwent a revision. In 1810 The University of Berlin was established. It was in this institution that theological education was dissected and categorized into convenient components.

> At the beginning of the nineteenth century the University of Berlin was designed to reflect the "research university" along the lines of the Enlightenment vision of education. In this respect, it intentionally defined itself against the earlier model of *paideia* that had characterized earlier ecclesial forms of education (and pre-Christian Greek education as at Athens) and instead emphasized a critical, orderly, and disciplined science of research. That is, no texts or ways of reading them were seen to be authoritative, either because of spiritual authority or traditions deeming them so. Rather, all texts were to be critically scrutinized, using methods that were accessible to all rational men, and methods that could allow the repeating of tests to authenticate of [sic] establish results.[18]

It took Friedrich Schleiermacher's reframing of theology as a necessary discipline for the education of professional clergy. Schleiermacher determined to keep the study of theology in the university by arguing that its purpose was for the preparation of clergy. "Schleiermacher (1768–1834) proposed a curriculum in which theology would be studied under these headings: philosophical theology, dogmatic theology, and pastoral theology."[19]

The German model shifted the focus on theological education, from theology as the study of God that resulted in wisdom, toward an academic exercise on the journey toward a clerical profession. While the German model was establishing its subjects with practical theology as the practical

16. González, *The History*, 43.

17. Farley, *Theologia*, 60–61.

18. D'Costa, "Missiology," 215–16.

19. González, *The History*, 106.

application of the theoretical theological courses, other European schools for a time maintained a focus on paideia. Professor and Academic administrator at North Park Seminary, Linda Cannell summarizes the situation, "The German system, with its emphasis on research and professional training, concentrated on the advancement of the discipline while deemphasizing (though not excluding) the development of character. English educators, while not denying the importance of research, retained the ideal that a university education should first shape the character of the student."[20]

Shaping pastoral students during this time was done largely through an apprenticeship system. However, as the German model of theological education became established, apprenticeship started to wane. Cannell describes apprenticeship's challenges: "The dominant model for professional education through the seventeenth and eighteenth centuries was apprenticeship. This mode ultimately proved unworkable as the complexity of the knowledge base of the profession increased and as the number of willing masters decreased. The professional had enough to do without taking on an apprentice."[21] This shift away from apprenticeship happened at Yale. The university established a divinity school in 1822. The primary reason for the change, according to Ronald Bainton, was "the inadequacy of the apprenticeship system . . . Parish ministers were too busy to conduct school." Bainton explains, "the apprenticeship system had been replaced by a professional school." It was the era of professional schools, medicine, law, and divinity.[22]

In early nineteenth century Canada, the fledgling Anglican Diocese of Toronto itself used an apprenticeship model. They soon moved toward a hybrid system with the establishment of the Diocesan Theological Institute in Cobourg, Ontario. Historian William Westfall describes its focus on nurturing cultured clergy through community integration and apprenticeship:

> When a number of the clergy who had been trained at Cobourg looked back on their experience, it was these qualities that they recalled most fondly. They appreciated the independence they had enjoyed within a strong academic environment. They had enjoyed acting out their future roles and relished their stature within the local community. Known rather affectionately as "the school of the prophets," the Diocesan Theological Institute was remembered as

20. Cannell, *Theological Education Matters*, 141.

21. Cannell, *Theological Education Matters*, 198.

22. Bainton, *Yale and the Ministry*, 80–81.

a place where candidates for holy orders were treated not as mere students but as gentlemen in the making.[23]

However, this institution and its apprenticeship model were not to last. The school was closed, and the students moved to Trinity College in Toronto for Anglican clerical formation. The geography was not the only change. Pedagogy also shifted. Summing up the changes in the institutions, Westfall writes:

> There can be no doubt that the new program of theological training lengthened the period of time devoted to formal education (from three years to five) and perforce increased the cost of becoming a clergyman. It also defined this period of training with much more precise (and less flexible) academic markers: at Cobourg, one went forward when one was judged ready; at Trinity, progress was linked to passing a series of formal examinations.[24]

In the end, Westfall describes the shift away from clergy formation via apprenticeship toward a more Berlin, intellectual model, as "misguided."[25] This way of educating clergy represented a movement away from the formation of virtuous individuals whose character and identity demonstrated their wisdom toward a focus on obtaining prerequisites and requirements for graduation. In addressing modern theological education Justo González says it like this, "Instead of a process of formation of the whole person, the theological curriculum becomes a series of courses, much as a series of requirements to fulfill, and the formation of the candidate for ministry moves to the background."[26]

The Association of Theological Schools and Theological Education Today

In 1918 a handful of Theological School presidents convened in Cambridge, Massachusetts to address questions they had in common including, "what is a theological seminary, how are people (mainly men) admitted to it, how does a theological school relate to the broader world, to the academy, to the

---

23. Westfall, "Some Practical Acquaintance," 57.
24. Westfall, "Some Practical Acquaintance," 59.
25. Westfall, "Some Practical Acquaintance," 62.
26. González, The History, 113.

church?"[27] This gathering was the beginning of an association of schools that became The Association of Theological Schools (ATS).

The ATS comprises two separate corporations: The Association, providing support for schools, and the Commission on Accrediting, offering accreditation. They promote the improvement and enhancement of graduate theological schools in Canada and the United States, which includes 270 schools, 74,500 students, and more than 7,200 faculty members.[28] The ATS is the body that maintains the standards and guidelines that govern the direction and values of most theological schools in North America.

Before exploring the role of virtue and identity formation in students on their way to becoming clergy, it is important to review ATS's standards. In June 2020 new ATS accreditation Standards were formally approved. The updated Standards replace the 1996 Standards, that had been amended in 2012 in part to address shifts toward online education.[29] In the 2012 Standards, the section dealing with education for pastoral formation and virtue is found under the heading "Basic program oriented toward ministerial leadership" and states, "[programs] provide opportunities for formational experiences through which students may grow in those personal qualities essential for the practice of ministry—namely, emotional maturity, personal faith, moral integrity, and social concern (ES.1.2.1)."[30] The updated 2020 Standard, "Standard 3. Student Learning and Formation" relates to student formation and reads as follows:

> Theological schools are communities of faith and learning centered on student learning and formation. Consistent with their missions and religious identities, theological schools give appropriate attention to the intellectual, human, spiritual, and vocational dimensions of student learning and formation. Schools pursue those dimensions with attention to academic rigor, intercultural competency, global awareness and engagement, and lifelong learning. Schools support student learning and formation through appropriate educational modalities and policies.[31]

While both standards address formation, neither addresses virtue specifically. The 2012 standard uses terms such as "emotional maturity" and

27. Miller, "A Community of Conversation," 3.
28. Association of Theological Schools, "About ATS."
29. Blossom, "Piecing Together."
30. Association of Theological Schools, *Educational Standard.*
31. Association of Theological Schools, *Standards of Accreditation.*

"moral integrity" which tend to be closely related to virtues such as self-control and patience. However, the 2020 draft revision says nothing about necessary individual qualities or traits to be developed in theological school students. The formation of virtue could fit into the human and spiritual dimensions of learning referenced in the first part of the paragraph but the ways of nurturing these dimensions are through means that do not have a clear link to virtues such as love for others and inner peace. This movement of ATS away from clearly defining things such as fostering virtues and a self-differentiated identity in theological students is not a surprise. In the 1950's, ATS commissioned a study reviewing the state of theological education. H. Richard Niebuhr's book, *The Purpose of the Church and Its Ministry* was one of the fruits of that study. In a chapter entitled, "The Idea of a Theological School," Niebuhr lays out the concept of, "the theological school as intellectual center of the Church's life."[32] Niebuhr saw the role of the theological school as being primarily academic in its association with the church. The enlightenment focus on the centrality of the intellect is evident in his two-pronged purpose of the school:

> As the center of the Church's intellectual activity, animated by the Church's motivation and directed by its purpose, the theological school is charged with a double function. On the one hand it is that place or occasion where the Church exercises its intellectual love of God and neighbor; on the other hand it is the community that serves the Church's other activities by bringing reflection and criticism to bear on worship, preaching, teaching and the care of souls.[33]

Farley, on the other hand, pushes back against a purely academic view of the theological school. His critique points toward the inclusion of paideia. According to Farley, post-Enlightenment "education means a communication of the many regions in which scholars and scientists divide up the cognitive universe. Absent from this view is the ancient Greek ideal of culture (*paideia*) according to which education is the 'culturing' of human being in *aretē* or virtue."[34]

There is a growing sense that theological schools are struggling with clarity about their purpose and knowledge about what needs to be done in the future. Linda Cannell describes the challenge in these terms:

32. Niebuhr, *The Purpose of the Church*, 107.
33. Niebuhr, *The Purpose of the Church*, 110.
34. Farley, *Theologia*, 152.

The consensus of the contemporary literature is that theological education is in crisis. The analysis of the problem is that seminaries have failed to produce the desired product, a skilled leader, or that the purpose of theology is not understood and therefore the theological curriculum is in disarray. The representative perspectives from Farley, Vanhoozer, Liefeld, and Wilkes suggest that theological education is ineffectual if all that is produced is knowledge of a set of propositions, polished skills, or a well-stocked mind.[35]

The formation of the mind is important in theological education. However, character is also important, perhaps even more so. For clergy training, knowing what to believe must be coupled with knowing how to live out and practise faith. Bonnie Miller-McLemore, Professor of Religion, Psychology, and Culture, describes the importance of training how people should respond and act in the world:

> Those who come into the [practical theology] classroom must leave better prepared to do something, whether that be to listen, worship, preach, lead, form, teach, oversee, convert, transform, or pursue justice. They need theology know-how. They need more than just the capacity to "*think* theologically" (the focus of plenty of books on reflective practice and the heart of many treatises on practical theology), but also the capacity to "*practice* theology" by putting theology into action through one's body on the ground.[36]

Theological education has focused on finetuning the minds of students while the other aspects of formation are part of extracurricular activities. This, according to Hwa Yung, should not be. He writes, "If theology is fundamentally pastoral and missiological, then the primary emphasis cannot be academic training and inculcation of skills alone. It must also pay at least equal attention to the moulding of the character and spirituality of the trainee."[37] If there is a concern for the formation of more than just the mind in theological education, should there be concern for the surge in the design and delivery of online theological courses?

35. Cannell, *Theological Education Matters*, 43.
36. Miller-McLemore, "Practical Theology and Pedagogy," 173.
37. Yung, "Critical Issues," 77.

ONLINE THEOLOGICAL EDUCATION

The Rise and Rapid Adoption of Distance
Education in Theological Schools

In the late twentieth and early twenty-first centuries, as theological schools struggled to define themselves and their mandates, technological changes opened ways for institutions to expand their distance education departments to include something that was only starting to emerge in the world of higher education—online learning. Linda Cannell describes various reasons for this development:

> Advances in technology, the demands of an increasingly mobile and diverse population, economic realities, emphases on the democratization of education, dissatisfaction with traditional modes, and concerns for institutional growth and/or survival are among the issues that have sparked renewed interest in distance education through the 1980s and into the 1990s. Factors of schedule conflicts, costs, family responsibility, and professional commitments have encouraged the development of distance education options, especially as adult students are less willing to be uprooted from their jobs or families for extended periods.[38]

These realities made online education an ideal medium for theological schools to deliver content, but would online courses and programs receive ATS approval?

In 1999, The Association of Theological Schools granted approval to two schools to offer MA degrees mostly online. After the initial experiment, the floodgates were opened, and theological schools moved quickly toward Internet course offerings:

> The first mostly online MDiv (limited to two- thirds of the degree) was not approved until 2002, but the online trickle quickly became a strong stream, if not a flood. Between 2002 and 2007, some 70 schools began offering online courses—roughly a fourth of the membership. Between 2007 and 2012, another 40 schools went online for a total of 110, with 85 of them (a third of the members) offering courses online on a regular basis.[39]

---

38. Cannell, "Review," 6.
39. Tanner, "Online Learning at ATS Schools: Part 1," 1.

In order to study the effectiveness of online education and given the rapid uptake of Internet learning in higher education generally, the ATS received funding to assist member schools in embracing online learning:

> In 2014, Lilly Endowment, recognizing the rapidly changing face of higher education in general and theological education in particular, gave a grant to the ATS to assess current and developing educational models and practices among ATS member schools, identify their most promising aspects, and assist member schools in implementing new and innovative models.[40]

In a 2017 report from the director of Accreditation and Institutional Evaluation at ATS, Tom Tanner describes the speed with which ATS institutions shifted their educational locus toward online courses. He suggests:

> The pivot point in the Association's online history came in 2012, when the standards were revised to allow more online learning. That revision . . . eliminated the residency requirement for academic MA degrees and reduced the residency requirement for MDiv and professional MA degrees, including an option for an exception that permitted those degrees to be offered completely online. The very first completely online MDiv and professional MA programs were not approved until August 2013.[41]

The push toward integrating more Internet courses allowed schools to reach more students and showed an increasing appetite for this mode of education. Tanner writes, "Today, nearly two-thirds of our 273 member schools have online offerings. More than half have substantive online offerings, and more than a fourth offer entire degrees completely online."[42] The virtual genie has been let out of the bottle and there is no going back. In looking forward, Tanner sees this mode of education only growing:

> The Association's history of growth with online learning appears poised to continue for some time. As just noted, seminary online enrollment (i.e., those taking at least one course online) has mushroomed from zero students 20 years ago, to nearly 8,000 students 10 years ago, to 14,000 five years ago, to more than 23,000 students today. If recent trends continue, *a majority of ATS students may be enrolled online within a few years*; one-third already are (vs. one-tenth 10 years ago). What is even more striking about our recent

40. Miller and Scharen, "(Not) Being There," 18.
41. Tanner, "Online Learning at ATS Schools: Part 1," 1.
42. Tanner, "Online Learning at ATS Schools: Part 1," 1.

history is that during the last decade, when overall ATS enrollment declined by 11%, ATS online enrollment grew by 195%.[43]

Since ATS schools have largely embraced this medium of course delivery there must be advantages when compared to in-class courses. Along with advantages, there are deficiencies. Both will be examined in greater detail in the following section.

The Strengths and Deficiencies of Online Theological Education

Online education is defined in a myriad of ways, but Canadian educator who has published extensively about online education D. Randy Garrison provides one of the most helpful descriptions of what he calls e-learning. He defines it as follows: "E-learning is formally defined as electronically mediated asynchronous and synchronous communication for the purpose of constructing and confirming knowledge."[44] Through the course of this book, the terms "online," "Internet," and "Web-based" when coupled with terms such as "learning," or education" will be used interchangeably and in keeping with Garrison's definition of e-Learning. The term "learning management system (LMS)" will be used to describe software applications used by schools to deliver online education.

The rise in online learning has been accompanied by a growing body of research into its educational effectiveness. In order to explore how character virtues and self-differentiation can be taught using an online medium, it is important to first explore the strengths and deficiencies of the medium for education in general as well as looking at the strengths and deficiencies of online *theological* education specifically.

The Strengths of Online Learning

There are a variety of reasons why higher education institutions are generally positive and find online learning attractive. Linda Cannell found that schools have a number of reasons for optimism. Summarizing her findings, she describes the following:

> Distance education, and its accompanying technology, is attractive
> to higher education because it seems to address the challenges of

43. Tanner, "Online Learning at ATS Schools: Part 1," 2.

44. Garrison, *E-Learning in the 21st Century*, 2.

declining enrollments, increasing costs, the potential market of adult professionals, pressure from corporations, institutional competition for faculty or increased sharing of faculty, and increasing global access to technology.[45]

While these are reasons to celebrate within the administrations of higher education institutions, what about student experiences? Does Internet education offer a high-quality learning environment for students? Does online learning allow for creative and critical engagement with learning material? The answers to these questions appear to be, "yes."

Online education practitioners Anderson, Archer, and Garrison have done extensive research into the use of the Internet for the delivery of education. They have developed a compelling model for online education called the Community of Inquiry (COI).[46] It integrates cognitive and social learning elements using a three-fold method of ensuring social presence (peer-to-peer interaction), cognitive presence (individual thought process), and teacher presence (teacher-student interaction) are maintained in an online educational experience. In considering the strengths of online education their research and findings are important.

Research indicates that the loss of traditional community dynamics allows for enhancements in areas such as creativity and critical thinking. Garrison, Anderson, and Archer suggest that the online setting appears to offer an advantage over face-to-face learning in sourcing material and generating solutions.

> Newman, Webb and Cochrane (1997) found significant differences between computer conference and face-to-face seminars in critical thinking. More specifically, computer- conferencing students more often brought in outside material and linked ideas to solutions while face-to-face students were slightly better at generating new ideas. Consistent with this finding, computer-conferencing students were found to be less interactive. Students said less but the level of critical thinking was higher.[47]

Beyond an enhanced ability to draw in external resources and heightened levels of critical thinking, there are additional advantages offered by an online medium that are not available in a traditional classroom. In the digital world, for example, time becomes flexible, learning resources can

45. Cannell, "Review," 6.

46. See Garrison et al., "Critical Inquiry."

47. Garrison et al., "Critical Inquiry," 93.

be accessed quickly and easily, and various learning formats can be used to suit student and teacher needs. Terry Anderson lists these and other features of Internet learning:

> The most compelling feature of [the online] context is the capacity for shifting the time and place of the educational interaction. Next comes the ability to support content encapsulated in many formats, including multimedia, immersive environments, video, and text, which gives access to learning content that exploits all media attributes. Third, the capacity of the Net to access huge repositories of content on every conceivable subject—including content created by the teacher and fellow students—creates learning and study resources previously available only in the largest research libraries, but now accessible in almost every home and workplace. Finally, the capacity to support human and machine interaction in a variety of formats (ie. text, speech, video, and so on), in both asynchronous and synchronous modalities, creates a communications-rich learning context.[48]

Randy Garrison describes one of the greatest advantages of online coursework: the value of written work for yielding thoughtful and critical reflection on ideas. He writes:

> There is sufficient evidence to suggest that writing has some inherent and demonstrable advantages over speech when engaged in critical discourse and reflection. One obvious advantage is the permanent record afforded teachers and researchers. This, of course, contrasts with the ephemeral nature of discussions in face-to-face classroom environments. Furthermore, face-to-face conversation is generally less systematic, more exploratory, and less attentive to others' views.[49]

In addition to a permanent, well-organized record of learning and a seemingly greater attention to others' views, communicating ideas and thoughts using the written word, something inherent in e-learning, also appears to enhance learning and communication. Garrison argues:

> Text-based communication provides time for reflection. For this reason, written communication may actually be preferable to oral communication when the objective is higher-order cognitive learning. Some of the literature does, in fact, suggest that written

48. Anderson, "Teaching," 344.
49. Garrison, E-Learning in the 21st Century, 16.

communication is very closely connected with careful and critical thinking (Applebee, 1984; Fulwiler, 1987; White, 1993). These authors suggest that it is the reflective and explicit nature of the written word that encourages discipline and rigor in our thinking and communicating.[50]

While written communication and its results are clearly a boon for online education, education based on writing alone misses critical tools. The social aspects are also important. Can the Internet offer a social "place" where students and teachers can experience community together? Thomas Hawkins offers an insightful perspective on Internet community:

> Can community really exist if we are not face-to-face in a classroom? Is community possible in a virtual environment? The ancient Greeks had two words for "place": *topos* and *chora*. *Topos* referred to physical location or the actual geographic features of a place. *Chora,* on the other hand, was an older term that described more the subjective meaning or "feel" of a place. According to Plato, *chora* unifies the physical and moral. It captures the sensuousness and energy of a place. Plato believed that *chora* could be known only through myth and story, not through pure reason.[51]

Social Media demonstrate that community can exist through written interactions online. How does this happen in the absence of so many non-verbal cues? Offline, people use vocal inflections, facial expressions, and hand gestures to communicate. Can this sort of communication happen in text? Randy Garrison suggests that it can. He writes, ". . . students can and do overcome the lack of non-verbal communication by establishing familiarity through the use of greetings, encouragement, paralinguistic emphasis (e.g., capitals, punctuation, emoticons), and personal vignettes."[52] Garrison, Anderson, and Archer also describe the way non-verbal communication can enhance social presence online for groups that never meet face-to-face. "The lack of visual cues may present particular challenges to establishing social presence. However, Kuehn (1993) and Walther (1994) describe how participants develop techniques, such as the use of emoticons or other unconventional symbolic displays, to add affective components to computer-mediated dialogue."[53]

50. Garrison et al., "Critical Inquiry," 90.
51. Hawkins, "From the 3r's to the 3w's," 175.
52. Garrison, *E-Learning in the 21st Century*, 32.
53. Garrison et al., "Critical Inquiry," 95.

In addition to offering creative ways of using a written medium to provide social cues, Internet courses act as a place where students are able to participate equally, without discrimination based on personality traits. Whereas a classroom may favour students who are more vocal, online classes gives everyone a space to be heard. Anita Louisa Cloete describes heightened participation writing thus: "Classroom-based education often provides a forum for extrovert learners to participate, while introverts find it difficult to participate, resulting in difficulty in allocating marks for participation. Online education, however, provides an environment where all and often marginalised voices could be heard, contributing to a higher participation of students as well as collaborative learning."[54]

While these examples are common to Internet education generally, there are strengths for theological schools specifically. It is to these aspects we now turn.

The Strengths of Online Learning for Theological Schools

Theological schools have been facing difficult days. With fewer students considering vocational ministry and a societal turn toward higher education as a vehicle to employment, schools have been suffering. Internet based learning, however, has provided a light in the darkness through increasing enrollment for schools. In their 2017 report on the state of online education in ATS institutions, Miller and Scharen describe the uptick in new students registering for online courses: "For schools that are heavily tuition driven, the pursuit and retention of students is a never-ending quest and, just as extension sites once held out the promise of expanding enrollment, online courses and degrees appear to be a boon for admissions officers."[55] Echoing those same sentiments, Tom Tanner writes, "To be sure, going online is no guarantee of enrollment growth, but it clearly seems to increase the odds."[56]

While enrollment appeared on a list of biggest benefits, it was not top of the list for Academic Deans. According to a 2016 Association of Theological Schools survey of Academic Deans:

> Among the biggest benefits of online education, these were the top five responses: (1) 99% said it gives students more flexibility,

54. Cloete, "Technology and Education," 5
55. Miller and Scharen, "(Not) Being There," 22.
56. Tanner, "Online Learning at ATS Schools: Part 1," 2.

(2) 81% said it reaches more students, (3) 66% said it helps students learn in their own contexts, (4) 46% said it helps reduce the cost for students, and (5) 45% said it enhances the school's global outreach. The lowest rated benefit was 'helps reduce costs for the school,' chosen by only 14% of the respondents. That is consistent with the comments noted above about cost savings being more for students than for institutions. Among the dozen or so open-ended comments submitted, about half highlighted the increased accessibility provided by online learning, and about half highlighted the improvement in learning that occurs online. As one respondent noted, teaching online "helps faculty members think through their educational goals and processes," with another adding "it increases student engagement in the course."[57]

Online education allows students the flexibility to live far from school yet still enjoy the benefits of learning from their choice of theological school. Students at a distance are not the only ones taking advantage of online courses. Internet education has opened up more choices and options for all students. Flexibility, especially for students with families, is a main advantage. Miller and Scharen describe the shift online:

> Offering courses online is another way to meet students' needs. Some schools developed such options intentionally for students who live far from campus only to find that residential students were also eager to avail themselves of this option because of work conflicts or family needs. On some campuses, the majority of students enrolled in online classes in fact live locally.[58]

Online education allows students across the country more choices, but it also opens the learning doors to students from around the world. In this way, Miller and Scharen see the democratization of theological education as another benefit. "How many committed, talented individuals feel called to ministry and yet have, in years past, been stymied by where they live and their limited financial means? Clearly, online programs democratize theological education, much as the printing press democratized Luther's writings in sixteenth-century Germany."[59]

In addition to the benefit of bridging the geographic distance, online theological education appears to be a more cost-effective way of educating.

---

57. Tanner, "Online Learning at ATS Schools: Part 2," 3.

58. Miller and Scharen, "(Not) Being There," 22.

59. Miller and Scharen, "(Not) Being There," 23.

This is not so much about the learning management system reducing the costs associated with consumables and physical space and more about sheer numbers of students that enroll in an online course. "Almost one-third of respondents (30%) to the ATS deans' survey had looked at the cost-effectiveness of their online courses or programs, and 46% said that a clear benefit of online education was helping to reduce the cost for students."[60]

A central component of preparation for pastoral ministry has been the requirement for residential education. That expectation has meant that students have lived in a campus based residential community. According to Miller and Sharen's report, that might not be the best educational paradigm:

> There are a growing number of people in theological education who believe that training for ministry is more effective if students remain in their context (i.e., not uprooting them to move to a residential campus or to take classes in a traditional classroom). Two-thirds of deans on the ATS deans' survey said that online education helped students learn in their own context. There is no question that better integration between classes and the "real world" happens more quickly and more organically if students remain in their context.[61]

The Deficiencies of Online Learning

While the benefits of learning online are clear, not everyone agrees that Internet education is as helpful as it has been described. The following research highlights the challenges that schools face in offering Internet courses and programs.

A general concern is that the online medium promotes inequality in education. Martha McCormick raises an alarm about the potential colonial-ization that occurs when students learn online. She writes, "I am concerned that the relationship between the Internet (as a technology of information) and diverse cultures is a colonizing one. I believe there are inconsistencies between the insights of postcolonialism and the Internet, so highly and yet often mistakenly praised as a great equalizer."[62] She points to the source of online education boundaries and questions the conventions and habits that are being promoted as being colonializing at their core:

60. Miller and Scharen, "(Not) Being There," 23.

61. Miller and Scharen, "(Not) Being There," 23.

62. McCormick, "Webmastered," 76.

My challenge to internet culture resides in the fact that Internet users are so willing to abide by regulations whose source can never be clearly located and whose values go unquestioned, and they are also so willing to punish rogue users who commit infractions against administrative apparatuses that are manifestations of deep-seated linguistic and cultural conventions and habits. This trend bears an uncomfortable resemblance to the heyday of colonialism, in which colonialist power was actually consolidated by everyday folks under the guise, for example, of giving the "natives" a proper English education.[63]

Echoing similar concerns about the potential for colonialization, O'Sullivan and Palaskas write, "Information and communication technologies (ICTs) tend to increase gaps in power and wealth, allowing those in certain groups to strengthen their control over others. In this way, it is possible to marginalize communities as opposed to empowering them."[64]

Aside from "cultural conventions and habits" that reside in the online medium there are also obstacles when students are largely anonymous. In a traditional educational setting, students show up to participate in class and write exams. In an online context, there is no guarantee that the registered student is the one showing up and doing the work. This is a significant issue for Massive Open Online Courses (MOOCs). MOOCs are exactly as their title describes: their enrollment can be in the millions, they are open source, and online. There are numerous challenges for schools producing MOOCs but one issue of relevance is the possibility of MOOCs being used to nurture character virtues. Pike and Gore assert that these courses are contexts where rates of dishonesty and a lack of stick-to-it-iveness among students is high. They describe MOOCs as a challenged medium for quality educational experiences:

Despite the large investment in MOOCs and their platforms by the various providers, MOOCs have not yet evolved enough to provide a number of important pedagogical elements, including thorough peer assessment methodologies and tools for dealing with plagiarism and online cheating. In addition, MOOC platforms have generally failed to provide high, stabilised retention rates, robust business models, resoundingly engaging learning design or presentation without technical difficulty.[65]

63. McCormick, "Webmastered," 86.
64. O'Sullivan and Palaskas, "The Political Economy," 45.
65. Pike and Gore, "The Challenges," 154.

MOOCs appear to fail when it comes to student retention: "One of the largest challenges facing MOOCs is undoubtedly engagement, with poor engagement undoubtedly contributing to poor completion rates."[66] Interpersonal connection is important in classroom settings but all the more in e-learning contexts. When student engagement is lacking online, learners become isolated. Marjorie Kibby highlights social isolation and other drawbacks of online education:

> The drawbacks of online learning have been extensively discussed and include the social isolation which students feel without face-to-face contact with tutors and other students; bandwidth, browser and software limitations which can restrict instructional methods, and increase student frustration; the costs that may be involved in server access, downloading and printing; the constraints on providing valid and reliable assessment; and the need for students to be self-motivated and self-directed.[67]

The technological limitations and accompanying frustrations from slow Internet connections and video lags are no secret. Everyone has experienced the irritation from technological glitches. Anecdotally, during a meeting with my doctoral supervisory committee to defend my thesis proposal, which happened to be the initial stage of writing this book, three of us attempted to connect in Toronto with my supervisor who was in Australia. The connection was poor and as a result my supervisor was unable to facilitate the meeting. The other committee members were required to carry on the meeting and near the end of our time, the connection improved. When it comes to Internet learning, the best pedagogical plans can be cut off at the knees by a bad connection. Nevertheless, online courses that integrate synchronous video connections provide a great deal more than those that are exclusively text based. Garrison, Anderson, and Archer highlight the face-to-face oral communication medium as 'rich'. While they see critical thinking happening best outside an oral context, they do note the value of paralinguistic cues as being important to oral communication. They write, "Oral communication in a face-to-face context provides multiple non-verbal or paralinguistic cues such as facial expression and tone of voice. Socially and emotionally, face-to-face oral communication is a rich medium."[68]

---

66. Pike and Gore, "The Challenges," 156.
67. Kibby, "Hybrid Teaching," 87.
68. Garrison et al., "Critical Inquiry," 90.

When the online connection deteriorates the medium shifts from 'rich' to 'poor' and that can only be considered a deficiency in learning.

The Deficiencies of Online Learning for Theological Schools

Since I have been identifying some deficiencies of online education generally, it's important to look at online theological education specifically. Most issues raised appear to be common to all online educators and not specifically theological. There are, however, concerns that are unique to theological educators such as whether or not the medium can be used to nurture spiritual formation in students. While there are a number of articles written about facilitating spiritual formation online, there is nothing written about how learning management systems can be used to cultivate virtue in pastors. Instead, most of the research is focused on social and cognitive aspects of e-learning. What follows is an overview.

In an article by then director of Accreditation at ATS, Tom Tanner identifies five issues facing online theological education:

> Among the chief challenges of online education, these were the top five: (1) 60% cited training faculty to teach online, (2) 56% cited incorporating good instructional design, (3) 51% cited doing formation online, and (4/5) 34% cited "building relationships" and "addressing the technology have's and have not's." Tied for last (with only 20% citing) were "getting faculty acceptance" and "school's ability to afford the technology needed." Among 18 open-ended comments, concerns varied widely, but faculty training and suitability of the online format for certain students or courses were cited by about half.[69]

According to the Association of Theological Schools' survey of deans, there are a number of reasons for faculty reluctance to embrace online teaching:

> Faculty at some schools view online teaching with great distrust and apprehension. Other schools find faculty divided between those eager to board and those who are reluctant to set foot on the train. Their reasons vary from the practical ("I don't know how to do it") to the pedagogical ("How can I teach X to students who are not sitting in my classroom?") to personal ("I don't have time") to

69. Tanner, "Online Learning at ATS Schools: Part 2," 4.

institutional ("We don't have the resources") to the social ("How can we form community if students aren't on campus?").[70]

While having to learn new ways of teaching online is a concern for faculty, the quality of relationships with students is another. One of the important components of residential models of theological education is the mentoring that happens between teachers and students. This is more than conversation between two parties. It entails embodied experiences where one learns from the other. Edwin Chr. van Driel, Professor of Theology at Pittsburgh Theological Seminary questions the ability of theological schools to offer this sort of learning using Internet courses:

> If education is understood as a form of apprenticeship in which the students learn by imitating the master craftsman, one has to ask to what degree this form of education is compatible with on-line delivery. Apprenticeship presupposes a "thick" relationship. The apprentice follows the craftswoman around. He does not just receive formal instruction, but he observes the craftswoman at work and joins in. The question is *whether* in an online environment the relationship between teachers and learners can be thick enough for apprenticeship to flourish.[71]

Van Driel highlights another consideration for a medium that leaves the campus behind. He raises questions about broadening student exposure to ecclesial differences. Most denominations ordain clergy to function as part of the broader church rather than one specific congregation. The residential theological school has provided a means by which students with minimal exposure to churches outside their own are given a wide exposure in their residency and chapel experiences in seminary. Van Driel sees this broader exposure as difficult to replicate online.

> Traditionally, residential seminaries function as the community where candidates for ministry are ecclesially formed in an awareness of their place in the wider church. Students who may know only one, or a few, local congregations are brought together with fellow ordination candidates rooted in very different locations— geographically, socioeconomically, racially, culturally, and theologically. By going to chapel together, eating in the common room, living communally in the dorms, joining in family play dates, and sharing personal joys and woes, these students learn what it will

---

70. Miller and Scharen, "(Not) Being There," 27.
71. van Driel, "Online Theological Education," 72.

mean to serve together in one church. In that sense, the formative nature of the residential campus is a holistic experience. Students are not just ecclesially formed by what happens in the classroom but also, and maybe equally importantly, in the relationships that are being formed in the communal life on campus.[72]

Philosopher Hubert Dreyfus outlines a variety of challenges with Internet learning and apprenticeship.[73] In chapter 3, a thorough description of Hubert Dreyfus's criticisms of online learning will be explored. For now, it is enough to introduce Professor of Media Studies, Charles Ess as he draws on Dreyfus' concern with the inability of the online platform to effectively provide a central element of liberal arts education: "I concur with Dreyfus' argument that distance education cannot achieve the highest goals of liberal arts learning—specifically, Aristotle's phronesis or practical wisdom."[74] For Ess and Dreyfus the Internet does not provide an avenue for virtue formation in learners, a theme that will be explored deeply in chapter 4. Since virtue formation is central to liberal arts learning and theological education, to neglect the formation of the soul in virtue is to focus education on peripheral learning rather than what Ess calls "a specific theme" that is foundational to education: "I want to lift up a specific theme in Socrates' teaching as a foundational element of liberal learning: namely, the recognition that the pursuit of human excellence (*aretē*) or virtue must always come first."[75]

The Place and Role of Online Theological Education in ATS Accredited Institutions

In his 2017 article focused on online learning at ATS schools, Tom Tanner describes the survey results from theological schools, revealing the significant span of e-learning:

> Almost half (45%) of the respondents *offer degrees that are either completely or mostly online.* The most frequent programs offered completely online are the academic MA (28%), the professional MA (13%), and the MDiv (12%). The most frequent programs offered mostly online are the professional MA (35%), the MDiv (31%), and the academic MA (21%). A handful of schools also

72. van Driel, "Online Theological Education," 77.

73. See, for example, Dreyfus, *On the Internet.*

74. Ess, "Liberal Arts," 118.

75. Ess, "Liberal Arts," 120.

offer other degrees completely or almost completely online, e.g., the DMin, ThM, and PhD.[76]

An article published in 2019 by ATS' Director of Research and Faculty Development states, "As of this year, 163 (62%) ATS schools are approved to offer distance education."[77] Clearly, online education has gained a foothold in the majority of accredited theological schools. The question is no longer about whether this format should be accredited. Rather, the most relevant question is whether virtue and self-differentiation can be taught using this format. If so, to what extent?

With ATS endorsing and encouraging schools to further embrace online learning there is an unaddressed gap. The gap is in the area of "formation." ATS has clear definitions around academic requirements for accreditation, as noted earlier in this chapter. However, when it comes to formation, the ATS has determined to let individual schools define it for themselves. Eliza Brown was part of an ATS group researching how spiritual formation looks in an online course or program. She describes the process of an ATS committee letting go of standardizing formation and leaving this in the hands of schools:

> Among the most daunting challenges is how formation is defined and measured in an online learning environment. The peer group's consensus is that formation must be defined for each school according to its mission and the goals for each particular degree program. The group is identifying tools and processes for schools to use in measuring formation, which it will assess and present as part of its final report.[78]

Perhaps spiritual formation, with its focus on nurturing virtue and identity development, is seen as less important than the cognitive and academic elements that have standardized assessments. Not so says Deborah Gin, an ATS representative. She writes, "In many ways, formation is central to theological education. While it is true that schools define formation differently—based on ecclesial, theological, or cultural context—the development of mind, heart, character, spirituality, habits, and skills within community is at the core of theological education."[79] If this is the case then should there

---

76. Tanner, "Online Learning at ATS Schools: Part 2," 2.

77. Gin et al., "Forum," 74.

78. Smith Brown, "Accessible, Effective," 3.

79. Gin et al., "Forum," 73.

not be a way to assess whether someone is growing and maturing in their formation? It seems odd that schools and even individual instructors are left to operate with their own definitions of formation, while that same ambiguity would not be permitted to define what distinguishes academic excellence from mediocrity.

ATS' hands-off posture regarding spiritual formation allows scholars and academic administrators to define formation in a variety of ways, allowing for definitions that do not include virtue or the development of a healthy sense of self-differentiation. Therefore, the literature on Internet based spiritual formation does not rely on common metrics. Diane Hockridge summarizes this finding when she writes, "It appears that the term 'formation', while frequently used both in theological education literature and in everyday theological language, remains variously understood and variously practised within the theological education sector."[80] This leads to significant variance in definitions of formation. For example, Roman Catholic priests follow the *Program of Priestly Formation*, which states:

> Formation, as the Church understands it, is not equivalent to a secular sense of schooling or, even less, job training. Formation is first and foremost cooperation with the grace of God. In the United States Conference of Catholic Bishops' document *The Basic Plan for the Ongoing Formation of Priests*, a reflection on St. Paul's words in 2 Corinthians 3:17-18 leads to a description of formation. "The apostle Paul marvels at the work of the Holy Spirit who transforms believers into the very image of Jesus Christ, who himself is the image of God. This grace of the new covenant embraces all who have joined themselves to Jesus Christ in faith and baptism. Indeed, it is sheer grace, all God's doing. Moved by that grace, however, we make ourselves available to God's work of transformation. And that making ready a place for the Lord to dwell in us and transform us we call formation."[81]

Alternatively, G. Brooke Lester, a professor at Garrett Evangelical Theological Seminary, focuses on formation from a constructivist perspective. He describes formation as a synthesis of prior experiences with new insights. He states, "In any formational encounter, a learner is not only arriving at understandings, knowledge, and skills, but on the way towards that is also and necessarily being 'on-boarded' into some community. Formation, then,

---

80. Hockridge, "What's the Problem," 27.

81. United States, *Program*, 28.

always involves transformation towards community."[82] This definition incorporates a social aspect but says very little about the sort of community that individuals are being transformed towards. It may or may not involve a movement toward the virtues of love or generosity. Likewise, nothing is stated about shaping one's identity apart from the community, as self-differentiation necessitates.

With such varied understandings of formation, it appears nearly impossible for theological schools to purposefully build toward a goal and have accountability for accomplishing that goal, even if it is something as foundational as virtue and self-differentiation.

82. Gin et al., "Forum," 78.

2

The Internet and Education
The Use of Technology and Its Effects on Learning

TECHNOLOGY IN EDUCATION: A NEUTRAL TOOL OR ACTIVE AGENT?

THEOLOGICAL EDUCATORS HAVE PUBLISHED very little research studying the impacts of Internet technology on student formation.[1] Instead, they have focused for the most part on finding the best ways to leverage technologies to reach and teach students online. In the process they have neglected to ask a simple question: how might technology itself affect student formation? For institutions that value pastoral skill development and virtue formation, in addition to academic excellence, the unasked question seems like a glaring omission. The most obvious reason for its absence is that technology is viewed as a neutral educational tool. Learning management systems and the gadgets used to connect students and teachers in virtual classrooms are but another pedagogical development to assist educators. Except, what if these pedagogical developments create subtle, undetected changes for teachers and learners? This chapter will aim to show that technology is not a neutral tool to be used by a teacher to accomplish the same ends as a face-to-face context like a classroom. Rather, technology influences the teacher, students, and learning content in surprising ways. I will argue that digital devices, and their accompanying ways of operating, can be experienced similarly to that

1. Three exceptions are Kelsey, "Spiritual Machines," Ellingsen, "Neurobiological Data," and van Driel, "Online Theological Education."

of the interaction one has with a person. The experience with technology itself shapes social behaviors and ways of thinking.

Technology as Non-Neutral

As described in chapter 1, most proponents of online education see technology as just another pedagogical apparatus. Some appreciate it, others do not. Regardless of their comfort with it, most e-learning technologists believe that digital instruments function as neutral pedagogical devices.[2] Others, like Martin Heidegger, view technology as having agency and life-like qualities. Heidegger writes, "Everywhere we remain unfree and chained to technology, whether we passionately affirm or deny it. But we are delivered over to it in the worst possible way when we regard it as something neutral."[3] Heidegger, writing in a pre-cell phone age, saw the essence of modern technology as a "challenging revealing." In his book, *The Question Concerning Technology and Other Essays*, he describes the danger of modern technology: "Under the dominion of this challenging revealing, nothing is allowed to appear as it is in itself."[4] This chapter will extend Heidegger's idea that modern technological instruments are non-neutral to include computers and digital media. His insights, as well as the insights of others, have important implications for human "being" in light of the increasing demand for online course delivery in theological education.

Heather Kanuka provides some help to explore concepts related to modern machinery and devices. She offers a framework by which to categorize perspectives on technology. She highlights three views of technology and human engagement:

> The first position is referred to as *uses determinism*. This view pertains to the instrumental uses of technological artefacts and, correspondingly, the uses effects on technological artefacts and society. The second position is referred to as *technological determinism*. This view focuses on the forms and effects that technological artefacts have on uses and society. The third position is referred to as *social determinism*. This view asserts that social contexts and cultures affect forms and uses of technological artefacts.[5]

2. See Dahlberg, "Internet Research" and Kanuka, "Understanding E-Learning," 96.
3. Heidegger, *The Question Concerning Technology*, 4.
4. Heidegger, *The Question Concerning Technology*, xxix.
5. Kanuka, "Understanding E-Learning," 95–96.

As noted above, most online educators, the ones that see technology as a neutral tool, fall into the category of *uses determinism*. This position sees technology as an implement in the hands of human beings or, more specifically, as an instrument to be used by educators focused on examining ways to use digital tools to enhance learning. This is the bent of most journal articles focused on helping educators navigate the world of online learning. The nexus of this chapter, however, will be on highlighting Kanuka's second position, the forms and effects that technological artefacts have on uses and society. This perspective views technology as a shaper of humanity and human systems. It is held by several scholars, one of the most prominent being Marshall McLuhan. Addressing the ways media shape culture, he writes, "All media work us over completely. They are so pervasive in their personal, political, economic, aesthetic, psychological, moral, ethical, and social consequences that they leave no part of us untouched, unaffected, unaltered. The medium is the massage."[6] Arguing that technology plays a central role in human and societal development has a profound impact in an increasingly interconnected world. If technology is seen, not simply as a useful tool for shaping human thinking and acting, but as something that "works us over completely" as McLuhan says, theological educators should exercise vigilance. Given that theological education has traditionally focused on forming the identity and character of pastoral students, if the medium itself is teaching students, then it is important to understand what sort of shaping results from technology's influence in online theological education. To begin, it will be helpful to explore the human-computer relationship.

The Human-Computer Relationship

In the mid-1960's, MIT professor Joseph Weizenbaum composed a computer program that allowed a person to type a portion of a conversation into a computer and the computer would generate a response. He stumbled into findings that shocked him. Having programmed the computer to function based on Rogerian psychotherapy, he found that users related to his computer, called DOCTOR, as if it were human rather than a computer. He writes:

> I was startled to see how quickly and how very deeply people conversing with DOCTOR became emotionally involved with

6. McLuhan and Fiore, *The Medium Is the Massage*, 26.

the computer and how unequivocally they anthropomorphized it. Once my secretary, who had watched me work on the program for many months and therefore surely knew it to be merely a computer program, started conversing with it. After only a few interchanges with it, she asked me to leave the room. . . . people were conversing with the computer as if it were a person who could be appropriately and usefully addressed in intimate terms.[7]

Based on his observations of human interactions with his computer, Weizenbaum concludes:

What I had not realized is that extremely short exposures to a relatively simple computer program could induce powerful delusional thinking in quite normal people. This insight led me to attach new importance to questions of the relationship between the individual and the computer, and hence to resolve to think about them.[8]

Weizenbaum came to the realization that technology shapes human beings even when that outcome is not programmed into the system. The human-computer relationship takes on a life of its own. As a person discloses thoughts and asks questions to certain machines, the machine's response alters the person and causes them to become more deeply connected and related to it. If one computer, programmed to use Rogerian psychotherapy, could induce a feeling of intimacy toward a machine in a person, what about all the other technological devices running in society? Weizenbaum writes:

Many machines are automatic in the sense that, once they are turned on, they may run by themselves for long periods of time. But most automatic machines have to be set to their task and subsequently steered or regulated by sensors or by human drivers. An autonomous machine is one that, once started, runs by itself on the basis of an internalized model of some aspect of the real world. Clocks are fundamentally models of the planetary system. They are the first autonomous machines built by man, and until the advent of the computer they remained the only truly important ones.[9]

Weizenbaum's example of the clock highlights an important aspect of human relationships as they pertain to things we create. We create technological devices to function in certain ways in order to make our lives easier or more efficient. However, we also become bound to them and shaped by

7. Weizenbaum, *Computer Power and Human Reason*, 6–7.

8. Weizenbaum, *Computer Power and Human Reason*, 7.

9. Weizenbaum, *Computer Power and Human Reason*, 24.

them. Weizenbaum's clock reference is a nod to philosopher Lewis Mumford, who had earlier laid a philosophical foundation. In his book *Technics and Civilization*, Mumford described the clock as "... the foremost machine in modern technics . . . it marks a perfection toward which other machines aspire."[10] Neil Postman also draws on Lewis Mumford's clock musings to describe the way a piece of machinery changes human perception of the world. Picking up on Mumford's description of how the clock's role creates the concept 'moment to moment', Postman highlights something Mumford observed in *Technics and Civilization*:

> "The clock," Mumford has concluded, "is a piece of power machinery whose 'product' is seconds and minutes." In manufacturing such a product, the clock has the effect of disassociating time from human events and thus nourishes the belief in an independent world of mathematically measurable sequences. Moment to moment, it turns out, is not God's conception, or nature's. It is man conversing with himself about and through a piece of machinery he created.[11]

Creating the clock meant that human beings could be in relationship, and be formed by that relationship, with a machine. In some ways it allowed more precise measurements and data to be used and collected to increase societal efficiency. In other ways it allowed for a dependency on the machine to supply something to society. Life became more oriented around and ordered by the technology. This ordering caused humans to learn new ways of using technology to further industrialize the world thus further ordering human societies around those technologies. Heidegger writes about this ordering in *The Question Concerning Technology and Other Essays*. Using forceful terms like "setting-upon" and "challenging-forth," he describes how nature became a tool in the hands of humanity. Depicting the human-technology relationship, he references a hydroelectric dam 'set upon' the Rhine River to 'challenge-forth' unseen energy:

> That challenging happens in that the energy concealed in nature is unlocked, what is unlocked is transformed, what is transformed is stored up, what is stored up is, in turn, distributed, and what is

10. Mumford, *Technics and Civilization*, 15.

11. Postman, *Amusing Ourselves*, 11. Postman references Mumford's *Technics and Civilization* but does not cite the page number. The actual reference for Postman's quotation is Mumford, *Technics and Civilization*, 15.

distributed is switched about ever anew. Unlocking, transforming, sorting, distributing, and switching about are ways of revealing.[12]

He goes on to describe what happens when technology is used to order creation, "the setting-upon that challenges forth thrusts man into a relation to that which is, that is at once antithetical and rigorously ordered."[13] This ordering is a distortion of nature. Technology, therefore, is changing the river and revealing something new but what is revealed is unnatural. Elsewhere, Heidegger describes the setting upon that challenges forth as an "expediting." "It expedites in that it unlocks and exposes. Yet that expediting is always itself directed from the beginning toward furthering something else, i.e., toward driving on to the maximum yield at the minimum expense."[14] This revealing, focused on "furthering something else," stands in stark contrast to Heidegger's revealing of another kind: "*poiēsis*, which lets what presences come forth into appearance."[15] For Heidegger, technology reorders creation toward certain ends, including humanity and human societies, which in turn changes the essence of being, including human being. Technology alters humans in ways that cause us to function more like the technology and less like creative, wise beings. As relational ties between humans and technology strengthen, our natural ways of being human change. Weizenbaum, like Heidegger, describes the interaction of humans with technology as a movement toward making people more machine-like:

> "The scientific man has above all things to strive at self-elimination in his judgments," wrote Karl Pearson in 1892. Of the many scientists I know, only a very few would disagree with that statement. Yet it must be acknowledged that it urges man to strive to become a disembodied intelligence, to himself become an instrument, a machine.[16]

Educator and media theorist Neil Postman suggests that humans are becoming more like machines as the computer is further integrated into society. Of particular significance to online theological education is Postman's suggestion that even spirituality is shaped by the computer. These themes

12. Heidegger, *The Question Concerning Technology*, 16.

13. Heidegger, *The Question Concerning Technology*, 27.

14. Heidegger, *The Question Concerning Technology*, 15.

15. Heidegger, *The Question Concerning Technology*, 27. Heidegger defines *poiēsis* as "a bringing-forth, e.g., the bursting of a blossom into bloom.", 10.

16. Weizenbaum, *Computer Power and Human Reason*, 25–26.

will be explored later in this chapter and at other parts of this book but for now, Postman's portrayal of humanity is revealing:

> The fundamental metaphorical message of the computer, in short, is that we are machines—thinking machines, to be sure, but machines nonetheless. It is for this reason that the computer is the quintessential, incomparable, near-perfect machine for Technopoly. It subordinates the claims of our nature, our biology, our emotions, our spirituality. The computer claims sovereignty over the whole range of human experience, and supports its claim by showing that it "thinks" better than we can.[17]

If, according to Heidegger, human engagement with and use of technology has the power to change the essence of being itself, and if, according to Postman, the computer and its many digital applications are subverting human emotion and spirituality, then why are theological educators so quick to integrate technology in teaching? Perhaps their questions and concerns are focused on the wrong areas.

Learning at the "Hands" of Computers

As noted in the previous chapter, most theological educators and administrators are attuned to enhancing online teaching rather than asking how the platform might be affecting the learner. Encouragement from the Association of Theological Schools for institutions to adopt online education or be left behind makes it difficult to take time for discernment, especially as the ATS continues to find new and creative ways to help schools move in that direction.[18] This push is happening amid limited research into how online learning may be making humans less human. Perhaps the dearth of research is because technology is viewed as a neutral tool. Or, maybe the lack of theological research is due to technology narrowing the field of questions that people think to ask. The data and information collected by computers, smartphones, and tablets are oriented toward certain ends and not others. Therefore, while humans assume greater freedom, given the useful ways computers collect and store information, freedom also means interacting with stored data becomes more and more limited. Brent Waters, author of *From Human to Posthuman*, writes:

17. Postman, *Technopoly*, 111.

18. See, for example, Tanner, "Online Learning at ATS Schools: Part 2." Also, Smith Brown, "Accessible, Effective."

The adage that computers do not impose their ways upon their users is misleading, because it hides an imposing destiny in a guise of instrumental neutrality. By reassuring ourselves that the computer does not impose its ways upon us, we have already succumbed to the imposition of its destiny. The computer, for example, promises greater freedom in creating and organizing data in accordance with our goals and purposes. Yet computers can only be used in a limited number of ways for creating, storing and classifying this information, thereby forming the goals and purposes that it purportedly serves in an instrumental manner. The resulting "freedom" is illusory, because the computer, like any technology, constrains the range of choices its users can make within the limited parameters of its imposed destiny.[19]

Stated another way, Weizenbaum writes:

A computing system that permits the asking of only certain kinds of questions, that accepts only certain kinds of "data," and that cannot even in principle be understood by those who rely on it, such a computing system has effectively closed many doors that were open before it was installed.[20]

Online learning platforms are narrowing the field of creativity and praxis of teaching simply because they accept only certain kinds of inputs and data. What might that mean for teaching and learning in pastoral programs? Internet platforms are not designed to address the emotional and spiritual aspects of a learner's development. However, these are precisely at the core of Christian formation. As learning has shifted toward online environments, theological schools, administrators, and educators have been trying to build the same sort of learning experiences with new tools, hoping the outcomes will be the same. In the meantime, major, yet often unrecognized, shifts have taken place. Whereas teachers used to have the freedom to design courses using creative means such as field trips, retreats, and in-class exercises that involved moving around and interacting, now educators are limited by technology that might mimic some experiences but the experience of learning collectively in one another's presence is lost. Additionally, educational platforms (e.g., Moodle, Google Classroom, Blackboard, etc.) limit the ways students and teachers interact: They restrict nuanced assessment by providing a host of tools to "help" instructors grade submitted

19. Waters, *From Human to Posthuman*, 127.
20. Weizenbaum, *Computer Power and Human Reason*, 38.

work using precise instruments (e.g., online rubrics, etc.), yet those same tools require them to work with the program's narrow design selections. Additionally, online educational platforms can be used to limit learners. Teachers may "mute" students during video class meetings. This is an impossibility in a common physical space inhabited by teacher and students. It would appear as though the tools have become the instructors and the instructor has become a tool. While writing this chapter, I was given the opportunity to teach a graduate course at the University of St. Michael's College via Zoom. Since it was my first time instructing for the school, I was assigned a faculty mentor to act as guide and helper. My mentor had a strong background in online teaching and had much to offer by way of helpful advice. During our meeting he made a surprising comment. He said, "When teaching online, the student's center of attention is not the instructor but Quercus [The University of Toronto's online teaching and learning environment]."[21] In a traditional learning context, the center of a student's attention is the teacher. In an online learning context, students interact almost entirely with the learning platform rather than the teacher. They receive announcements, course information, assignments, and pre-recorded lectures via the educational platform. Course requirements such as forum reflections and assignments get uploaded through the learning platform. Likewise, the teacher interacts more with the learning platform, uploading assignments, lectures, announcements, and grading assignments rather than through direct contact with students.

What happens to student learning and formation when technology becomes the center of the student's attention? It highlights the quotation referenced above by Weizenbaum about technology and elimination of human judgements. For all that the efficiency technology provides, there are downsides. Neil Postman describes what happened in medicine when the stethoscope was invented. This brilliant device allowed physicians to get more accurate diagnoses of people's problems—to hear more clearly what was happening inside the body. However, for all the newfound gains, the invention of the stethoscope changed patient care:

> Imposing an instrument between patient and doctor would transform the practice of medicine; the traditional methods of questioning patients, taking their reports seriously, and making careful observations of exterior symptoms would become increasingly

21. A comment made by Dr. Jean-Pierre Fortin during a Zoom conversation, August 6, 2020.

irrelevant. Doctors would lose their ability to conduct skillful examinations and rely more on machinery than on their own experience and insight.[22]

Postman goes on to suggest that modern physicians have indirect relationships with patients that are predominantly mediated through technical machines. He writes:

> By the turn of the [twentieth] century . . . medical practice had entered a new stage. The first had been characterized by direct communication with the patient's experiences based on the patient's reports, and the doctor's questions and observations. The second was characterized by direct communication with patients' bodies through physical examination, including the use of carefully selected technologies. The stage we are now in is characterized by indirect communication with the patient's experience and body through technical machinery. . . . It is to be expected that, as medical practice moved from one stage to another, doctors tended to lose the skills and insights that predominated in the previous stage.[23]

Few would argue that advances in medical technology, even at the expense of physician skill, is a negative development. However, the decline of experiential or somatic knowledge is worth noting, especially when roles such as that of pastor, which rely on personal experience and knowledge of God as central elements for the work of ministry, are being filled by those educated using an online medium. Could a Web interface such as Quercus act like a stethoscope? Could it open up new ways of learning, yet impede the growth of embodied knowledge that is crucial for clerical ministry? Pastoral work has been traditionally understood in service terms and has required the pastor to be an embodied presence of love and service who communes with God among the people. William H. Willimon, professor, theologian, and United Methodist Church pastor, points to the important role of serving people. He describes the pastoral role in terms of service when he pens these words:

> Those whom we designate as "ministers" are, in the New Testament, *diakonoi*, Paul's favorite title for Christian leaders, derived from the Greek word for "service" (1 Cor. 12:4–30). Significantly,

22. Postman, *Technopoly*, 99.
23. Postman, *Technopoly*, 101.

it is the same word that is the root for "butler" and "waiter," terms that have a greater edge to them than "ministry."[24]

The Roman Catholic standard for ordained ministry highlights embodied presence to an even greater degree. Drawing attention to Jesus Christ as the model, the following is written in the *Program of Priestly Formation*: "Priests are called to prolong the presence of Christ, the One High Priest, embodying his way of life and making him visible in the midst of the flock entrusted to their care."[25] With a shift toward online learning, there is a risk that the embodied skills of pastoral ministry become stifled and even deadened like those of modern day, tech-dependent, physicians. As embodied pastoral skills become dulled and inactive, the vacuum once occupied by somatic pastoral practice, may become filled by something useful but not particularly theological, *viz.*, data.

Divine Data

The pastoral role hinges on being attentive to God and one's congregation members. Yet, advances in technology have facilitated a modern pastoral ministry shift away from direct experience with human beings toward tools and data that keep people interested in and attracted to worship.[26] The tools and data may cede results, such as more people showing up for worship or additional "likes" on a Facebook page, but the outcome is more quantifiable data. This is also the case in educational contexts. Studies showing the effectiveness of online education by, for example, the increase in student enrollment, shows an orientation toward numbers: Students equal numbers and numbers equal data. The reliance on data and numbers, as opposed to valuing human experience and intuition, is addressed by Weizenbaum:

> This rejection of direct experience was to become one of the principal characteristics of modern science. It was imprinted on western European culture not only by the clock but also by the many prosthetic sensing instruments, especially those that

24. Willimon, *Pastor*, 35.

25. United States, *Program of Priestly Formation*, 9.

26. In the introduction to his book, Eugene Peterson describes American pastors as "a company of shopkeepers . . . preoccupied with . . . how to keep customers happy, how to lure customers away from competitors down the street, how to package the goods so that the customers will lay out more money." Instead, Peterson writes, "The pastor's responsibility is to keep the community attentive to God." Peterson, *Working the Angles*, 2.

reported on the phenomena they were set to monitor by means of pointers whose positions were ultimately translated into numbers. Gradually, at first, then ever more rapidly and, it is fair to say, ever more compulsively, experiences of reality had to be representable as numbers in order to appear legitimate in the eyes of common wisdom.[27]

Numbers do add legitimacy, but they also shift the focus away from humanity and the essence of embodied life toward economic considerations. Robert Tilley, a lecturer at the Catholic Institute of Sydney, sees the subtle influence of Capitalism in the quest for data and the abstraction from lived reality it creates:

> A culture based upon an economy informed by usury . . . will increasingly subordinate all things, including humanity and the Humanities to a system of value and meaning that privileges mathematics. The logic demands that all things be *quantifiable* in terms of maths if there is to be an absence of friction—if Capitalism is to be triumphant. As far as possible, "presence" will be simulated by being translated, via mathematics, into a *virtual* presence, a process which requires that identity be abstracted from essence.[28]

A society that values numbers, efficiency, and disembodied presence is concerning. The dependence on data means a decreasing dependence on traditional human traits. Traits such as discernment and wisdom, developed through a lifetime of experiences, including love, loss, and failure, cannot be captured in data nor learned through education oriented toward numbers, efficiency, and outcomes. These realities seem to be more in keeping with what some refer to as a posthuman reality brought about through a future merging of humans and computers. In an article that touches on the dangers of a posthuman reality, Travis Kroeker addresses the deficiencies of data. Speaking about the powers and principalities at work in technology, Kroeker describes a focus on data as something that shifts attention away from the core of what it is to be human:

> How is it that our human quest for liberation and happiness ends up in such a tawdry and dehumanizing vision of totalitarian, mechanistic disembodiment that is nevertheless celebrated as the benevolent salvation of the future? I suggest it has something to do with the fact that we think we will magically crack the code

27. Weizenbaum, *Computer Power and Human Reason*, 25.
28. Tilley, "Opposing the Virtual World," 72.

of life through the collection of data. This is a Faustian bargain. Data lacks sanctity and goodness; to be sure, it takes attention away from our moral and spiritual sensibilities, which are developed and communicated through a different sort of language—the language of symbol, narrative, and the ordering of love, justice, beauty, and goodness.[29]

Character virtues, such as love and goodness, have very little to do with data. Hence, a focus on orienting theological education toward outcomes established by data places the development of human virtues at risk. Beyond the way data usage changes learning, it also changes how individuals relate. In his leadership book, *Failure of Nerve*, family therapist and ordained rabbi Edwin Friedman sees danger for those preparing for leadership yet fixated on data. He suggests that the presence of a non-anxious person strengthens leadership to a greater degree than methods informed by the latest data. He argues that data and numbers may do more harm than good when a leader focuses on them rather than operating out of a sense of calm and common sense. Friedman argues that the modern fixation on data is causing problems with differentiation:

> The capacity of leaders to distinguish what information is important depends less on the development of new techniques for sorting data than on a leader's ability to avoid being driven by the regressive anxiety that is often the source of the unregulated data proliferation to begin with.[30]

Self-differentiation, the ability of an individual to avoid being driven by regressive anxiety, is a core trait of pastoral leaders as will be seen in the next chapter.[31] Yet, like the physician's stethoscope, an over-reliance on data could mean that pastoral differentiation gets lost in the pursuit of finding the right solution or technique to alleviate congregational anxiety. This, in turn, raises the leader's anxiety level and could drive them deeper into what Friedman calls a data deluge. He suggests:

> Despite its anxiety-provoking effects, the proliferation of data also has an addictive quality. Leaders, healers, and parents "imbibe" data as a way of dealing with their own chronic anxiety. The pursuit of data, in almost any field, has come to resemble a form of substance

29. Kroeker, "Technology as Principality," 172–73.

30. Friedman, *A Failure of Nerve*, 97.

31. See Friedman, *Generation to Generation*, Richardson, *Becoming a Healthier Pastor*, and Richardson, *Creating a Healthier Church*.

abuse, accompanied by all the usual problems of addictions: self-doubt, denial, temptation, relapse, and withdrawal. Leadership training programs thus wind up in the codependent position of enablers, with publishers often in the role of "suppliers."[32]

Considering the effect of the proliferation of data on the educational system, the shift toward online learning could be considered as a step in the right direction. After all, computers categorize and create pathways to access information. Yet, what if the construction of the platforms built to access information is being driven by societal anxiety? This may be a hidden reality that occurs without most educators, administrators, and students noticing. Friedman playfully describes higher education institutions as possessing an overdeveloped societal brain, unaware of its embodied anxiety influencing its profession. He offers this provocative perspective:

> If we were to conceive of the academic institutions of our civilization as its "cortex" then a parallel process could be seen in society at large. Data that are being published may be magnificently formulated and accurate, but they will still be of little help in producing change because they are irrelevant to the larger emotional processes driving that "cortex" to produce all the data. Actually . . . the emotional and the theoretical can be connected in such a way that even when thinking processes are articulated in the most logical manner, they could be driven by emotional processes that are really quite mad.[33]

Theological schools may be caught in the rush to produce high quality online courses and programs based on sound data. The risk, in the end, is the loss of human formation in the image of God as learning becomes increasingly contingent on digital technologies developed in an anxiety-fueled cycle of production. Is there an alternative to this madness?

The pedagogy of Paulo Freire stands as an example of a way of educating that is distinct from Friedman's anxious institutions. Oriented toward the learner's context rather than starting with data, Freire's liberating pedagogy emerged from his work as an educator among the poor of South America. As an example of this liberating learning, Freire describes how in teaching people to read and write he began by entering their world, trying to understand words and meanings according to the "unlettered" people. This is apparent in his interaction with his family cook named Maria, a

32. Friedman, *A Failure of Nerve*, 98.
33. Friedman, *A Failure of Nerve*, 130.

Portuguese woman who could not read or write. He started by showing her pictures of a boy with the Portuguese term for "boy" captioned beneath. Then, he repeated the process each time removing certain letters from the term and asked her what was missing.

> At the beginning of my experiments in Brazil, I thought about the possibility of developing a method that would permit "unlettered" people to read and write with ease. I tried to place some symbols associated with words in people's consciousness without their being aware of it. The next step is to critically challenge these concepts in order to rediscover the association between certain symbols and words so as to help people recollect them in the course of learning to read and write.[34]

As seen in this excerpt, Freire was interested in understanding what certain words and concepts meant to the people in their context. Those terms became the launching point for learning, both for him as an educator and the "unlettered" students. Freire discovered that learning with the oppressed, rather than teaching things to the oppressed, liberates both teacher and learner and shifts power differentials. He describes traditional education as "banking education," turning students, "into 'containers,' into 'receptacles' to be 'filled' by the teacher."[35] The "data" or learning content held by the teacher caused students to maintain a posture of passivity. Freire believed all education was political, with the banking model maintaining a system whereby educating the uneducated to be passive receptacles prevented them from believing they have power to think and act for themselves. In the words of Brazilian educator Moacir Gadotti, "[Freire] thought education would need to prepare [unlettered people] to make critical choices about alternatives proposed by the elite so that, eventually, they could forge their own path."[36] His alternative to this oppressive form of learning is problem-posing education, where students and teacher work to discover and transform the world around them. Freire saw the work of teachers and learners co-creating as important to the process of human development.[37] This stands in stark contrast to a system built on data, information, and outcomes. For example, when data is the starting point, the administrators and educators themselves become "containers to be filled" and data

34. Torres, *Diálogo*, 30. As cited in Lownds, "Wake up," 89–90.
35. Freire, *Pedagogy of the Oppressed*, 72.
36. Gadotti, "Freire's Intellectual," 35.
37. Freire, *Pedagogy of the Oppressed*, 81.

becomes the oppressor. Data ignores the context and experiences of individuals. It is received and passed on in an abstract form. Freire presents a different starting point, a place which cannot be derived from abstracted data: the generative theme.

> The generative theme cannot be found in people, divorced from reality; nor yet in reality, divorced from people; much less in "no man's land." It can only be apprehended in the human-world relationship. To investigate the generative theme is to investigate people's thinking about reality and people's action upon reality, which is their praxis. For precisely this reason, the methodology proposed requires that the investigators and the people (who would normally be considered object of that investigation) should act as co-investigators.[38]

Freire worked against the dehumanizing educational practices that oppressed the poor. While he writes about human oppressors, his way of understanding oppression promoted by education systems could be equally applied to digital platforms used for online learning. Freire writes, "In order to achieve humanization, which presupposes the elimination of dehumanizing oppression, it is absolutely necessary to surmount the limit-situations in which people are reduced to things."[39] In order to fully understand how data and information became separated from lived experience in the first place, the role of media and concepts such as "figure" and "ground" must be addressed. For that we turn to Marshall McLuhan.

MEDIA, THE INTERNET, AND THEIR EFFECTS

The Medium is the Message (Media 101)

Media theorist, Marshall McLuhan, coined the now famous phrase "the Medium is the Message" as a perspective on media that calls attention to what happens behind the scenes of communication technologies. His insights are important in an age when the rapid development and use of media tools for the delivery of education occurs at an ever-quickening rate. W. Terrance Gordon, Professor Emeritus at Dalhousie University, writes about McLuhan's concern for getting caught up in the pace of technological change:

---

38. Freire, *Pedagogy of the Oppressed*, 106.

39. Freire, *Pedagogy of the Oppressed*, 103.

Media are powerful agents of change in how we experience the world, how we interact with each other, how we use our physical senses—the same senses that media extend. They must be studied for their *effects*, because their interaction obscures those effects and deprives us of the control required to use media effectively.[40]

In order to understand why studying the effects of media is important, the evolution of media itself should be understood. McLuhan suggests that, a long time ago, when humans learned to read and write, attention shifted away from multisensory instruction toward learning that highlighted vision to the exclusion of the other senses. He writes, "Primitive and pre-alphabet people integrate time and space as one and live in an acoustic, horizonless, boundless, olfactory space, rather than in visual space."[41] This horizonless and boundless space was interrupted by the invention of devices that could transmit messages using pictures and words. Just as the development of the clock changed the concept of time, the shift to visual media opened up new possibilities and changed how humans thought, not just about words but also about space. Gordon describes it like this:

Print culture intensified the effects of the older technology of writing... Writing transformed space into something bounded, linear, ordered, structured, and rational. The written page, with its edges, margins, and sharply defined letters in row after row, brought in a new way of thinking about space.[42]

This new concept of the environment meant that the page replaced the acoustic space, formerly occupied by someone speaking. The printing press created an ordered way of seeing letters separated by precise spaces in uniform shapes. Then, as literacy increased, a private, interior world developed as reading became popular. McLuhan writes,

Printing, a ditto device, confirmed and extended the new visual stress. It provided the first uniformly repeatable "commodity," the first assembly line—mass production. It created the portable book, which men could read in privacy and in isolation from others. Man could now inspire—and conspire. Like easel painting, the printed book added much to the new cult of individualism. The

---

40. Gordon, *McLuhan*, 107.

41. McLuhan and Fiore, *The Medium Is the Massage*, 57.

42. Gordon, *McLuhan*, 92.

private, fixed point of view became possible and literacy conferred the power of detachment, non-involvement.[43]

McLuhan sees the printing press creating distance between humans. Formerly, acoustic space required the messenger and the one receiving the message to be in the same space. The new media, books, allowed the message to become detached from the messenger and context, and the reader to become detached from the embodied presence of another and the shared space once occupied together.

Where the introduction of books separated the reader's need for an embodied speaker, online platforms are changing the medium of learning yet again. The acoustic space of the classroom and the solitary experience of book learning is being replaced by screens. New technologies are extending the reach of the classroom and now image becomes central. One of the greatest dangers of this new educational medium is the potential loss of an ability to differentiate oneself from the image, since, unlike books and classrooms, media screens reveal some things but leave others hidden. McLuhan uses the story of Narcissus to describe the ease with which one can ignore the surroundings and focus on the image:

> In discussing the myth of Narcissus, McLuhan begins by pointing out the common misrepresentation in which Narcissus is said to have fallen in love with *himself*. In fact, it was his inability to recognize his image that brought him to grief. He succumbed to the same numbing effect that all technologies produce, if the user does not scrutinize their operation. Technologies create new environments, the new environments create pain, and the body's nervous system shuts down to block the pain. The name Narcissus comes from the Greek word narcosis, meaning numbness.[44]

This concept of new environments causing pain can be seen, for example, in the recent phenomenon of screen exhaustion. With the rise of the Coronavirus, the use of Zoom for work meetings, social engagements, and school has increased. The result? Technological and social overload. The effect has become commonly known as Zoom fatigue. According to a BBC news article published in 2020, Zoom fatigue occurs: 1) because of the need for extra focus on social cues and body language of those on the screen; 2) because silence, during online video conversations, makes people anxious;

---

43. McLuhan and Fiore, *The Medium Is the Massage*, 50.

44. Gordon, *McLuhan*, 109.

and 3) because being "on camera" produces anxiety.[45] Zoom exhaustion is one example of the way modern technology fatigues people. It is largely due to the use of platforms to perform in-person tasks. However, like Narcissus, most people are failing to see that the Internet has changed the medium of connection and the new way of connecting is changing people in ways that are being investigated only minimally and in retrospect.

The idea of scrutinizing the operation of technologies in order to prevent people from succumbing to their numbing effects, according to McLuhan, begins with recognizing two concepts of media: figure and ground. Originating in Gestalt psychology, figure-ground is a way of seeing objects (figure) as distinct from their background (ground). In the example of Zoom fatigue, people see the faces of their friends and co-workers (figure), but they are unaware of the environments of the others and the Zoom platform itself (ground). According to McLuhan, people tend to observe the figure and not see the ground. Gordon writes:

> By then [McLuhan] had fully realized that the great potential of figure/ground analysis lay in its application to media ("radio service is ground, whereas radio program is figure"), to the unnoticed environments they create (the restructuring of cityscape and landscape alike under the effect of the automobile), and to the equilibrium of the human senses altered by technology (mankind given an eye for an ear with the advent of television).[46]

One of the many challenges of online learning technology can be captured in McLuhan's figure-ground metaphor. Figure-ground helps the study of online education's effects in two ways: First, in examining the relationship between the curriculum (figure) and the online platform/program used (ground) to access the content; and second, the relationship between the learner (figure) and their educational context (ground). Addressing the curriculum and online platform first, educators and students alike tend to focus on the content being delivered through online courses (figure) without questioning and determining how the platform or technology (ground) shapes it. By way of example, anyone that has lectured in a classroom and then tried lecturing on Zoom quickly discovers that the speaking script and tone of voice (figure) can be the same, but it changes when delivered via an online platform (ground). The second way figure-ground is important for online education is in the relationship between the learner and their context

45. Jiang, "The Reason."
46. Gordon, *McLuhan*, 129.

that is not shared with the other students in their online class. Online education permits the teacher and students to learn course content (figure) while learning in very different contexts (ground). This could be likened to what happens at a sporting event or concert, where everyone is collectively sharing and participating in an experience that cannot be replicated via video. In an educational context, the classroom represents the venue where everyone gathers for the collective experience. When participating in online education, the ground of the classroom is lost when individuals learn in their own, distinct contexts. This is less of a concern for online courses that allow for interaction between teachers and students. However, this is a serious concern if the course is uploaded content or a livestream that does not permit interactivity. The pedagogical issue is around Freire's generative theme; when the learner's context is not considered, expect passive students. If the ground is not considered, learning becomes oppressive and abstracted from student reality. It becomes focused on data and figures, it does not allow the teacher to experience a shared context (ground) with the learners, and it calls the learner's attention away from their own context toward the abstract narrative of the teacher being mediated by technology. When the ground is ignored, reality becomes further removed from embodied human life. Citing McLuhan again, Gordon writes, "logic itself is a technique for omitting the *ground* in favor of dealing only with figures, a process which the Schoolmen and Descartes handed on to the mathematical logicians of our time. There is a single appetite to reduce all situations to more and more ethereal quality."[47] In the end, Canadian cultural critic and novelist Douglas Coupland attempts to summarize McLuhan's thinking about the medium, which is the "ground" in the figure-ground discussion. Coupland writes, "Marshall's ultimate message might well have been that the body is the medium and trumps all else."[48]

McLuhan is not alone in noting that technologies create new environments and those new environments can be destructive to learning and even humanity. In the introduction to *Technopoly*, Postman writes,

> Stated in the most dramatic terms, the accusation can be made that the uncontrolled growth of technology destroys the vital sources of our humanity. It creates a culture without a moral foundation.

47. Gordon, *McLuhan*, 137–38.
48. Coupland, *Mashall McLuhan*, 204.

It undermines certain mental processes and social relations that make human life worth living.[49]

Postman warns about the uncontrolled growth of technology. Its growth must be examined for the impact on human societies, in the same way that McLuhan's interpretation of Narcissus reveals the character's naïve inability to recognize the environment, thereby leading to his downfall. The downfall comes because the numbing effect of the image obscures the ground. In some ways, Narcissus' obsession with the image did not allow him to see that he was being prevented from seeing the ground. Gordon, referencing McLuhan, offers a helpful analogy to show how technology produces constraints, such as the one experienced by Narcissus, while at the same time opening new opportunities that were otherwise unavailable. He uses the concept of the bicycle and car being an extension of the foot.

> Whether you are pedaling a bicycle or speeding down the freeway in your car, your foot is performing such a specialized task that you cannot, at that moment, allow it to perform its basic function of walking. So, although the medium has given you the power to move much more quickly, you are immobilized, paralyzed. In this way, our technologies both extend and amputate. Amplification becomes amputation. The central nervous system reacts to the pressure and disorientation of the amputation by blocking perception. Narcissus, *narcosis*.[50]

While online education extends some things—such as the face of the teacher into the home or office of the student or the opportunity for far away students to type thoughts and ideas for discussion—the pressing question is, what is lost? What has been amputated by online education?

Embodied Wisdom and the Incarnation

The global coronavirus pandemic accelerated the massive shift of higher education institutions toward online learning. As I write, schools across Canada have closed their doors and mandated that all classes be moved to online platforms to conclude the Winter 2020 semester. As of the Spring 2021, most courses have been moved online. To play with McLuhan's metaphor, if classroom learning were a foot and online learning a car, what used

49. Postman, *Technopoly*, xii.
50. Gordon, *McLuhan*, 109.

to be a helpful medium for extending education over great distances (the car) is now being used by everyone, regardless of the physical distance. The streets of higher education have become clogged with learners idling in vehicles of online learning (or, as McLuhan might quip, idol-ing vehicles of online learning!) and the pedestrian parks and trails of natural, embodied, learning have been closed. The acoustic space of the classroom where students and teacher inhabited and experienced an environment together has been exchanged for multiple, individual, environments and a fixation on words, images, and sounds emanating from screens.

The shift to online learning has unsettling theological implications. The most significant is the diminishment of Christology, specifically the doctrine of the Incarnation. According to Brent Waters, "The Incarnation is the mainstay of Christology."[51] God becoming human situates God's message of love in an enfleshed medium. The incarnation alone elevates the value of the human person and materiality as a whole. It humiliates concepts of "being" that downplay physicality. Yes, if the incarnation is so important in Christian theology, how is it that the disincarnating experience of online education has been so readily embraced by theological educators? How can theologians instill the value of the incarnation in students through a disincarnating medium? James K. A. Smith states, "The way we inhabit the world is not primarily as thinkers, or even believers, but as more affective, embodied creatures who make our way in the world more by feeling our way around it."[52] The likely reason online educators are not seeing this disconnect is that they understand technology and e-learning to be useful and neutral educational instruments.

As noted in the previous chapter, there are great benefits to certain aspects of online education. However, there are drawbacks, and the subtle erosion of embodied, communal life and learning is one of them. Even the media guru, Marshall McLuhan, could see the difficulty of digital media for the Christian faith. Gordon describes McLuhan's dis-ease with electronic technology:

> The effect of electronic technology that most troubled McLuhan personally, because of its implications for Christianity, was the loss of the physical body: "One of the effects of instant speed is that the *sender is sent* . . . That is, man has become essentially discarnate in

---

51. Waters, *From Human to Posthuman*, 106.
52. Smith, *Desiring the Kingdom*, 47.

the electric age. Much of his own sense of unreality may stem from this. Certainly it robs people of any sense of goals or direction."[53]

McLuhan saw the disconnect between what people watched on their screens and how they lived. That "discarnate" experience, producing a sense of unreality, leads to a loss of meaning. Meaning and purpose are themes at the heart of human spirituality. For technology and media to alter the perception of reality of what it is to be human without more critical engagement with Christian theologians and those promoting online theological education, is concerning. Regent College Professor Craig Gay, author of *Modern Technology and the Human Future* writes:

> From the point of view of the Christian religion, then, modern technology's diminishment of ordinary embodied human existence poses a very serious problem. If the Christian proclamation of the incarnation signals the divine intention to redeem, restore, and ultimately to glorify embodied human beings, then clearly anything that undermines, enfeebles, or otherwise diminishes ordinary embodied human being must be at odds with the divine purpose. We must decide, then—given its evident trajectory—whether modern automatic machine technology qualifies for this kind of censure.[54]

Being human is not a reality determined by technology and computers. For the Christian Church and theological schools, it is rooted in a person. That person is God incarnate, Jesus Christ. In the God-became-human person, Jesus Christ, the value of human embodiment reached a definitive juncture. Craig Gay writes:

> The incarnation of Jesus Christ is nothing if not a colossal endorsement of embodied human being, of the very walking, talking, eating, sleeping, working, loving way of being-in-the-world that we presently and ordinarily enjoy. And although we are to be clothed in immortality at the resurrection of the dead, we will even then be recognizably embodied. After all, the resurrected Christ walked with, talked with, ate with, and was handled by his astonished disciples. "Look at my hands and my feet," he said to them. "It is I myself! Touch me and see; a ghost does not have flesh and bones, as you see I have" (Lk 24:39). True, the Christian tradition has from time to time lost sight of the significance of human

53. Gordon, *McLuhan*, 136–37.
54. Gay, *Modern Technology*, 14.

embodiment, but in the face of the *dis*-embodying bent of modern technology, there is clearly an urgent need now to remember it.[55]

Gay proposes that the reason the Protestant church has forgotten the significance of Christ's incarnation and its implications for human embodiment is a diminished value of the sacraments. He writes:

> It is perhaps not surprising that modern Protestant believers have not been particularly sensitive to the threat modern automatic machine technology poses to human embodiment. Our experience of the world has been so disenchanted—or, more accurately, desacramentalized—that we tend to see little in ordinary embodied existence that discloses the life of God. A kind of mechanical frame of mind has prevented us from seeing that the entire world, including our own lives, participates in and proceeds moment by moment from the living God, the God "in whom we live and move and have our being" (Acts 17:28). We have apparently also forgotten that when "the Word became flesh and made his dwelling among us" (Jn 1:14) this both vindicated and immeasurably exalted ordinary embodied human existence.[56]

Sacramentality requires embodied human beings to value physicality. James K. A. Smith believes that a renewed sacramental embrace of the world helps human beings caught in a Platonic dualism where the mind and body are at odds.

> Our essential embodiment will keep interrupting our Platonic desire to do away with the body, will keep interrupting itself into our dualistic discourses to remind us that the triune God of creation traffics in ashes and dust, blood and bodies, fish and bread. And he pronounces all of it "very good" (Gen. 1:31). This liturgical affirmation of materiality is commonly described as a sacramental understanding of the world—that the physical, material stuff of creation and embodiment is the means by which God's grace meets us and gets hold of us.[57]

If God meets human beings in, as Smith describes, "the material stuff of creation" then how do online platforms contribute to the God-meeting-humanity in nature? E-learning may end up being a very helpful medium for theological education but discernment, leading to real, embodied

---

55. Gay, *Modern Technology*, 153.

56. Gay, *Modern Technology*, 220.

57. Smith, *Desiring the Kingdom*, 141.

engagement with teachers, students, and Christ, must be central to the process, as will be seen in the following chapters. Robert Tilley writes:

> A Christian and biblical education must be one that is oriented to real presence: the real presence of a teacher, of a classroom, of challenge and demand—indeed of struggle and sacrifice. The medium must correspond to the message and as the message is predicated upon the real presence of God in Christ incarnate, in Christ embodied, in his body the Church, then the medium of teaching this must embody real and substantial presence.[58]

The Good News of the Incarnation of Jesus Christ is at the heart of pastoral formation. Learning through embodied engagement with teachers and students in a shared context is something that has been part of theological learning throughout history. The impact of this sort of learning on faith and wisdom is known. Much less is known about the effect of Internet usage on human life and development. An initial exploration of the findings concludes this chapter.

The Internet and its impact on human beings

By now it should be clear that the focus of this chapter has been on the way that technology, a non-neutral medium, affects human beings. The final aspect to investigate is exactly how Internet usage and interaction with online platforms affect people. The following outlines the ways Internet use affects the social well-being of a person and the cognitive functioning of the brain.

The Internet and Social Well-being

Pastoral work is social and communal. It requires interacting with people as a servant and embodied representative of Jesus Christ. Therefore, clergy education should be oriented toward helping individuals learn how to engage with others. Do online contexts lend themselves to learning social interactions? In some ways they do. From "tweets" to "snaps" to "likes," the Internet provides ways of bringing people into more frequent contact than ever before. Yet the research shows something sinister lurking beneath the social media frenzy. Findings about Internet usage show that it contributes to feelings of isolation and sadness. Hubert Dreyfus writes, "Researchers at

---

58. Tilley, "Opposing the Virtual World," 83.

Carnegie Mellon University were surprised to find that, when people were given access to the World Wide Web, they found themselves feeling isolated and depressed."[59] The authors of the study referenced by Dreyfus concluded that, "The most important finding is that greater use of the Internet was associated with subsequent declines in family communication."[60] The study, conducted in the early days of the Internet, studied families with no prior in-home Web access before and after they were given computers with Internet access. Researchers discovered that new social relationships were established after the Web was introduced to the home, but not to the same degree as embodied relationships:

> Most of these new relationships are weak. MUDs, listservs, newsgroups, and chat rooms put people in contact with a pool of new groups, but these on-line 'mixers' are typically organized around specific topics, activities, or demographics and rarely revolve around local community and close family and friends.[61]

While Internet usage may contribute to finding a broader social network of friends, those relationships do not seem to translate into collective social engagement or closer family bonds. One longitudinal study of teenagers found that not only are bonds weaker between people when interacting online, the young people in the study also became sadder:

> Consistent with past research, heavy use of the Internet and video-games was positively related to increases in depression. However, this relation was also consistent with the withdrawal hypothesis that young people who experience depressive symptoms increase their use of media and desist from social and physical activity.[62]

Whether social isolation leads to greater Internet use or Internet use leads to greater social isolation, the outcome is the same: higher rates of depression. Sharon Horwood and Jeromy Anglim researched the phenomenon of technostress, a term describing the almost constant need to attend to attention-grabbing devices like smartphones and social media sites:

> One explanation for the experience of technostress is that continuous access to, and demand for attention from, social networking sites, supply of news and information, work activities, and various

59. Dreyfus, On the Internet, 2.

60. Kraut et al., "Internet Paradox," 1025.

61. Kraut et al., "Internet Paradox," 1019.

62. Romer et al., "Older Versus Newer," 618.

forms of entertainment result in cognitive-emotional preoccupation with the agent of delivery, the smartphone.[63]

What makes their observation important is their description of the smartphone as an agent of delivery. In this sense, they have captured McLuhan's figure-ground concept of media by looking beyond the content of the applications and media on the phone and seeing the phone itself as a participant in elevating human stress. Leonard Reinecke et al. take a different approach to technostress. Their paper views Internet technology and its corresponding media as contributing to perpetual distraction and procrastination. Their research points to the potential for serious mental health implications:

> In sum, our findings confirm the pivotal role of everyday Internet use for procrastination and its psychological effects. This study thus significantly extends the findings of prior research by demonstrating that the negative effects of procrastinatory media use go beyond negative self-related emotions such as guilt and are associated with an increased risk of more serious psychological health-impairments. Furthermore, our findings also have important implications for research on problematic Internet use and Internet addiction.[64]

Most of these studies focus on younger people who tend to spend more time gaming and on social media applications. The findings may very well be skewed and not reflect the reality of students oriented toward pastoral ministry. Today, ministerial students may not be as engaged in these kinds of problematic activities. However, assumptions about ministerial students may not be true in the future. Levels of Internet usage continue to grow among all people. As young people and mature students enter seminary with more attachments to technology and higher levels of Internet usage, the psychological effects of the Web will grow for all ages. A student's capacity to discern appropriate limits for their Internet usage will likely decline as access to the Internet and its applications continues to grow. Therefore, educators should not assume that future students will enter seminary with the same abilities to moderate their Web habits and usage as they do today.

To conclude this exploration of how Internet use affects social well-being, an imaginative look to one person's utopian future provides a witty take. Written long before the World Wide Web, former president of the University of Chicago, Robert Hutchins, described his university vision.

63. Horwood and Anglim, Problematic Smartphone Usage," 2–3.

64. Reinecke et al., "Permanently Online," 873.

The University of Utopia offers a poignant reminder that technology, promoted as a gateway to human leisure, may actually be destructive:

> [The Utopians] are of two minds about gadgets. On the one hand, they notice with interest that these devices have in many cases increased the leisure available to the people. One the other, they observe with some alarm that the charm of these devices promotes infantilism in the population, that their multiplication may consume a disproportionate share of the resources and energies of the country, and that some of them, because of the horrible sounds or pictures they are capable of emitting, or because they are dangerous when in motion in large numbers, may be destructive of the leisure that they could create and even of life itself.[65]

Hutchins' writing captures the early impact of television and vehicles on human life. Little did he realize that many of his observations would become exacerbated by Internet and social media ubiquity. His observations, about leisure and social well-being, are only one part of the impact. The mind is also being changed in ways that have lasting consequences.

The Internet and the Brain

Overall, research shows a negative correlation between large quantities of time online and cognitive affects. This is especially evident in patterns of smartphone use. While the previous section looked at the effect of Internet use on social well-being, including increased rates of loneliness and depression, this section will examine changes in cognitive functioning. I will say more in chapter 4, but for now, the following research offers an introduction to the way device usage changes the brain. In an article entitled, *"The Online Brain": How the Internet May Be Changing Our Cognition*, Joseph Firth et al. write:

> Even when not using the Internet for any specific purpose, smartphones have introduced widespread and habitual "checking" behaviours, characterized by quick but frequent inspections of the device for incoming information from news, social media, or personal contacts. These habits are thought to be the result of behavioural reinforcement from "information rewards" that are received immediately on checking the device . . . The variable-ratio

---

65. Hutchins, *The University of Utopia*, 18–19.

reinforcement schedule inherent to device checking may further perpetuate these compulsive behaviours.[66]

Firth et al. go on to summarize the damaging effects of media multi-tasking:

> Nonetheless the literature, on balance, does seem to indicate that those who engage in frequent and extensive media multitasking in their day-to-day lives perform worse in various cognitive tasks than those who do not, particularly for sustained attention.[67]

Smartphone usage and device checking alter the way the brain behaves. Nicholas Carr has written several books on this subject. He has discovered that the way the Web is designed alters human functioning. His findings will be explored more fully in chapter 4 but by way of introduction, Mark Ellingsen, Professor of Church History, has written an article about online education based on Carr's findings:

> What happens to these brain dynamics when most of our education is online (and especially when we spend most of our waking hours this way)? The prefrontal cortexes of the brain are not focused just on linguistic and memory functions. All the regions of the brain get in the act. Over time, this will lead to weaker neural connections among these brain functions. In its place, extensive activity among all brain regions is the order of the day. This has the virtue of keeping the entire brain active. But the cost is concentration and memory (and intelligence).[68]

The brain remains active simply due to human interaction with digital devices. What lessons about sabbath and rest (or the lack thereof) might technology be teaching? Perhaps some of the classical spiritual disciplines, such as sabbath and meditation, may become things of the past as online education reshapes human behavior patterns. Ellingsen continues:

> Nicholas Carr's conclusions seem vindicated: heavier online use is making us more shallow, more caught up in the present moment and its patterns, less transcendent in our thinking and behaviors. And as these trends become increasingly accepted as the *only* modern way to communicate and think (for Internet education is the way of our schools), as they consequently more and more shape the brains of our heirs, there may be less aptitude and less place for

---

66. Firth et al., "Online Brain," 120.
67. Firth et al., "Online Brain," 121.
68. Ellingsen, "Neurobiological Data," 7.

deep thinking, aspirations, and emotions that only emerge from meditative encounters with what transcends us.[69]

Ellingsen reminds readers that online usage affects students negatively, yet it is the way of our schools. His sobering look at Internet education in light of research findings leads him to posit, ". . . students focusing on a text, a lecture, or watching one television screen retain information better than those who study the same phenomena through multimedia and/or Internet modes of viewing."[70] Ellingsen concludes, "For the present, suffice it to note that there is hard data indicating that at least some seminary students do not learn as well when the instruction is interrupted, as it is on the Internet."[71] Interrupted learning is likely not helpful for anyone, let alone seminary students. Yet, it is the way theological schools have chosen to adapt in order to stay relevant in the future. The results for pastoral education will be graduates with very different skills and behaviors than those instilled historically. Education itself will be radically different than embodied apprenticeships or classroom mentoring of previous eras. In the midst of students studying online, one of the most interesting and new dynamics to watch will be the relationship of the pastor to electronic media. Will future clergy make the mistake of McLuhan's Narcissus or will they recognize their image? The degree to which the Internet can be used to nurture self-differentiation in students is the subject of the next chapter.

69. Ellingsen, "Neurobiological Data," 10.

70. Ellingsen, "Neurobiological," 4–5. Ellingsen's conclusions arise from Bergen et al., "How Attention Partitions," Hembrooke and Gay, "The Laptop," Rockwell and Singleton, "The Effect."

71. Ellingsen, "Neurobiological Data," 5.

3

Internet Education and Bowen Family Systems Theory

Chronic Anxiety, Self-Differentiation, and Pastoral Skill Development

As NOTED IN THE previous chapter, Douglas Coupland summarizes Marshall McLuhan's theory using these words: "the body is the medium that trumps all else."[1] In the classroom, teachers are the medium through which almost all teaching originates. Online education, however, shifts the locus of teaching, displacing the human educator. On the Internet, students engage *directly* with the formational digital interface and *secondarily* with other learners and the teacher. Human educators are no longer even required for some programs of online learning.

In this chapter, I posit that the online interface acts as a sort of mediator or third party in the learning process, affecting students differently than a traditional classroom. In the same way that a three-person relationship might function with two people sharing tighter emotional bonds and the third watching from the outside, online learning provides the context for technology to act as one of those entities. The previous chapter demonstrated that a digital device or online program serves as a non-neutral party in the online learning context. It explored ways that social interactions and the brain are changed through online engagement. This chapter

1. Coupland, *Mashall McLuhan*, 204.

proposes that technology acts in ways that decrease levels of positive self-differentiation in students. I will rely on psychiatrist and theorist, Murray Bowen and his family systems concepts, to explore the emotional dynamics involved in self-differentiation. I will begin by describing Bowen Family Systems Theory with a particular focus on his concepts of triangulation, differentiation of self (DoS), and societal emotional process. Each concept will be defined and then applied to the human-technology relationship with particular attention to implications for online theological education. Furthermore, this chapter examines the extent that online education can be used to nurture pastoral skill development.

TECHNOLOGY AND BOWEN FAMILY SYSTEMS THEORY

Bowen Family Systems Theory is a therapeutic model developed by Murray Bowen. Bowen theory arises from the emotional dynamics he observed as he worked with families. By observing family interactions, he developed eight interlocking concepts—three of which provide helpful lenses for viewing the interplay between humans and devices/interfaces—triangulation, differentiation of self, and societal emotional process. Before examining these concepts, I will define the term "anxiety," a foundational word in Bowen's concepts.

Anxiety and Bowen Family Systems Theory

Counsellor and educator Peter Steinke describes the term "anxiety" as coming from concepts of "squeezing" and "choking":

> Taking a look at anxiety's family tree, you get a sense of its power to affect your life. The great-grandfather is *ango*, which means "to press together." Our English word for anxiety derives from the Latin *angere* (to cause pain by squeezing). In almost every language, the word for anxiety comes from a word signifying wind or air, choking or strangling, or the physical area of the neck. A common symptom for those who suffer anxiety disorders is the difficulty of breathing.[2]

Steinke goes on to parse out the differences between acute and chronic anxiety:

2. Steinke, *Uproar*, 16.

Acute anxiety, being time-bound and situational, has a lesser effect on your functioning. Momentarily you lose your poise, but you regain it quickly. Chronic anxiety is always set to go off. No matter what issue is being contested, what interpretation is being discussed, or what idea divides people, the anxiety alarm is ready to sound. Essentially, the chronicity relates to a person's inability to regulate one's own emotional capacities. Instinct has a headlock on intent.[3]

The regulation of chronic anxiety in an emotional system is central to Bowen's concepts of triangulation, self-differentiation, and societal emotional process. The temporary nature of acute anxiety can be helpful, such as the release of adrenaline to flee a dangerous situation or help conquer a new step in skill development. However, chronic anxiety is systemic and leads to emotional regression. Edwin Friedman writes:

The kind of anxiety Bowen was referring to is not what is usually meant by therapists or psychologists who are diagnosing individuals nor the existential "angst" of philosophers—the anxiety that is a byproduct of being mortal, the fact that we are neither omniscient not omnipotent. Nor is it the anxiety that is meant by political commentators who refer to our era as "an age of anxiety," pointing to economic worries or fears of violence or nuclear holocaust—although it might include such fears. Chronic anxiety is systemic; it is deeper and more embracing than community nervousness. Rather than something that resides within the psyche of each one, it is a regressive emotional process that is quite different from the more familiar, acute anxiety we experience over specific concerns.[4]

Friedman goes on to further clarify the concept of anxiety in a system by stating:

The issues over which chronically anxious systems become concerned, therefore, are more likely to be the focus of their anxiety rather than its cause. . . . Assuming that what a family is worried about is what is "causing" its anxiety is tantamount to blaming a blown-away tree or house for attracting the tornado that uprooted it.[5]

3. Steinke, *Uproar*, 18.
4. Friedman, *A Failure of Nerve*, 58.
5. Friedman, *A Failure of Nerve*, 59.

Steinke describes the telltale signs of a chronically anxious system and how the people within that system tend to behave. He draws on five of Friedman's reactions and adds two of his own:

1. emotional reactivity replaces careful thought;

2. the herding instinct is strong (circle the wagons, strength in numbers, groupthink);

3. blame displacement (finding the scapegoat);

4. wanting a quick fix (for the reduction of unpleasant anxiety);

5. weakened leadership (failure to take a stand and disappoint some segment of the system);

6. secrecy (never on the side of growth or challenge); and

7. invasiveness (boundary violations).[6]

Anxiety is a chronic, emotional response that appears in systems of all kinds, from families to nations.

Triangulation

Bowen theory asserts "that the triangle, a three-person emotional configuration, is the molecule or the basic building block of any emotional system, whether it is in the family or any other group."[7] Usually, the triangle involves a two-person relationship where the third functions to stabilize the others. When conflict arises between two people there is a strong likelihood that at least one will reach out to a third party for help. This bid for help serves to alleviate chronic anxiety and bring balance back to the relationship. Peter Titelman, a contemporary practitioner and researcher of Bowen Family Systems Theory, describes how this transfer of anxiety happens in a triangle:

> Triangles can function to reduce the anxiety of one or more members of a family, or any other emotional system, when the stability of a comfortable closeness/distance between two individuals is thrown out of balance. The unbalanced emotional system can be stabilized through the transfer of anxiety by involving a third individual.[8]

6. Steinke, *Uproar*, 28.

7. Bowen, *Family Therapy*, 373.

8. Titelman, *Triangles*, 29.

Michael Kerr, the current director of the Bowen Center for the Study of the Family, clarifies how drawing a third party into an anxious relationship serves to spread anxiety around:

> When anxiety increases, a third person becomes involved in the tension of the twosome, creating a triangle. This involvement of a third person decreases anxiety in the twosome by spreading it through three relationships. The formation of three interconnected relationships can contain more anxiety than is possible in three separate relationships because pathways are in place that allow the shifting of anxiety around the system.[9]

While much has been written about Bowen's triangulation in therapeutic contexts, very little has been done to apply this concept to the human-computer relationship.[10] Michael Kerr and Monica McGoldrick are two researchers that have noted the possibility of non-human parties to be triangulated into a relationship. Kerr writes:

> A live third person is not required for a triangle. A fantasized relationship, objects, activities, and pets can all function as a corner of the triangle. For all the facets of a triangle to be played out, however, three live people are usually required.[11]

Similarly, Director of the Multicultural Family Institute Monica McGoldrick describes the possibility of triangulating technology into a relationship:

> Triangulating occurs with things other than people as well. A spouse's investment outside the family may be in work, hobbies, alcohol, pets, the Internet, and so on, but the impact is the same. It often happens that the closer the husband gets to the job, the alcohol, or the Internet, the more negative the wife becomes toward both him and the object of his "affection." The more negative the wife becomes, the closer the husband moves toward the triangulated thing.[12]

---

9. Kerr and Bowen, *Family Evaluation*, 135.

10. One exception is a Master's thesis that looks at the drama triangle, a variation of Bowen's triangle concept that attaches roles of villain, victim, and rescuer to the parties involved. While these roles could be relevant to a human-computer relationship, the thesis author focused on these roles as they arise among online students and their teacher rather than focusing on the technology itself as taking on one of the roles. See Gerlock, "Sense of Community Online."

11. Kerr and Bowen, *Family Evaluation*, 136.

12. McGoldrick et al., *Genograms*, 178.

The most significant aspect of concern in any emotional triangle is the growing presence of chronic anxiety in the system. As will be examined in detail below, anxiety is one of the signs that a triangle will form in a relationship. Brian Majerus and Steven Sandage highlight how chronic anxiety in an individual can cause them to shift their attention to another party:

> Anxiety may be exhibited in both individual and communal expressions, including emotional cutoff/fusion, triangles, and overfunctioning. Triangles are a means of relating where one avoids dealing with the anxiety of conflict with another person by relating to a third party.[13]

While technology is not alive, programs and devices act in ways that are highly responsive to human action and can serve to lower or raise anxiety. For example, if I am anxious about expectations in a meeting for which I am running late and I do not have the address, I can simply ask my phone or computer to take me there. The device responds almost instantly with a route to the destination, which slightly lowers the underlying anxiety I feel about letting down my colleagues. Likewise, if I am feeling disappointed after a conflict with my teenager, I can triangulate in a wi-fi enabled household device, asking it to play my favourite song. It will comply with my request immediately, which lifts my mood in the process. This responsiveness, similar to Weizenbaum's computer in chapter 2, demonstrates how technology can function in a way that changes the emotional state of an individual, thereby momentarily reducing anxiety. These examples are ways that devices may serve to lower individual anxiety when linked to expectations of others and self. However, as will be seen in the following example, not all actions mediated by technology de-escalate unease.

Returning to Michael Kerr's description of triangulation, he highlights the "insider" and "outsider" emotional dynamics at play:

> When anxiety in the emotional field of a triangle is low, two people are comfortably close (the insiders) and the third is a less comfortable outsider. This is not a static system; even during calm periods it is in constant motion. Both insiders continually make adjustments to preserve their comfortable togetherness, lest one become uncomfortable and form a togetherness with the outsider. The outsider is not idly standing by, but continually attempts to form a togetherness with one of the insiders.[14]

13. Majerus and Sandage, "Differentiation of Self," 43.

14. Kerr and Bowen, *Family Evaluation*, 136.

Psychologist Sherry Turkle provides a frightening yet profound example of a time when she got herself into a situation of seeking "comfortable togetherness" with technology. Remembering Kerr's description above, notice the emotional dynamics at play as Turkle describes how she and her colleague entered a room to study a human tracking robot named Cog.

> Trained to track the movement of human beings (typically those objects whose movements are not constant), Cog "noticed" me soon after I entered the room. Its head turned to follow me, and I was embarrassed to note that this made me happy—unreasonably happy. In fact, I found myself competing with [my colleague] for the robot's attention. At one point, I felt sure that Cog's eyes had "caught" my own, and I experienced a sense of triumph. It was noticing me, not its other guest . . . Cog had a face, it made eye contact, and it followed my movements. With these three simple elements in play, although I knew Cog to be a machine, I had to fight my instinct to react to "him" as a person.[15]

While interactive robots stretch the human-technology relationship beyond the scope of this book, Turkle's example shows that technology can, in fact, be triangled into human relationships and work in ways that change human emotional dynamics. When Turkle and her colleague entered the room, they were comfortable insiders. Soon thereafter, the insider/outsider dynamics described by Kerr began. If mood altering changes happen between humans and robots, is it safe to assume that triangulation happens with online interfaces and devices as well? The answer is, yes. In a classroom context, there may be triangulated relationships between students and teachers or within a group of students such as when a teacher may appear to favour one student, or a group of students, as "insiders" and the remaining student "outsiders" triangulate in their parents or the dean. However, when education shifts online, there is a new entity in the mix. That "thing" plays a powerful role in the educational process. According to McLuhan's theory, the medium itself is the educator. When learning online there are still peers and a teacher, but technology occupies a central role in the triangle, a role that is impossible to ignore. Therefore, while students continue to think and absorb information online as in a classroom, emotional operations are regulated differently. While *mental* processes may continue to function normally, student *emotional* processes are a different matter. In other words, students may perform very well in terms of managing course

15. Turkle, *Alone Together*, 84.

material and expectations online while their emotional processes suffer. High performing students (as understood from a cognitive/mental process perspective) may become tied (from an emotional process perspective) to the online interface or device in ways that are unknown to their teacher and peers. This emotional tie, between human and device, represents a lack of self-differentiation and has significant repercussions for online students.

Differentiation of Self

Pastor and counselor Ronald W. Richardson describes differentiation of self as a concept derived from the behavior of cells:

> How do we define differentiation of self? The term comes from biology; cells develop from an amorphous, undifferentiated conglomerate into highly differentiated cells with specific functions or identities within the larger organism, but the cells remain connected to one another, communicating with one another while functioning somewhat independently. One simple way of defining differentiation is as an ability to be closely connected with just about anyone we choose and still be a self, still maintain a sense of one's own functional autonomy with the close relationship.[16]

Bowen's concept deals with the human ability to separate thinking from feeling. Bowen writes:

> Undifferentiated people hardly distinguish thoughts from feelings; their intellects are so flooded with feeling that they are almost incapable of objective thinking . . . Because they are less able to think clearly, undifferentiated people react emotionally—positively or negatively—to the dictates of family members, science, culture, and religion. These people have little autonomous identity . . . In contrast, differentiated people are able to take definite stands on issues because they are able to think things through, decide what they believe, and then act on those beliefs.[17]

While Bowen's definition may appear "antifeeling," Richardson cautions against that conclusion:

> Bowen's family of origin work is not antifeeling [sic] or anti-emotional or simply "intellectual." The words feeling and emotion mean

16. Richardson, *Becoming a Healthier Pastor*, 56.

17. Bowen, *Family Therapy*, 350.

different things in terms of the theory. Emotionality is the more all-encompassing word and refers to more than just our feelings. It includes our instincts and drives—for example, our automatic functioning, most of which is beyond our awareness. Research has demonstrated how our blood pressure, skin temperature, and galvanic skin response go up and down during the seconds, minutes, and hours of our relationships with others, but we have no awareness of this. Our physical body is probably connected to our relationship system in ways we have not yet considered.[18]

Peter Titelman describes differentiation of self as, "the variation in an individual's capacity to be an individual while functioning as part of a group. Differentiation can be described as the variation in one's ability to act for oneself without being selfish while being able to act for others without being selfless."[19] Therapist Edwin Friedman defines differentiation as:

> The capacity of a family member to define his or her own life's goals and values apart from surrounding togetherness pressures, to say "I" when others are demanding "you" and "we." It includes the capacity to maintain a (relatively) nonanxious presence in the midst of anxious systems, to take maximum responsibility for one's own destiny and emotional being.[20]

While self-differentiation was not a term Erik Erikson used, the developmental psychologist's use of the term "identity" describes the essence of self-differentiation. Erikson writes, "The term 'identity' expresses such a mutual relation in that it connotes both a persistent sameness within oneself (selfsameness) and a persistent sharing of some kind of essential character with others."[21]

The Relevance of Differentiation of Self for Pastoral Ministry

According to United Church Bishop, William Willimon, self-differentiation is required for pastors and churches because the nature of Christian ministry functions largely counter to prevailing social norms:

---

18. Richardson, *Becoming a Healthier Pastor*, 63.
19. Titelman, "The Concept of Differentiation," 25.
20. Friedman, *Generation to Generation*, 27.
21. Erikson, *Identity and the Life Cycle*, 109.

Because the Christian ministry is significantly *countercultural*, at some odds with the predominate culture, including the very first cultures of Israel and Rome in which we found ourselves, we must guard against styles of Christian leadership that are essentially accommodationist.[22]

According to Ronald W. Richardson, differentiated church leadership is important for congregational health. He proposes:

The level of differentiation of the leaders in the church is a crucial variable in how well that particular church will run its communal life, deal with the inevitable challenges and crises that come to it, and accomplish its mission.[23]

Maintaining a differentiated self is a ministerial requirement, given the need to take countercultural stands and nurture healthy congregations. Self-differentiation is important for the pastor to know how to draw away from the crowd and be utterly alone or stand non-anxiously in the midst of a chaotic church. Bonhoeffer describes this balance in his book, *Life Together*, stating, "Let him who cannot be alone beware of community. He will only do harm to himself and to the community." He then goes on to write, "But the reverse is also true: Let him who is not in community beware of being alone. Into the community you were called, the call was not meant for you alone."[24] This concept of being comfortable when alone *and* with others, even when they are anxious, is an attribute of good, self-differentiated, pastoral leadership. Bowen describes the dual responsibility toward oneself and others like this: "A person working toward responsibility in self is always aware of his responsibility to others. As he devotes primary energy to self, he automatically becomes more responsible toward others, and less irresponsibly overinvolved with others."[25] Ronald Richardson describes a pastor's ability to differentiate him/herself as, "*the* basic requirement for good leadership in the church and the major marker that distinguishes better and poorer leaders."[26] In his book, *Generation to Generation*, Edwin Friedman writes about the need for self-differentiation in religious leadership. Defining the basics of self-differentiation, he writes:

22. Willimon, *Pastor*, 70.

23. Richardson, *Creating a Healthier Church*, 177.

24. Bonhoeffer, *Life Together*, 77.

25. Bowen, *Family Therapy*, 449.

26. Richardson, *Creating a Healthier Church*, 86.

If a leader will take primary responsibility for his or her own position as "head" and work to define his or her own goals and self, while staying in touch with the rest of the organism, there is a more than reasonable chance that the body will follow. There may be initial resistance but, if the leader can stay in touch with the resisters, the body will usually go along.[27]

Becoming self-differentiated as a pastor is not simply a good leadership strategy, it signifies Christian maturity. In the words of Majerus and Sandage, *"Differentiation of Self* (DoS) represents another relational construct that is promising for conceptualizing spiritual maturity."[28] Ronald Richardson echoes a similar perspective when he writes, "Differentiation is a way to humility, as well as to wisdom.[29]

Since the concept of self-differentiation is critical in pastoral ministry, it is important that it is learned as part of a pastor's education, be it online or otherwise. Yet, with the turn toward Internet education for pastoral formation there are two challenges to self-differentiated learning. The first is the challenge of self-differentiation when one stays in a poorly differentiated system and the second is the growth of anxiety in online students.

Learning Differentiation of Self when Online Students are in Poorly Differentiated Systems

The first challenge relates to students that stay in their home context. As noted in chapter one, a significant benefit of online learning for theological students is the flexibility it provides. Namely, learners may remain in their own contexts rather than being uprooted to move to a residential school.[30] According to Miller and Scharen, this arrangement allows students to integrate their knowledge into the "real world" more quickly.[31] This situation is less of a concern for older students, a group that happens to be the fastest growing segment among ATS school enrolees, as the need for a destabilizing event, such as moving away from one's family of origin, may not be as critical. However, the majority of students in ATS schools are still under

27. Friedman, *Generation to Generation*, 229.

28. Majerus and Sandage, "Differentiation of Self," 42.

29. Richardson, *Creating a Healthier Church*, 183.

30. See Miller and Scharen, "(Not) Being There"; and Tanner, "Online Learning at ATS Schools: Part 2."

31. Miller and Scharen, "(Not) Being There," 23.

thirty.[32] Miller and Scharen fail to consider the possibility of younger students living in poorly differentiated systems. In a residential model of theological education, most students leave home to enter a new network of relationships at school.[33] This serves as a destabilizing experience that requires students to stand apart from their families of origin. If students remain in their contexts to learn online, their opportunity to step outside their family system, and ultimately, move into deeper levels of spiritual maturity, may be threatened.

In his book, *Stages of Faith*, James W. Fowler describes, "an ordering of the predictable phases of growth in faith" as a person develops.[34] Fowler's term for the young adult stage is called Individuative-Reflective faith. According to Fowler, this is the stage when one "must begin to take seriously the burden of responsibility for his or her own commitments."[35] To frame it in Bowenian terms, this is a time of learning self-differentiation. Fowler describes this faith stage as learning to distinguish oneself from the values of one's childhood and discovering one's own sense of inner authority and self-definition. In Fowler's words, "The two essential features of the emergence of [Individuative-Reflective faith], then, are the critical distancing from one's previous assumptive value system and the emergence of an executive ego."[36] While these two developmental steps may occur without a change in life situation, they are traditionally associated with substantial life change that creates something of a disorienting effect, which then leads to a broadened understanding. This sort of disruption usually happens for adolescents when they attend university or college. Fowler sees moving away from home as a possible catalyst that opens the door toward a more Individuative-Reflective faith:

> By virtue of the college experience, travel or of being moved from one community to another, many persons undergo the

32. Brown and Meinzer report that the over-50 age group is the fastest growing segment of students enrolled in ATS accredited schools. The under thirty-year crowd is the largest (30% of students) and the 50-plus group is the second largest (22% of students). See Brown and Meinzer, "New Data."

33. van Driel describes residential theological schools as "a community where candidates for ministry are ecclesially formed . . . Students are not just ecclesially formed by what happens in the classroom but also in the relationships that are being formed in the communal life on campus." van Driel, "Online Theological Education," 76–77.

34. Fowler, *Stages of Faith*, 38.

35. Fowler, *Stages of Faith*, 182.

36. Fowler, *Stages of Faith*, 179.

relativization of their inherited world views and value systems. They come face to face with the relativity of their perspectives and those of others to their life experience.[37]

Students who critically distance themselves from their presumptive value systems become better differentiated. When that happens with ministerial students, they are better equipped to navigate themselves and their future congregations through the complexities of life. Finding ways to create distance from poorly differentiated systems is only one of the difficulties involved in nurturing self-differentiation online. The second challenge is not only a possible issue for younger students, but for all online students.

"Emotional Fusion" with Devices and Lower Levels of Self-Differentiation

The second challenge facing pastoral students seeking to learn self-differentiation online is the medium itself. The use of a technological device appears to be encouraging a fused relationship between the learner and the gadget. Monica McGoldrick describes "emotional fusion" and its effect on relationships. As noted above with reference to triangles and technology, the same could be stated about devices and fusion:

> Family members in fused or poorly differentiated relationships are vulnerable to dysfunction, which tends to occur when the level of stress or anxiety exceeds the system's capacity to deal with it. The more closed the boundaries of a system become, the more immune it is to input from the environment, and consequently, the more rigid family patterns become. In other words, family members in a closed, fused system tend to react automatically to one another, practically impervious to events outside the system that require adaptation to changing conditions. Fusion may involve either positive or negative relationships; in other words, family members may feel very good about each other or experience almost nothing but hostility and conflict. In either case, there is an overdependent bond that ties the family together.[38]

McGoldrick's description of emotional fusion is written with family members in mind. However, it could be equally true about the relationship of a person to a technological device. The behavioral changes that humans are

37. Fowler, *Stages of Faith*, 179.
38. McGoldrick et al., *Genograms*, 18.

undergoing due to devices, referenced in chapter 2, appears to point toward "emotional fusion." Even though there is a risk of "emotional fusion" between humans and devices, the growing ease and accessibility of education with those devices should lead to less student anxiety. However, that does not appear to be the case.

While it might be tempting to believe online education reduces student anxiety, the research on student use of devices and online technologies appears to indicate the opposite. Returning again to the concept of chronic anxiety and Family Systems, the concept of self-differentiation is tied to anxiety. Majerus and Sandage, professors at Bethel Seminary, sum up the role of anxiety in Bowen's concept of differentiation of self succinctly, "At the core of the challenge of DoS/maturity is the influence of *anxiety*."[39] Furthermore, Majerus and Sandage write:

> In studies with adolescents, DoS has been negatively correlated with chronic anxiety and test anxiety (Peleg-Popko, 2004), mental health problems (Cavazzi, 1993), drug use and high-risk sexual behavior (Knauth, Skowron, & Escobar, 2006) and positively correlated with cognitive performance (Peleg-Popko, 2004) and academic engagement (Knauth et al. 2006).[40]

Clinical psychologist Susan DeCesare focused her doctoral research on determining whether anxiety and depression could be expected from a poorly self-differentiated person. Similar to Majerus and Sandage, she concluded her research stating, "Overall, the current study suggests that among student sample [sic], [the lack of] self-differentiation was the best predictor of both depression and anxiety."[41] Put simply, according to Bowen's theory, when someone is not well differentiated then anxiety is the natural result. In other words, these researchers show that DoS and anxiety are linked. What about research on DoS, anxiety, and the Web? Is there any research exploring Bowen's DoS and the Internet? The answer is yes. In a fascinating study looking at the relationship between Bowen's differentiation of self and Major Depressive Disorder, Melisa Elieson and Linda Rubin assessed levels of differentiation in clinically depressed and nondepressed populations. These nondepressed populations comprised a student sample and an Internet sample. Similar to DeCesare's findings, they also found that "depression

---

39. Majerus and Sandage, "Differentiation of Self," 43.

40. Majerus and Sandage, "Differentiation of Self," 44.

41. DeCesare, "Anxiety and Depression," 58.

and differentiation of self had an inverse correlational relationship."[42] What makes Elieson and Rubin's study such a strong contribution to online student formation research is their discovery that the online sample group showed lower levels of differentiation of self than the student sample. At the conclusion of their research, Elieson and Rubin state:

> In this study, researchers hypothesized that there would be no significant difference on measures of differentiation between the traditional student sample and the Internet sample. Results showed that Internet participants were significantly less differentiated than were student participants.[43]

Their findings appear to suggest those who function at lower levels of differentiation are drawn toward online engagement. These findings alone are grounds for theological educators shifting pastoral learning and formation online to stop and reconsider the limits of Internet learning. However, their findings unearthed something even more troubling. Not only was the Internet sample group less differentiated than the student sample, they were more poorly differentiated than the clinically depressed sample. Elieson and Rubin write:

> Interestingly, the Internet sample had significantly lower levels of differentiation than did the clinically depressed sample. One explanation for this finding is that Internet users truly have lower levels of differentiation than those with clinical depression. Consistent with this finding, Kraut, Patterson, Lundmark. Kiesler, Mukopadhyay, and Scherlis (1998) found that greater use of the Internet was associated with decreased family communication, increased loneliness, and increased depression. Based on this conclusion, Internet users may experience increased depression plus other symptoms of maladjustment. Individuals with lower levels of differentiation may experience more psychological dysfunction as they have fewer resources for handling stress (Griffin & Greene, 1999). Theoretically, those with low differentiation tend to be less flexible, less adaptable, and more emotionally dependent on others.[44]

Elieson and Rubin postulate why the Internet may be a safe haven for the poorly differentiated:

42. Elieson and Rubin, "Differentiation of Self," 125.
43. Elieson and Rubin, "Differentiation of Self," 137.
44. Elieson and Rubin, "Differentiation of Self," 135.

Possibly, as stress levels increase, those with lower levels of differentiation may find relief in the anonymity of the Internet. The Internet allows people to interact without the high social involvement, commitment, and emotional intensity of more direct communication. Perhaps those with lower levels of differentiation take refuge in the Internet during times of stress. Shapiro (1999) indicated that those who have reduced social contact might turn to the Internet to replace missing social interaction. Parks and Floyd (1996) suggested that people generally feel less close in online communication than in real world relationships. Those with lower levels of differentiation of self have difficulty balancing emotional distance and togetherness in relationships (Bowen, 1978). The Internet may provide a more comfortable forum for interacting with others while maintaining distant emotional boundaries.[45]

In a dissertation written to address differentiation of self and cell phone usage along young people, Annie Smith arrived at similar findings to those of Elieson and Rubin: technology and DoS do not appear to mix well. Smith writes:

This dissertation is an important first step in answering Walsh, White, and Young's (2010) call to researchers and clinicians to develop interventions that encourage young people to develop broader identities than their cell phone personas. By demonstrating that higher levels of differentiation of self are related to decreased cell phone involvement, this research begins to build a path for the tools and constructs used by family systems clinicians to address cell phone dependence, particularly among young adults.[46]

Based on the above research, it appears that cell phone and Internet usage are not conducive to promoting self-differentiation. For online theological education programs designed to deliver education via the very tools that appear to promote lower levels of differentiation, this could be problematic. Pastoral education should help students become effective and non-anxious congregational leaders, not promote stronger ties to technology that lead to higher levels of anxiety. Technology is useful for many things but nurturing self-differentiated students is not one of them. If anything, results of Internet usage on emotional well-being reveal concerning trends in anxiety levels. Anxiety negatively affects many things, but Peter Steinke's statement is of particular importance. He writes, "Anxiety affects your functioning in many

45. Elieson and Rubin, "Differentiation of Self," 136.
46. Smith, "The Cell and the Self," 93.

negative ways [including] decreasing your capacity to learn."[47] If, as discovered by Elieson and Rubin, those who gravitate toward online participation have lower levels of self-differentiation, and if anxiety is a sign of a poorly differentiated student, could technology be playing a role in lowering DoS levels and raising anxiety? McGoldrick's research, that devices and technology can be triangled into a relationship, appear to suggest people can become "emotionally fused" with technology. As cited earlier she writes, "The more closed the boundaries of a system become, the more immune it is to input from the environment." Does technology have the potential to "close the boundaries of [the learner's system]" and create an "emotionally fused" relationship between student and device, thereby disrupting the development of healthy self-differentiation? If so, a poorly differentiated ministerial student could develop a stronger relationship with technology than people. Furthermore, that attachment to technology could strengthen as disappointments among congregants grow, an inevitability every seasoned pastor knows. In what follows, Sherry Turkle's reflection on alterity, a trait closely linked to differentiation, shows how an "emotional fusion" with technology plays out. Her example of robot companionship shows a human-technology enmeshment that has obvious similarities to a poorly differentiated, tied-to-technology student, taking ministerial studies online:

> The first thing missing if you take a robot as a companion is *alterity*, the ability to see the world through the eyes of another. Without alterity, there can be no empathy. Writing before robot companions were on the cultural radar, the psychoanalyst Heinz Kohut describes barriers to alterity, writing about fragile people—he calls them narcissistic personalities—who are characterized not by love of self but by a damaged sense of self. They try to shore themselves up by turning other people into what Kohut calls *selfobjects*. In the role of selfobject, another person is experienced as part of one's self, thus in perfect tune with a fragile inner state. The selfobject is cast in the role of what one needs, but in these relationships, disappointments inevitably follow. Relational artifacts (not only as they exist now but as their designers promise they will soon be) clearly present themselves as candidates for the role of selfobject.[48]

Current selfobjects for those enrolled in online theological education programs are not robot companions but devices with apps and browsers. These

47. Steinke, *Uproar*, 18.
48. Turkle, *Alone Together*, 55–56.

portals allow students to avoid what Turkle calls their "fragile inner state." Left unchecked, these poorly differentiated students could be graduating from online theological school programs, entering into congregational ministries, and attempting to form their congregations into selfobjects. With technology's rapid evolution, the ability of a student to become more self-differentiated using an online medium appears naïve at best and futile at worst.

Societal Emotional Process and Technological Saturation

As shown above, the interplay of student anxiety and Internet usage could be a limited problem with select individuals who lack self-differentiation. However, what if the problem is larger than individual behaviors? What if the issue of chronic anxiety and technology stems from a lack of differentiation within society as a whole? With social media and access to breaking news at our fingertips, human interconnectedness and a fear-of-missing-out (FOMO) are at an all-time high. This leads to a society in a differentiated slide. Writing pre-Internet, Bowen describes his concept of societal emotional process and makes a case for a whole society in the midst of regression:

> The members of society are fused into each other and are more emotionally dependent on each other, with less operating autonomy in the individual. Emotional events are more similar to the "within an ego fusion" than to events between relatively autonomous people. A relatively differentiated self can live a more orderly life whether alone, or in the middle of the human pile. A poorly differentiated person is not productive alone. Powerful emotional "togetherness" forces draw him into the discomfort of fusion, with the impingement of self on self and the counter mechanisms to deal with too much closeness.[49]

Bowen's assessment, when read in light of human-technology dynamics discussed in chapter 2, comes close to addressing the ever growing human-technology relationship using the language of self-differentiation. His assessment is that self-differentiation is not simply a matter within families or individual relationships but within society as a whole. As people become more dependent on devices for learning, or any aspect of life, all of society regresses and everyone becomes less well differentiated.[50]

---

49. Bowen, *Family Therapy*, 440.

50. See section "'The Internet and its Impact on Human Beings" in chapter 2.

Theological School Anxiety—Choose-your-own-adventure

Individual anxiety has been explored above, particularly the kind linked with those experiencing lower levels of DoS and its relationship to online devices. Societal regression is a much larger problem, affecting civilization as a whole and it may exist at the level of institutions such as theological schools. Regression surfaces in theological schools in the same way it manifests in individuals, through chronic anxiety. Chronic anxiety may grow in schools facing declining enrolment, rising costs, and the real possibility of being left behind and offline. The urgency to change in order to stay viable becomes pressing.[51] Chronic anxiety, rather than theological reflection, may start to govern decisions about program shifts and the suitability and limits of technology in human formation. For example, some theological schools are trying to recruit by focusing on the sorts of things students themselves want to learn, allowing the recently enrolled to customize their education.[52] On the one hand, this encouraging shift empowers students and liberates them to make choices. However, there is a problem. Students may not know what they should be looking for, in courses and programs, to prepare them for the pastoral life. This choosing-in-ignorance method could lead to very narrow and limited education. Edward Tenner, using search engines as an example, describes how choosing without really knowing could lead to a narrowed perspective:

> The real problem is that search engines as they exist—even ones limited to supposedly more reliable information like Google Scholar—are inefficient ways to absorb an unfamiliar subject. The user needs the very knowledge that he or she is hoping to find—an idea going back to Plato's dialogue Meno, which raises the question of how a person can learn without already knowing. To make things worse, uninformed people don't always recognize their ignorance. Some of them, according to research by the social psychologists Justin Kruger and David Dunning, are sometimes

51. Two books released in 2019 address the present challenges facing theological schools and the need to change to be relevant in the future. See Valentín, *Looking Forward with Hope*; Wheeler, *Disruption and Hope*.

52. For example, Nick Carter proposes a "passport" for seminary students that would allow them to be "free to find and secure an education in a host of places and at an affordable price." Carter suggests that faculty would still need to approve the courses taken but he does not provide a clear understanding for how faculty would get to know the student they are advising or be able to assess the quality of programs and courses at other schools. Carter, "A House Built on Sand," 83.

firmest about topics they know least about. Another investigator, Brendan Nyhan, found that many people confronted with acknowledged facts challenging their views respond by reaffirming their positions. Search engines aid this tendency by making it easy to find information confirming just about any opinion. So, despite Google's original declared mission statement of organizing the world's information and making it useful, it can be no better than the knowledge and attitudes of users. The outcome is that fewer than 9 percent of all Google searchers look beyond the first page of results, and about a third choose the top-rated link.[53]

While Tenner describes picking and choosing links using search engines, could the same be said for ministerial students choosing courses to gain pastoral knowledge? In a traditional MDiv program, more than half of the courses are predetermined requirements, with the rest being electives.[54] This provides a course of study that exposes the student to a broad range of subjects. As programs shift toward requiring fewer pre-determined courses and offering more electives, Tenner's search engine problem may surface in programs of pastoral formation. This choose-your-own-adventure learning may mean that students forego the less appealing courses, ones that could end up loosening a student's entrenched position, thus maintaining a narrowed perspective in the long run.

Course selection is not the only example of how chronic anxiety may be governing theological school decisions. As noted earlier, students may choose to stay in their home contexts for a variety of good reasons. However, they may lose out on an opportunity to differentiate themselves from their families of origin and faith communities. Rather than innovating ways to aid students in their journey toward self-differentiation, many theological schools are making fairly rapid pedagogical changes, as outlined in chapter 1, toward online learning models. According to Bowen, this plays precisely into the theory of institutional regression:

53. Tenner, *The Efficiency Paradox*, 56.

54. In January 2021, I did a quick search of two MDiv programs: the school where I was enrolled, St. Michael's College—Roman Catholic (Basilian), and an evangelical seminary in Toronto, Tyndale University. Both had more than half the program comprising prerequisite courses. This is not the case everywhere. The school where I received my M.A., McMaster Divinity College (MDC), has an MDiv that does not have a single required course but a series of electives that must be taken within broader categories such as "Biblical studies," "Ministry studies," "Theological studies" with a specialization in one of five areas. Clearly MDC has started down the path of offering an education that is more customized by individual students.

> There are striking analogies between regression in a family and regression in larger social groups and society. Regression occurs in response to chronic sustained anxiety, and not in response to acute anxiety. If there is regression with acute anxiety, it disappears when the anxiety subsides. Regression occurs when the family, or society, begins to make important decisions to allay the anxiety of the moment.[55]

Could it be that decisions to shift learning online by theological schools might be rooted in attempts to alleviate "chronic sustained anxiety"? With the onslaught of the COVID-19 pandemic, all institutions responded to the acute anxiety of the moment. While moving all courses online was a necessary and important step for schools to maintain student engagement and learning, that response to the sudden change does not necessarily make it a preferred future educational mode. As argued, there is evidence that the human-device relationship leads to higher levels of anxiety and lower levels of self-differentiation. Could the unwillingness to consider other options for pastoral formation be due to Bowen's concept of societal emotional process and the challenge it is for school administrations, accrediting bodies, and professors to differentiate themselves from social forces? Turning again to Edwin Friedman and his theory, that a fixation on data can render institutional leaders ineffective, he addresses the effect of chronic anxiety:

> the greatest mental health problem in America today may be substance abuse of data. If the data deluge puts all leaders on an anxious treadmill of pursuing more information in order to "stay on top of things," the pursuit of information also offers family and institutional leaders and healers an easy escape from having to deal with society's chronic anxiety as well as their own personal being.[56]

The antidote to the treadmill of chronic anxiety, according to Friedman, is nothing short of the same steps to freedom from a substance addiction. He suggests the following keys:

> Facing the pain of anxiety and growth, not denying the emotional processes that erode self-differentiation, being willing to risk and be vulnerable—these are the keys to overcoming the addiction to data, as well as the way to avoid being overwhelmed by the data deluge.[57]

---

55. Bowen, *Family Therapy*, 277.

56. Friedman, *A Failure of Nerve*, 114.

57. Friedman, *A Failure of Nerve*, 116.

Bowen's concept of societal emotional process and the movement toward lower levels of differentiation has relevance with respect to the way technology is shaping humans, as outlined in chapter 2. The technological shift toward a world that becomes less and less differentiated from technology appears to be part of Google's plan. Poorer levels of differentiation make it difficult to take principled stands and to think differently than others, while staying connected to them. One may assume this to be the case when technology fulfills the role of "the other." While Google founders, Sergey Brin and Larry Page, are not seeking to promote a poorly differentiated population, their description of Google's vision of an "artificial brain" certainly points to that end:

> "The ultimate search engine is something as smart as people—or smarter," Page said in a speech a few years back. "For us, working on search is a way to work on artificial intelligence." In a 2004 interview with *Newsweek*, Brin said, "Certainly if you had all the world's information directly attached to your brain, or an artificial brain that was smarter than your brain, you'd be better off."[58]

Brin and Page are not the only ones seeing a future where the undifferentiated human-machine relationship results in artificial brains. In an insightful article examining theological education and theological anthropology, David Kelsey draws attention to the blurring of human-technology lines as machines become "spiritual":

> "Spiritual machines"—the image is emblematic of a widespread view that intelligence and consciousness simply are software programs. They are installed in the neurological wiring of our brains. But brains are nothing but sloppy and physically vulnerable machines. Their programs can in principle be downloaded onto much more powerful and durable computers. In principle, Kurzweil claims, there is no reason why my consciousness and intelligence could not be downloaded onto a computer that would then be me, or a replication of me. Indeed, since the computer will be more powerful than my brain, it will be an enhanced replication of me. If being spiritual means being conscious, the machine would be a spiritual machine.[59]

---

58. Carr, *Utopia Is Creepy*, 239.

59. Kelsey, "Spiritual Machines," 8.

Kelsey's writing demonstrates how software engineers and inventors such as Kurzweil are forging ahead with plans for a world of human-machine enmeshment, a world where human-device differentiation is nonexistent.

As theological schools make further shifts toward online education for pastoral formation, a flag of caution must be raised. As more students, teachers, and theological schools off-load the challenging work of remembering, thinking, and problem-solving into the world of Google and learning management systems, the risk of undifferentiated learning grows. Is offloading thinking and consciousness to machines really problematic? The short answer is, yes. It eliminates the difficulty of thinking and creating that leads to difference. Robert M. Hutchins describes both thinking and art as "the highest activities of man"[60] before going on to say that they are also "activities of the most painful and difficult kind."[61] Thinking is hard work. Contemplation takes time and focus and leads to self-differentiation. Self-differentiated thinking ushers in new, creative, and diverse positions— some of which are unpopular. Hutchins' words, published first in 1953, speak to Bowen's concept of societal emotional process, applied to what he calls, "a popular university," where a lack of differentiation leads to the loss of independent thought. He writes:

> I do say that a university in which no unpopular opinions are heard or one which merges imperceptibly into the social and political environment can be presumed, until the contrary is proved, not to be doing its job. If a university is a center of independent thought and criticism, then a popular university is a contradiction in terms.[62]

What Hutchins says about the university should be obvious to theological schools. The way of pastoral education and formation, as earlier described by Willimon, should be naturally (or unnaturally) countercultural. However, when anxiety and a lack of differentiation govern institutions, the willingness to risk decreases and the hard work of thinking gets exported to observing what others are doing and relying on data for the way forward. Nicholas Carr sees the increasing dependence on Internet applications and computer programs as detrimental to independent and creative thinking. Originating from a 2003 study by Dutch psychologist Christof van Nimwegen, Carr describes the findings of a computer puzzle experiment that

60. Hutchins, *The University of Utopia*, 17.

61. Hutchins, *The University of Utopia*, 20.

62. Hutchins, *The University of Utopia*, 88.

required the user to move colored balls around using explicit rules. Some participants relied on software designed to help while other users had no such assistance:

> The more people depended on explicit guidance from software programs, the less engaged they were in the task and the less they ended up learning. The findings indicate, van Nimwegen concluded, that as we "externalize" problem solving and other cognitive chores to our computers, we reduce our brain's ability 'to build stable knowledge structures'—schemas, in other words—that can later "be applied in new situations." A polemicist might put it more pointedly: The brighter the software, the dimmer the user.[63]

As students rely more and more on Internet applications and computer-based programing, the risk to thinking in new and creative ways appears to be in jeopardy. This problem is not specific to theological schools, but all institutions focused on online education. For theological schools, this is an issue to be addressed, but it is not the most pressing obstacle. What is even more concerning than thinking and creating, independent of the world wide web, is the call to discipleship for Christians generally and pastors specifically and its seeming incompatibility with Internet technology.

THE CHALLENGE OF DISCIPLESHIP AND THE EFFICIENCY OF THE INTERNET

I have touched briefly on some aspects of pastoral ministry, but I have not addressed how pastoral formation takes place. In what follows, I will describe the importance of discipleship for pastoral formation. I will draw on the work of pastors and authors, Dietrich Bonhoeffer, Dallas Willard, and Richard Foster, to describe the importance of discipleship. I will then go on to highlight the work of Hubert Dreyfus, where he describes the limits of Internet learning for skills development. I will finish by outlining pastoral skills, suggesting that given Dreyfus' work, their development is limited in an online context.

As the hard work of thinking is passed to computers, theological education loses one of the principles at its core, the cruciform life. The way of the cross is a way of thinking and living that cannot be downloaded and requires a self-differentiated life. Dietrich Bonhoeffer describes this life as

---

63. Carr, *The Shallows*, 216.

a life of discipleship. In responding to the call of Jesus Christ, the disciple enters what Bonhoeffer calls, "a new situation":

> If we would follow Jesus we must take certain definite steps. The first step, which follows the call, cuts the disciple off from his previous existence. The call to follow at once produces a new situation. To stay in the old situation makes discipleship impossible.[64]

Bonhoeffer appears to suggest that the decision to "follow Jesus" results in two radical changes: a departure from one's previous way of living and entrance into "a new situation." According to Bonhoeffer, becoming a disciple requires a repositioning of one's whole life. Philosophy professor Dallas Willard describes discipleship to Jesus Christ as an act of following and imitating the way of Jesus. He writes:

> If we would live the life which God made us for . . . first, we must learn from him the reason why we live and why we do the things we do. Second, we must learn from Jesus, our "in-former," a new internal character: new "bowels," one old translation says . . . then he invites us to follow him into his practices, such as solitude, silence, study, service, worship, etc. . . . Then, we must learn of his positive interactions and involvements with us in the concrete occasions of our day-to-day activities.[65]

Willard's steps into a life of discipleship to Jesus are not simple or efficient. He argues that the disciple needs to, first, "learn . . . why" they act the way they do. Then, the disciple needs to "learn from Jesus . . . then follow him into his practices." Finally, the disciple must "learn of Jesus' involvements with us." Each step of Willard's discipleship process focuses on learning something new. Learning, to embody new practices, requires time, focus, and strong models of the life of faith he describes. Richard Foster begins his book, *Celebration of Discipline*, with a call to become a deep person. He addresses the issue of a faith that is not grounded or tethered. He writes: "Superficiality is the curse of our age. The doctrine of instant satisfaction is a primary spiritual problem. The desperate need today is not for a greater number of intelligent people, or gifted people, but for deep people."[66] Foster describes twelve classical spiritual disciplines that are intended to open the pathway for growth and maturity. No one in the first century or

---

64. Bonhoeffer, *The Cost of Discipleship*, 62.

65. Willard, *The Great Omission*, 20–22.

66. Foster, *Celebration of Discipline*, 1.

earlier would have had to ask how to "do" the disciplines because they were embedded in the culture, modeled through embodied relationships, and picked up by observation.[67] Foster's description of submission is a particularly radical example of what was being taught by the master to the disciples. Foster says:

> It is impossible to overstate the revolutionary character of Jesus' life and teaching [on submission]. It did away with all the claims to privileged position and status. It called into being a whole new order of leadership. The cross-life of Jesus undermined all social orders based on power and self-interest. . . . Jesus called his followers to live the cross-life. "If any man would come after me, let him deny himself and take up his cross and follow me" (Mark 8:34). He flatly told his disciples, "If any one would be first, he must be last of all and servant of all" (Mark 9:35). When Jesus immortalized the principle of the cross-life by washing the disciples' feet, he added, "I have given you an example, that you also should do as I have done to you" (John 13:15).[68]

Bonhoeffer, Willard, and Foster provide ways of understanding discipleship as challenging, self-denying, and requiring time and effort to learn. Can Foster's life of submission be learned and demonstrated online? The world of technology is a world of efficiency.[69] Learning management systems seem to be designed for efficiency. Does that efficiency provide a context for learning discipleship to Jesus Christ? A cruciform life develops similarly to a skill or a trait, requiring time, effort, and sacrifice. The next obvious question is, can that life be developed online, using learning management systems?

Pastoral Skill Development Online

Philosopher Hubert Dreyfus focuses on a portion of his book, *On the Internet*, addressing whether skill development can be taught online. While pastoral skills—such as preaching, spiritual direction, prayer, worship leadership, and administration—are learned through formal courses and programs, there are also habits or character traits—such as patience, empathy,

---

67. Foster, *Celebration of Discipline*, 3.

68. Foster, *Celebration of Discipline*, 116.

69. For an excellent book on the dangers of the efficiencies of technology, see Tenner, *The Efficiency Paradox*.

and the ability to listen—that are implicit in the learning process and fundamental to a life of discipleship. Dreyfus' research on skill development reveals stages of learning, from someone at the very beginning to the person that has mastered the skill. Dreyfus' insights are compelling because he identifies the place where he believes Internet learning ceases to teach higher level skills.

Hubert Dreyfus' Stages of Skill Development[70]

Dreyfus describes the progression using the example of someone learning to drive. At the first stage, he calls the learner a *novice*. Here the student learns to recognize how fast they are going by looking at the speedometer. They are also given rules such as, when driving a manual transmission vehicle, shift to the next gear before the tachometer reaches the number four. Dreyfus calls the second stage, the *advanced beginner*. Here the driver begins to use engine sounds, rather than rules alone, to determine when to shift. The next step, stage 3, is where the learner gains *competence*. A competent driver on an off-ramp curve learns to pay attention to the speed of the car. The driver observes speed, surface condition, etc. in order to determine whether she is going too fast. She then has to make a series of decisions based on what she knows. A safe navigation around the curve spells relief, but if she goes into a skid she will be shaken. This stage is where Dreyfus believes the online platform of education reaches its limit. His rationale is simple. Engagement, involving the emotions and the body together, is difficult to reproduce online. To move beyond the stage of competence requires that the learners become emotionally engaged in the learning process. Citing an example from the field of nursing, Dreyfus writes:

> While it might seem that involvement could only interfere with detached rule-testing, and so would inevitably lead to irrational decisions and inhibit further skill development, in fact, just the opposite seems to be the case. Patricia Benner has studied nurses at each stage of skill acquisition. She finds that, unless the trainee stays emotionally involved and accepts the joy of a job well done, as well as the remorse of mistakes, he or she will not develop further, and will eventually burn out trying to keep track of all the features and aspects, rules and maxims that modern medicine

---

70. I have summarized Dreyfus' stages in this section. For a fuller look at the stages, see Dreyfus, *On the Internet*, 27–40.

takes account of. In general, resistance to involvement and risk
leads to stagnation and ultimately to boredom and regression.[71]

Dreyfus calls the next stage, *proficiency*. The learner gains an instinctual
and embodied sense of the experience. The proficient driver, approaching
the curve on a rainy day, may *feel in the seat of her pants* that she is going
too fast. She then must decide what to do. Valuable time may be lost in
decision-making, but the proficient driver is more likely to exit the curve
safely than the competent driver who spends additional time considering multiple factors. In this stage, embodied knowing happens before the
driver gathers evidence through observation. Dreyfus calls the fifth learning stage, *expertise*. In this stage, the expert driver not only feels in the seat
of her pants when speed is critical and too fast, she also knows how to
respond without calculating and comparing alternatives. What must be
done, simply is done. Dreyfus concludes his chapter on the stages of skill
development stating:

> Only emotional, involved, embodied human beings can become
> proficient and expert. So, while they are teaching specific skills,
> teachers must also be incarnating and encouraging involvement.
> Moreover, learning through apprenticeship requires the bodily
> presence of masters, and picking up the style of life that we share
> with others in our culture requires being in the presence of our
> elders. On this basic level, as Yeats said, "Man can embody the
> truth, but he cannot know it."[72]

Dreyfus sees risk-taking as paramount for student learning. If what is being
learned does not provoke an emotional response in the learner, it is safe to
assume it has not been learned. Dreyfus states:

> To become an expert, however, it is not sufficient to have worked
> through a lot of cases. As we have already seen in discussing the
> move from competence to proficiency, the cases must matter to
> the learner. Just as flight simulators work only if the trainee feels
> the stress and risk of the situation and does not just sit back and
> try to figure out what to do, for the case method to work, the stu-
> dents must become emotionally involved.[73]

71. Dreyfus, *On the Internet*, 32.

72. Dreyfus, *On the Internet*, 47.

73. Dreyfus, *On the Internet*, 38.

Dreyfus is not the only researcher addressing how computers may be hindering skill development. Just as Dreyfus notes the need for pilots to be under stress in order to learn, Nicholas Carr addresses another problem with computers and automation in the airline industry:

> As software assumes moment-by-moment control of the craft, the pilot is, as we've seen, relieved of much manual labor. This reallocation of responsibility can provide an important benefit. It can reduce the pilot's workload and allow him to concentrate on the cognitive aspects of flight. But there's a cost. Psychomotor skills get rusty, which can hamper the pilot on those rare but critical occasions when he's required to take back the controls. There's growing evidence that recent expansions in the scope of automation also put cognitive skills at risk. When more advanced computers begin to take over planning and analysis functions, such as setting and adjusting a flight plan, the pilot becomes less engaged not only physically but mentally. Because the precision and speed of pattern recognition appear to depend on regular practice, the pilot's mind may become less agile in interpreting and reacting to fast-changing situations. He may suffer what Ebbatson calls "skill fade" in his mental as well as his motor abilities.[74]

As the body weakens when muscles are not exercised, the mind and skills become dulled from lack of use. Online education for pastoral skill development and character formation may allow for underdeveloped skills to go unnoticed or a perpetual advanced beginner stage of pastoral formation. Formation takes time and, in conjunction with the Holy Spirit's work, struggle. Nicholas Carr argues that learning new skills and knowledge requires prolonged and focused effort:

> When we work hard at something, when we make it the focus of attention and effort, our mind rewards us with greater understanding. We remember more and we learn more. In time, we gain know-how, a particular talent for acting fluidly, expertly, and purposefully in the world. That's hardly a surprise. Most of us know that the only way to get good at something is by actually doing it. It's easy to gather information quickly from a computer screen—or from a book, for that matter. But true knowledge, particularly the kind that lodges deep in memory and manifests itself in skill, is

---

74. Carr, *The Glass Cage*, 57–58.

harder to come by. It requires a vigorous, prolonged struggle with a demanding task.[75]

As noted in chapter 2, the Web is designed to reward learned distractions such as "checking" behaviors. The Web has been shown to reduce levels of "sustained attention." These formational aspects are problematic for nurturing certain pastoral skills, such as contemplation and prayer. In the following chapter, I will address the way character virtues are developed and they will be linked to skill development. Beyond these behaviors, learning management systems do not allow for embodied risk-taking, as Dreyfus notes above. Risk-taking creates acute anxiety, which is temporary and helpful in learning skills. His focus on risk-taking and embodiment leads to becoming proficient at a skill. Character virtues, important for pastoral leadership and developed as skills, will be addressed in chapter 4.

Embodied Pastoral Skills

With a focus on the deficiencies of Internet learning for skill development, one question has yet to be addressed: what precisely is a pastor being trained to do? While there are many factors to consider in this question, I have chosen to highlight only two authors who see the pastoral role similarly: to help the congregation live as people of God.

In *The Purpose of the Church and Its Ministry*, H. Richard Niebuhr posits that the professional minister no longer serves primarily as priest or preacher but as pastoral director. Niebuhr states:

> In his work the pastoral director carries on all the traditional functions of the ministry—preaching, leading the worshipping community, administering the sacraments, caring for souls, presiding over the church. But as the preacher and priest organized these traditional functions in special ways so does the pastoral director. His first function is that of building or "edifying" the church; he is concerned in everything that he does to bring into being a people of God who as a Church will serve the purpose of the Church in the local community and the world.[76]

Performing the functions of Niebuhr's pastoral director require knowledge that goes beyond an intellectual understanding. His term "edifying" implies

---

75. Carr, *The Glass Cage*, 74.

76. Niebuhr, *The Purpose of the Church*, 82.

not only teaching the congregation how to live rightly but enacting and modelling what that looks like in practice. These are skills that develop through Dreyfus' stages and require emotional engagement.

Eugene Peterson possesses a slightly different take on what pastors are being trained to do. He sees the art of listening to God and people as being at the core of clergy work. In his book, *Working the Angles*, he laments the loss of this skill in contemporary church leadership yet sets forth a vision for what the pastoral office should be:

> The biblical fact is that there are not successful churches. There are, instead, communities of sinners, gathered before God week after week in town and villages all over the world. The Holy Spirit gathers them and does his work in them. In these communities of sinners, one of the sinners is called pastor and given a designated responsibility in the community. The pastor's responsibility is to keep the community attentive to God. It is this responsibility that is being abandoned in spades.[77]

Being attentive to God and keeping a community of people attentive to God is a challenge online. Relying on technology to learn how to listen to God may not be the best idea. Mentoring novice pastors to leave their technology at home may have a better effect. Edward Tenner writes about the power of a listening physician, even over drugs and devices, in the medical profession:

> Dr. Bernard Lown, winner of the Nobel Peace Prize, [has observed] that "the usual rules of efficiency are inverted in medicine. The more time a physician spends with patients, the more efficient he or she becomes. Listening costs next to nothing, and so is infinitely more cost-effective than drugs and devices." Listening is the key to the most effective and economical use of medical technology, and to avoidance of overtreatment. Limited as the stethoscope is, it also represents what research is beginning to recognize as the therapeutic power of touch.[78]

While an argument can be made that listening happens online, the "therapeutic power of touch," something equally important in medical and pastoral practice, is currently impossible to reproduce online. Things like Niebuhr's "edifying" and Tenner's "therapeutic power of touch" require embodied experts, to use Dreyfus' term, to model the skills and traits that

---

77. Peterson, *Working the Angles*, 2.

78. Tenner, *The Efficiency Paradox*, 198–99.

pastors are learning to practise and embody. Pastoral leadership is more than demonstrating a series of skills and character traits, it is reminding God's people how to be human, especially in light of the pull to become more machine-like, as outlined in the previous chapter. Learning how to be human requires the bodies of teachers to interact with the bodies of learners. David Kelsey summarizes the importance of teachers and learners embodied together coming to a deeper understanding of God:

> If we are best understood as personal organic bodies, then our bodies are inherently involved in our efforts to communicate ourselves as persons. In that case, learning and teaching inherently involve the organic personal bodies of teachers and learners. If coming to understand God involves deep changes in personal bodies, then teaching and learning that aims at deepening understanding of God inherently involves the organic personal bodies of both teachers and learners.[79]

The physical body is important. For student pastors to deepen their skills and knowledge of God, mature mentors are important. In the book, *For Life Abundant*, Christian Scharen's autobiographical chapter on learning to pastor draws on Hubert Dreyfus' research to describe the importance of seasoned pastoral guides:

> [Dreyfus'] stages of developmental learning imply that the "know-how" of expert individuals, whether drivers, plumbers, teachers, or pastors, is not innate, like a bird's ability to build a nest. Human beings have to *learn* to do things like this, usually through trial and error, and often by imitation of those more proficient.[80]

Scharen demonstrates that modeling by proficient and experienced pastors is necessary for learning. He argues that novices need to watch and learn from veteran ministers but also notes the grace that seasoned faith leaders can offer when addressing the blunders, missteps and mistakes of the inexperienced. He writes:

> Knowing that mistakes are normal and even necessary for learning at certain stages can help teachers and other guides to do their work well. Moreover, knowing which mistakes are normal and

---

79. Kelsey, "Spiritual Machines," 9.
80. Scharen, "Learning Ministry over Time," 284.

expected at various points along the way can be of great comfort and encouragement as young pastors learn.[81]

Pastoral skill development and character formation optimally happen through direct and embodied interactions between teacher-mentors and students. This arrangement lessens the chronic anxiety that comes when technology mediates the relationship. In the next chapter I will turn away from anxiety and skill development to address how virtue can be learned online.

81. Scharen, "Learning Ministry over Time," 288.

4

Growing Virtues (and Vices) Online

Sorting the Fruit of Technology
for Character Virtues

As THE PREVIOUS CHAPTER revealed, developing as a self-differentiated pastor requires a careful assessment of how technology may operate to lower levels of differentiation and raise levels of "emotional fusion" between person and device. Maturing as a ministerial student also requires time, practice, and embodied mentors. This chapter picks up where the previous one left off, addressing a parallel theme. Rather than addressing self-differentiation in pastoral development this chapter addresses another central tenet of ministerial work, character virtues. As will become clear, both self-differentiation and virtues are nurtured similarly to skill development. In both cases, technology offers some help for theological educators, but it comes with limits. The very root term "virtue" is found in "virtual" to refer to cyber activities. One refers to the highest attributes of humanity, the other refers to the appearance of something real without it physically existing. If, as discussed in chapter 2, technology possesses a formational character, moulding humans into more mechanical beings, and if that formation allows for chronically anxious and poorly differentiated learners to maintain their status as chronically anxious and poorly self-differentiated, then the next question is, what virtues (or vices) are nurtured by computer and internet usage? If technology itself has a formational character, can it be used to form student character in the image of Jesus Christ? Before exploring these questions, I will first define virtue and examine its place in theological education.

INTRODUCTION TO VIRTUE

Defining Virtue

In his book, *Character and Virtue in Theological Education*, Marvin Oxenham begins his exploration of virtues by grouping them into various categories. He organizes them as follows:

> Virtues have been classified and organized in different ways. We have, for example, the cardinal virtues of prudence, justice, fortitude and temperance. We have the Christian virtues of faith, hope and love. We also have moral virtues like kindness, compassion and generosity, civic virtues like decency, loyalty and diligence, and intellectual virtues like attentiveness, open-mindedness and curiosity. We then have some virtues which are foundational, such as prudence, constancy and love, and specific lists of virtues and vices like the seven capital vices of pride, envy, wrath, sloth/acedia, avarice, gluttony and lust and the corresponding seven capital virtues of humility, kindness, abstinence, chastity, patience, liberality and diligence.[1]

Aristotle's classification of virtues uses a simpler twofold approach highlighting distinctions between thought and character. He writes, "For some virtues are called virtues of thought, others virtues of character; wisdom, comprehension and intelligence are called virtues of thought, generosity and temperance virtues of character."[2] Expanding on this conception of virtue, Olli-Pekka Vainio highlights Aristotle's "practical wisdom," emerging from experience, as someone who is consistently able to find the mean between extremes:

> Virtue typically refers to a character trait that expresses some sort of excellence. This is what is meant by the Greek concept *arete*. Generally, the crucial feature of virtue is that it is a mean between two extremes, lack and excess. For example, a person is brave when she behaves neither cowardly nor foolhardily. Finding the mean

---

1. Oxenham, *Character and Virtue*, 25.
2. Aristotle, *Aristotle*, 215–16.

is often very hard, and this ability, which Aristotle calls practical wisdom (phronesis) is learned through experience alone.[3]

Shannon Vallor's description, linking virtue with excellence, also amplifies Aristotle's perspective. She describes a "moral excellence" view of virtue as longstanding and normative, "Thus the concept of 'virtue' as a descriptor of moral excellence has for millennia occupied a central place in various *normative* theories of human action—that is, theories that aim to prescribe certain kinds of human action as right or good."[4] She suggests that practical wisdom holds a central place in the understanding of virtue. According to Vallor, concrete situations are necessary in order to see someone's wisdom in practice. It is the practical application of wisdom in context that makes someone virtuous:

> ... the virtue of practical wisdom or *phronēsis* encompasses considerations of universal rationality *as well as* considerations of an irreducibly contextual, embodied, relational, and emotional nature—considerations that Kant and others have erroneously regarded as irrelevant to morality. From the totality of these considerations the virtuous person must make moral sense of each concrete situation encountered, and give an appropriate response. A successful moral response is distinguishable from a failed or inappropriate response *in practice*, and the reasons behind the success of that response can always be articulated after the fact. But the difference between moral success and moral failure can rarely, if ever, be deduced in advance from *a priori* principles.[5]

Vallor argues for specific and contextual applications of practical wisdom rather than universal principles. Therefore, virtue is not simply the implementation of general moral guidelines but action that is specific to a particular context and guided by the individual's sense of what is appropriate. Virtuous people act based on what their intuition *and* intelligence determine. Vallor writes, "Practical wisdom is the kind of excellence we find in moral experts, persons whose moral lives are guided by appropriate feeling and intelligence, rather than mindless habit or rote compulsion to follow fixed moral scripts provided by religious, political, or cultural institutions."[6] This way of being requires balance and discipline. Balance

3. Vainio, *Virtue*, 11.
4. Vallor, "Virtue Ethics," 2.
5. Vallor, "Virtue Ethics," 24–25.
6. Vallor, "Virtue Ethics," 25.

is knowing and avoiding pitfalls on either side of actions, what Aristotle calls the mean, and discipline is the ability to act with calmness even under extreme circumstances. Vallor asserts:

> Actions issuing from the moral habits of a virtuous person—that is, a person with practical wisdom—are properly attuned to the unique and changing demands of each concrete moral situation. In contrast, a person who is prone to thoughtless and unmodulated action is likely to go wrong as often as not. Thus moral virtue presupposes knowledge or understanding. Yet unlike theoretical knowledge, the kind of knowledge required for moral virtue is not satisfied by a grasp of universal principles, but requires recognition of the relevant and operative practical conditions.[7]

The virtuous person not only intellectually and rationally knows the right course of action, but intuitively acts on it. Vallor calls this possessing emotional and social intelligence:

> Moral expertise thus entails a kind of knowledge extending well beyond a cognitive grasp of rules and principles to include emotional and social intelligence: keen awareness of the motivations, feelings, beliefs, and desires of others; a sensitivity to the morally salient features of particular situations; and a creative knack for devising appropriate practical responses to those situations, especially where they involve novel or dynamically unstable circumstances.[8]

Virtue as practical wisdom is an intuitive way of living that transfers knowledge into action in a way that is seen by others as good and right. It is walking the talk. Doug Blomberg takes this approach in his book, *Wisdom and Curriculum*. He starts by exploring the use of the term "wisdom" when applied to objects rather than people, setting forth a meaning based in movement. He writes, "The Concise Oxford English Dictionary tells me that [the etymology of the term 'clockwise'] indicates 'a manner or a way of going.' It shows the way (OE *wisian*—originally, to 'make wise'), it points a direction."[9] Going further into the way of wisdom, Blomberg writes:

> Although the dictionary distinguishes this meaning of wise from that of the quality we attribute to persons, it is not difficult to see that they are not completely separable. Indeed, wisdom is also a way of going, a manner of being, an established direction and

7. Vallor, "Virtue Ethics," 26.
8. Vallor, "Virtue Ethics," 26.
9. Blomberg, *Wisdom and Curriculum*, 54.

pattern of living, as much if not more than a grasp of particular principles. Thus, when Jesus claims to be the way, the truth and the life (John 14:6), he is talking about a way of walking—the way of wisdom.[10]

Blomberg ultimately arrives at his summary of wisdom: "Wisdom is not a body of knowledge to be attained: it is a way of being."[11] This chapter focuses on developing this way of wisdom in those preparing for pastoral ministry. I will pay particular attention to nurturing character virtues, such as those found in the Apostle Paul's letter to the Galatians where he describes the fruit of the Spirit as "love, joy, peace, patience, kindness, goodness, faithfulness, gentleness, and self-control" (Gal. 5:22–23 NASB).

How Are Virtues Acquired?

Virtue as practical wisdom is a way of being. That Way, for theological educators, can be summarized in and through the life and teachings of Jesus Christ. How might the life of Jesus, that way of practical wisdom, be learned? Or, to ask it in another way, how are virtues of practical wisdom acquired?

Aristotle understood character virtues to be developed through repeated practice. Stating, "Virtue of character results from habit,"[12] Aristotle roots the development of virtues in continuous actions practised regularly. Aristotle posits that virtue does not originate in human nature—what modern science calls DNA—but is learned, much like an ability to play a musical instrument. Contrasting things acquired through nature to things acquired through habit, Aristotle writes:

> If something arises in us by nature, we first have the capacity for it, and later display the activity. This is clear in the case of the senses; for we did not acquire them by frequent seeing or hearing, but already had them when we exercised them, and did not get them by exercising them. Virtues, by contrast, we acquire, just as we acquire crafts, by having previously activated them. For we learn a craft by producing the same product that we must produce when we have learned it, becoming builders, for instance, by building and harpists by playing the harp; so also, then, we become just by

10. Blomberg, *Wisdom and Curriculum*, 54.
11. Blomberg, *Wisdom and Curriculum*, 170.
12. Aristotle, *Aristotle*, 216.

doing just actions, temperate by doing temperate actions, brave by doing brave actions.[13]

What Aristotle describes as virtue acquisition is the process of learning a trade or a skill. Matt Stichter agrees. In his book, *The Skillfulness of Virtue*, he argues that virtues are appropriated in the same way as expertise. Stichter opens his book by stating, "The acquisition of a virtue is a process of acquiring a skill. Expertise in a skill enables us to be reliably responsive to reasons and to act well in demanding situations, and acquiring expertise requires the motivation to hold oneself to high standards—all of which are elements we typically associate with possessing a virtue."[14] For Stichter, acting well in demanding contexts and holding oneself to high standards are strong rationale for linking virtue development with skill acquisition.

The Role of Others in Virtue Acquisition

If virtue is acquired in the same way as a skill, what role do people play in that learning development? According to Ross Thompson, embodied relationships are paramount. The development of virtue starts with the presence of another person. It begins in the very first relationship between parent and child. These first formative experiences lay the foundation for morality and character development. Thompson states:

> Virtue has developmental origins, therefore, in an intuitive premoral sensibility that emerges from early psychological understanding and its cultivation in the context of a parent-child relationship that builds on it—particularly positive relational experiences that afford mutual responsiveness, respect, and understanding. Any developmental account that overlooks these early influences risks misunderstanding the origins of moral awareness and of formative influences on moral character.[15]

Of particular interest is the role of positive relationships in virtue formation during childhood. Virtue acquisition, at this early stage in a child's life, occurs through direct and embodied contact with a trusted caregiver. This position parallels the findings of psychologist Erik Erikson. He describes basic trust as the first and most important ingredient of a healthy

13. Aristotle, *Aristotle*, 216–17.

14. Matt Stichter, *The Skillfulness of Virtue*, 1–2.

15. Thompson, "A Perspective," 297.

personality. How does one learn to trust? Erikson writes, "the *amount of trust* derived from earliest infantile experience does not seem to depend on absolute *quantities of food or demonstrations of love* but rather on the *quality* of the maternal relationship."[16] It appears that quality human relationships are of supreme importance in the development of virtue long before children learn to walk and talk.

> Trustworthy, nurturing, caregivers are essential in the earliest stages of virtue formation. However, they are not the only requisite. As one grows, habit and emotion play crucial roles as well. David James describes the core aspects of virtue formation as three facets: habit, emotion, and relationship. To the question about what is required in the acquisition of virtue, he submits: Persons acquire virtue at first through habit, then through other-directed emotional insights, and finally, through experiences of personal relationship and shared activities. All three are necessary for the complete acquisition of virtue, though each has been mistakenly put forward as sufficient by itself.[17]

According to James, habit, social relationships, and what he calls "other-directed emotional insights" work together. Knowing and doing the right things are not enough for the growth of virtue. Feeling and emotion must become involved and directed toward understanding others. James writes:

> I must know the other in her full concreteness if my feeling is to be directed toward her reality instead of my fantasy. Imaginative projection into the reality of the other, based on knowledge of the other, is essential to the existence of a benevolent virtue. In children this projective empathy may begin with fantasy play with dolls, then extend to care for pets, whose needs impose a stronger measure of reality on the developing child. Finally, moral feeling may gradually broaden and attach itself to playmates and other persons whose needs and reality must be understood before altruistic concern is possible.[18]

Human relationship is central to the acquisition of virtue. Not only are childhood experiences of a nurturing caregiver fundamental but learning to extend empathy and compassion back toward that caregiver or another human being is the way of nurturing and enacting virtue. It cannot be done

16. Erikson, *Identity and the Life Cycle*, 65.
17. James, "The Acquisition of Virtue," 102–3.
18. James, "The Acquisition of Virtue," 112.

through cognitive or intellectual pursuits alone. Virtue acquisition depends on feelings directed toward others when learning how to act rightly. Drawing on Aristotle, James writes:

> An adequate account of the virtue of compassion must go beyond the mere outward performance of actions corresponding to some moral precept or principle. For compassion is both a disposition to act in a certain way—to relieve suffering—*and* to feel in a certain way—to want to end suffering and to share the experience of the sufferer. It was obvious to Aristotle that if a man does not act from the right motive, he cannot be a good man. Moral character concerns both emotions and actions. There is more to the moral life and the worth of moral agents than a sense of duty. An ethic of principle's exclusive emphasis on actions motivated by reason should be rejected in favor of a neo-Aristotelian view which places emotions such as compassion at the center of the moral life.[19]

For right action to be virtuous, emotion plays a central role. Embodied relationships are also key to developing virtue and a flourishing life. Central to the growth virtue is what James calls "shared life together." This can be seen through James' reference to the villagers of Chambon where the whole community worked together to provide hospitality to Jewish children during the Second World War:

> Aristotle used the term philia or friendship to refer to all sorts of interpersonal relationships. Consider Nicomachean Ethics 1170a4-ll, where Aristotle says: "[P]eople think a flourishing person should live pleasantly. Now life is hard for a solitary person; for it is not easy to be continuously active apart by oneself, but this is easier together with others and toward them. So, [in living with others the flourishing person's] activity, which is pleasant in itself, will be more continuous, as it ought to be for a fully flourishing person." Aristotle here claims that friendship, as part of a good life, involves shared activities with others. Complete virtue in this way involves community and acting with others to produce good, just as the villagers of Chambon acted together to save Jewish children from the Holocaust.[20]

Summarizing James' understanding of the relationality of virtue acquisition, he writes: "Moral virtues involve distinctive operations of gradually educated practical insight and deliberation as well as motivating emotions

19. James, "The Acquisition of Virtue," 112–13.
20. James, "The Acquisition of Virtue," 116–17.

actively experienced through encounters of a person with others."[21] Or, to simplify James' theory, the acquisition of character virtues involves habits, emotions, and embodied relationships.

In *The Oxford Handbook of Virtue*, Nafsika Athanassoulis also confirms the role of relationships and emotions in the acquisition of virtue. Writing about Aristotle's take on practical wisdom, she states:

> Phronesis, then, is a type of know-how that is supported by a variety of abilities, from emotional maturity, to self-reflection, to an empathic understanding of what moves others, to an ability to see beyond the surface and understand the complexities of human behavior. These abilities develop gradually, over time, subject to favorable circumstances, but one by one they eventually form an impenetrable barrier, in Aristotle's words "[i]t is like a rout in battle stopped by first one man making a stand then another, until the original formation has been restored; the soul is so constituted as to be capable of this process."[22]

Virtue as practical wisdom is acquired through a process similar to skill development. However, virtue development diverges from learning a technical skill at one significant point: character virtues are relational at their core. Most skills require the learner to practise with objects and tools to gain expertise. Their skill can then be measured and assessed—such as Aristotle's craftsperson or harpist—through looking at what has been built or by listening to what is being played. Virtues cannot be assessed in the same way. Like the craftsperson or harpist, time and practice are also required by the person seeking to become virtuous or wise. However, the difference is that the expert or master skilled in wisdom is someone who *relates to others* in a virtuous way. Relationality is key. Human beings function both as models/teachers (harpists) of virtue but also as tools/subjects (harps). The master teacher must embody virtue for the learner and train the learner how to live virtuously. This is accomplished as the learner observes the master interacting with others. However, it is also learned as the master teacher relates virtuously with the student. The master and learner play and are played simultaneously as harpists and harps. They are encultured into virtue. In this climate of enculturation, embodied human relationships become teachers and subjects in the acquisition of virtue. The concept of an embodied culture of virtue is not something that can be

---

21. James, "The Acquisition of Virtue," 103.

22. Athanassoulis, "Acquiring Aristotelian Virtue," 424.

replicated online. Therefore, without the presence of another human be-ing acting virtuously, how would someone experience character virtues in the first place? Furthermore, even if they could experience virtues through memories and feelings of embodied experiences with a virtuous person, they would require another embodied human being with whom to practise becoming virtuous. The road toward becoming virtuous and wise begins with habituated practise of wise actions with and for others where emotion and feeling for others leads to action. With this understood, the next ques-tion is whether theological schools are contexts where habits, relationships, and emotions are being directed toward developing wise people.

VIRTUE IN THEOLOGICAL EDUCATION

It may come as a surprise but according to Marvin Oxenham, author of *Character and Virtue in Theological Education*, there have been very few articles written about virtue and theological education in the last 50 years. He insists:

> Browsing *Theological Education* from 1964 to 2017, I found a good stock of writing around spiritual formation, but only one article and one special supplement dealing specifically with character or moral education. Likewise, a combined keyword search in *The Journal of Adult Theological Education* for "character education" and "virtue" produced only seven articles, of which only one is really pertinent.[23]

Oxenham goes on to summarize his findings, "Overall, I think we can safely conclude that, in the last century or so, character and virtue educa-tion has not been an object of sustained attention in the literature on theological education."[24] Why such a dearth in writings about virtue in theological education?

Theological Education: Paideia or *Wissenschaft*?

The reason for the scarcity of writing on virtue is likely due to the modern educational focus that started in the universities of Berlin and became part of the fabric of pastoral education in North America. As outlined in chapter

23. Oxenham, *Character and Virtue*, 44.
24. Oxenham, *Character and Virtue*, 45.

1, modern theological schools moved away from a paideia focus, one that orients itself toward character and virtue formation leading to wisdom, to embrace German education's *Wissenschaft*, with its focus on pursuing knowledge through scholarship and its priority for training professional clergy. As Oxenham discovered in his literature review, paideia has not been the dominant focus of clerical education for some time. This shift is evident in an article by historian William Westfall describing the changes in Anglican clergy training in Upper Canada during the 1800's. He first cites an example of a more paideia-oriented apprenticeship. Drawing from a letter written in 1840 by The Rev. Featherstone Lake Osler about his program of clergy apprenticeship and his daily routine for those in training, he scribes:

> The following is the plan I pursue with regards to them. At 6 a.m. they meet in my study for Scripture reading. This engages them until half past seven, when we breakfast. Afterwards they study . . . until evening . . . . We take an early tea, after which I give them three hours to correct their exercises, hear them read &c. By this means none of my public duties [is] neglected, as I attend to [the students] when my outdoor . . . work is done . . . . On Sunday I send out two of them to . . . different outposts to read prayers, superintend the Sunday schools and visit the sick . . . . One I keep home to assist me in my central Sunday school.[25]

Westfall goes on to describe the evolution of Anglican clerical training from Rev. Featherstone Lake Osler's paideia methods to a slightly more formalized school setting in Cobourg, and then to the highly formalized institution, Trinity College in Toronto, where *Wissenschaft* became a focal point. Westfall recounts the loss of practical instruction as training shifted from Cobourg to Trinity:

> [Trinity College] seemed to downplay what Cobourg had done so effectively: provide candidates with "practical instruction in the labours of a missionary." After setting out in detail the academic requirements, the provisional statutes seemed to dismiss the importance of practical instruction, only expressing the hope that "arrangements [would] be made for giving the Theology Students some practical acquaintance with parochial duties." Furthermore,

---

25. Taken from Anne Wilkinson, *Lions in the Way: A Discursive History of the Oslers* (Toronto: Macmillan, 1956), 67. In Westfall, "Some Practical Acquaintance," 49.

this issue is not taken up in later revisions of the statutes, which drop even this passing reference.[26]

Westfall describes Trinity as being more focused on intellectual virtues than character and practical pastoral skill development. This is a far cry from Osler's small community of clergy students who accompanied their expert teacher through the rhythms of scripture study, prayer, and conversations over tea. As Oxenham discovered in his search for virtue-focused articles, the shift toward *Wissenschaft* has, indeed, been firmly established in theological institutions. These days, it appears, virtue and character formation are assumed to be developed before students arrive at theological schools as Ronald Mercier suggests:

> Most of our traditional models for theological education have presumed that a theological school could rely upon a "feeder culture" that would have formed both students and faculty members before they arrived. This assumption, one which [Edward] Farley and many others rightly note to be dangerous, allowed schools to focus on the distinctive elements needed for ministry, mostly academic learning and skill acquisition. These continue, for the most part, to be the heart of theological curricula and programs of study.[27]

With the assumption that students enrolling in theological schools have already been formed in churches and non-curricular methods, classroom learning focuses on intellectual development and academic assignments. However, not everyone agrees that this is how it should be. There are various perspectives about the role of theological schools in developing both intellectual and character virtues. The following are examples of two perspectives, one paideia and one *Wissenschaft*, in contemporary theological education debates.

Mike Harrison has written a relatively recent article arguing for character virtue formation in theological education. He examines the most important traits of Church of England clergy, detailing nine virtues. Describing their importance for Christian witness in the world, he outlines their value for British society:

> Nine qualities one might expect to see in the theologically educated: gratitude, joy, attention to beauty, responsiveness, humility, vulnerable learning, practiced listening, aware of the presence to

---

26. Westfall, "Some Practical Acquaintance," 59–60.
27. Mercier, "Balancing Formation," 320–21.

God, and leisured diligence—not an exhaustive list and inevitably
somewhat idiosyncratic. However, these characteristics are those
that might witness fruitfully in the culture in which we are set in
the 21st century. The focus is less on knowledge and skills (important as these are) as on character, reflecting both the missional
imperative to 'show the difference' following Jesus makes, and the
assumption of the ancient world that education is inculturation
(παιδεια) into a life of virtue (αρετη).[28]

He argues for a residential model of education to accomplish this paideia
education with the following rationale:

> An argument can be made for investment in places focused on
> clergy training for ministry here—one reason for residential
> training being to develop this theological education of praxis: a
> corporate rhythm of prayer and worship, community life in and
> through which we are challenged to share in the ways of God in
> our relationships, encounters and decisions.[29]

David Tracy, on the other hand, sees learning virtues in theological education, not as an immersion in a life of prayer and worship, but as a dialectical experience. For him, acquiring virtue in theological education is not a
process of enculturation but the logical exchange of ideas. Tracy sees the
act of conversation and debate leading to a deeper understanding of the
soul, something more at home in a *Wissenschaft* theological orientation. He
argues that the dialectical nature of learning is training of the soul:

> A theological education, grounded in continuous searching of the
> Christian classics, especially the Bible, open to the demands of
> inquiry become the demands of retrieval, critique, and suspicion,
> can become again a school for the training of the soul. That is how
> theological education began. That is how, I believe, it needs to see
> itself again. Otherwise even our noble contemporary attempts to
> teach "values" and "character-formation" may become trapped
> again in a mere individualism. To rethink theological education
> in our increasingly pluralistic and ambiguous global context is to
> rethink as well, not the 'individualist' model of the purely autono-
> mous self of Enlightenment modernity, not even, primarily, the
> classic notions of identity-formation through character of Aristo-
> tle and his successors. It is also to retrieve—critically, suspiciously,

---

28. Harrison, "What Do," 353.

29. Harrison, "What Do," 354.

even at times, but really—the Christian soul as the subject-in-process of the Christian identity.[30]

Educator Parker Palmer, while not a theological teacher, provides a helpful perspective. He uses the terms "soft" and "hard" for concepts that could fall under the understanding of paideia and *Wissenschaft* and suggests that both are important in education. The culture and context must provide an environment of trust and acceptance for dialectical exchange to produce fruit. He writes:

> The debate over educational reform has often been polarized between the apostles of the "hard" intellectual virtues and the disciples of the "soft" emotional virtues. It has been a fruitless debate because it has missed a simple point: the practice of intellectual rigor in the classroom requires an ethos of trust and acceptance. Intellectual rigor depends on things like honest dissent and the willingness to change our minds, things that will not happen if the "soft" values of community are lacking. In the absence of the communal virtues, intellectual rigor too easily turns into intellectual *rigor mortis*.[31]

If intellectual virtues, what Aristotle called virtues of thought—such as comprehension and intelligence—are exercised in *Wissenschaft*, and virtues of character—such as generosity and the fruit of the Spirit (Gal. 5:20–21)—find expression through paideia, then the next question is whether these two varieties of virtues can be nurtured online. It appears that *Wissenschaft* can be cultivated online but the culture and environment of paideia may be more difficult.

Examining the results of an Association of Theological Schools survey of graduating students shows the challenge of developing a paideia-focused environment where habit, emotion, and relationship work together to nurture virtue. The survey shows that, among other things, online students reported higher levels of spiritual development than on-campus students. However, when the results are viewed by looking at which group developed higher levels of virtues such as 1) empathy and compassion toward others, and 2) the development of what David James refers to as "acting with others to produce good" as noted above, the survey shows lower levels of development for online students. Every survey area that refers to others (i.e., respect for other religious traditions, empathy for the poor and oppressed, etc.)

---

30. Tracy, "Can Virtue Be Taught," 51–52.

31. Palmer, *To Know as We Are Known*, xvii.

shows lower levels of growth (the red/negative numbers in Fig. 1) for online students. So, while the results show online education is enhancing spiritual formation in students, it also reveals a reduction in empathy, compassion, and a community acting with other others to produce good for those same students.[32]

AREAS OF PERSONAL GROWTH [5 = highest]	MAJORITY ONLINE	MAJORITY ON-CAMPUS	DIFFERENCE
Enthusiasm for learning	4.42	4.17	+ .25
Respect for my religious tradition	4.22	4.16	+ .06
Self-knowledge	4.19	4.11	+ .08
Respect for other religious traditions	3.92	4.05	- .13
Empathy for poor and oppressed	3.78	4.00	- .22
Insight into troubles of others	3.85	3.98	- .13
Trust in God	4.30	3.95	+ .35
Self-discipline and focus	4.27	3.97	+ .30
Ability to live one's faith in daily life	4.20	3.88	+ .32
Strength of spiritual life	4.20	3.75	+ .45
Self-confidence	4.10	3.92	+ .18
Desire to become an authority in my field	4.03	3.87	+ .16
Concern about social justice	3.72	3.95	- .23
Clarity of vocational goals	3.86	3.80	+ .06
Ability to pray	3.64	3.37	+ .27

Results of 2015–2016 ATS Graduating Student Questionnaire Online vs. On-Campus Comparison (green = higher scores for online; red = lower scores for online)[33]

The survey reveals the challenge of defining spiritual formation and virtue development in theological education. Even though the "majority online" students self-reported higher levels of spiritual vitality, the social and communal aspects of virtue formation appeared lower among them. Again, this appears to show that some facets of virtue development, particularly those that are intellectual and interior, are suited to an online theological learning environment. However, character virtues that depend on relationships with others are not are readily developed online. Sherry Turkle describes this when she writes:

> In education, we said we would skip having in-person classes, because we could design online technology that would deliver

32. Tanner, "Online Learning at ATS Schools: Part 2."
33. Tanner, "Online Learning at ATS Schools: Part 2," 4.

a "personalized" class, pitched to each learner's skill level. But in the process, we often stopped asking what we really wanted students to get out of class. Is the class most important as a vector for the transmission of information? What about its role as a place where students learn to listen to each other? To empathize with each other? Those things don't easily happen if students are staring at screens.[34]

Learning Virtues Online

As noted in Chapter 1, several theological educators have fully embraced the transition from classroom instruction to Internet learning. Many see it as a step forward in teaching theology and student formation. Yet, their definition of formation seems unclear. It appears that many understand and write about it as a dialectical or dialogical experience that leads to transformation of the mind and life. This perspective on formation aligns well with the virtues of *Wissenschaft* rather than paideia. Others view formation as paideia, learning the way of wisdom and love through praxis. What follows are researchers and practitioners arguing that online learning management systems are appropriate and helpful platforms for student theological and pastoral formation. What will become clear is that the definition of formation for most is more aligned with *Wissenschaft* and the intellectual virtues it produces. Even those arguing for a paideia definition of formation appear to base their arguments on assumptions that dialogue leads to action. This again points back to a *Wissenschaft* model rather than a paideia model. I will first review arguments for *Wissenschaft* online, followed by arguments for paideia online.

Wissenschaft *Virtues Online*

In an article with a catchy title called, "What Would Kant Tweet," authors Ron Mercer and Mark Simpson suggest that scientific inquiry for theological learning can happen online. Pointing to the value of dialectics through things like online discussion groups they write, "Online learning should not be designed as just another modality for acquiring information. Instead, including a form of zetetic learning as proposed by Kant can make the classroom a dynamic formative environment for the fully online

---

34. Turkle, *Alone Together*, xxi.

student."[35] This theme of formation through dialogue is picked up by Mark Nicols. He concludes his article, looking at formational experiences of on-campus and online students, by writing, "A strong case can be made that optimal formation through theological education actually takes place when part-time students, already active in their local congregations, are empowered by theological ideas and dialogue."[36] These educators make a compelling case for formation through dialogue, a formation that nurtures *Wissenschaft* virtues.

Ros Stuart-Buttle also asserts a *Wissenschaft* orientation in her perspective of formation. She summarizes her research and experience as a Christian educator learning how to teach online by saying:

> [Online education] can achieve an authentic integration of pedagogy in a structured environment, where the role of the tutor still counts, and where quality materials can enrich religious knowledge and understanding as well as encourage the genuine reflection, articulation and collaborative interactions of the learning community.[37]

Stuart-Buttle suggests that a structured environment with good tutoring and quality materials can enhance the intellectual virtues of *Wissenschaft* such as knowledge and understanding. Mary Hess sees technology and media culture as ubiquitous, formational, and a necessary part of theological education. In her book, *Engaging Technology in Theological Education*, she states, "Media culture—which is increasingly digitally created and mediated—is the water in which all of us swim. It may even be, as Tom Beaudoin argues, the 'amniotic fluid' of younger generations."[38] Hess' admission that media culture "is the water in which all of us swim" sounds like paideia, especially when she argues for the use of technology as an important medium of expression. She writes:

> We need constantly to remind ourselves that learning—and thus the very specific learning that is graduate theological education—is at its heart about practice. We can do this in part by giving people access to digital technologies in ways that deconstruct

---

35. Mercer and Simpson, "What Would Kant Tweet," 17–18.

36. Nichols, "The Formational Experiences," 30.

37. Stuart-Buttle, *Virtual Theology*, 214.

38. Hess, *Engaging Technology*, 30.

instrumental assumptions and by encouraging expressive uses of digital technologies.[39]

Hess argues for the neutrality of technology, even arguing for the positive formational culture of the Net. However, her focus is on learning that leads to practice, rather than paideia and character formation. Hess sees the value of technology for the enhanced praxis of theological education in a media-saturated culture. Her orientation toward practice is another example of *Wissenschaft*, with its nexus of intellectual rigour and professional practice.

From these findings, it appears that certain types of e-learning provide ways for *Wissenschaft* virtues to be nurtured in students. The next question is whether character virtues can be developed online.

Paideia Virtues Online

In seeking to answer whether or not technology can "help cultivate that deeper theological wisdom that the Christian tradition expects of its pastoral ministers," Thomas Esselman answers "yes."[40] After reviewing his experience and that of his fellow faculty members engaged in online teaching, he asserts:

> I was particularly gratified to see how these adult learners used the online format to engage one another, especially in small groups. That spirit of mutuality and openness to learning, that ability to ask critical questions, and that willingness to take the lead in the reflection process characteristic of our face-to-face sessions carried over as they worked on the Web. The Web became more than just a storehouse of information or even a place in which to engage in critical dialogue; the Web became a tool for the ongoing development of the cohort as a wisdom community.[41]

Esselman highlights the mutuality and engagement in critical dialogue that occurred between students on the Web as a defining mark of a wisdom community. However, Esselman's assessment of deeper theological wisdom appears to look more like *Wissenschaft*, with its focus on dialogue and dialectics, as opposed to paideia. Beyond observing "a spirit of openness and

39. Hess, *Engaging Technology*, 32.
40. Esselman, "The Pedagogy," 160.
41. Esselman, "The Pedagogy," 166.

mutuality" he does not describe the practicalities of what he defines as a "wisdom community."

Ros Stuart-Buttle argues that Christian educators should be building communities of faith and that extends online as well. She suggests using learning management systems to model paideia virtues, writing:

> One way to do this is to become "wise caretakers" of the educational dimension of God's world and to use online learning technologies to model wisdom, truth, compassion, justice and peace in humility before the power of the Holy Spirit. Emphasis on such values may be a gift that the Christian community can bring to secular online education.[42]

While Stuart-Buttle's idea is noble, she does not offer any tangible examples of how such things as compassion or peace can be manifested online. Other researchers examining formation in learning, such as Jennifer Roberts, also make a case for developing what I would describe as paideia virtues in online contexts. Roberts asks, "The question that needs to be addressed is whether teaching in an online environment is possible when more than just content needs to be delivered. Can ethics, morals and spirituality be taught online—can we produce an OEH (Online Educated Human)?"[43] She determines that it can in fact be accomplished but her research and examples leave questions to be explored. Additionally, her conclusion contradicts her argument. Drawing on models of pre-Internet Distance Education studies as well as newer models such as Garrison, Anderson and Archer's Community of Inquiry model (outlined in chapter 1), she highlights that community, through *Wissenschaft* dialogue, can happen online. Additionally, she draws on a quantitative student survey showing that students self-report growing more in terms of spiritual formation from their congregation relationships than course materials. She ultimately concludes that a hybrid approach, using both online and in-class learning, is ideal.[44] Her questions focus on paideia but her answers, along with other researchers writing about online spiritual formation, do not address formation as paideia online and they fail to address the following: how does technology itself form the learner? Do traditional Distance Education programs develop paideia virtues in students? If so, how? And can responses from

---

42. Stuart-Buttle, *Virtual Theology*, 178.

43. Roberts, "Online Learning," 5.

44. Roberts, "Online Learning," 5–7.

students—who self-report on surveys—provide an accurate assessment of growth in virtues such as love, generosity, etc. in their lives?

One exception to the scarce supply of research on paideia's character and wisdom formation online is an article entitled, "Virtual Empathy?" in which educators Melinda Sharp and Mary Ann Morris make a strong case for teaching the soft virtue of empathy in a Web-based classroom. They describe observing empathy between students online through clear and focused instructions at the outset of a Web-based pastoral care course. They argue that, in providing clear instructions up front, they are creating a context where e-learning anxieties can be turned into empathy. Empathy can be expressed, they suggest, once helpful parameters are put in place. They cite an example of what they call "virtual empathy" in an online chat exchange as part of a role play for their pastoral care course. Their assertion, that empathy can be shown in an online course, is convincing. However, they do not go so far as to suggest that empathy can be taught and learned online, simply that they have found a way for it to be manifest through online chat features.[45]

Skill Development Online

While Dave Ward does not deal directly with teaching virtue in theological education online, he concedes that developing skills online is possible. Since the similarities of virtue acquisition and skill development have already been shown, Ward's research is relevant. He takes issue with some of Hubert Dreyfus' assertions, covered in chapter 3, about the Internet not being a context that allows for the development of skilful expertise among subjects. He writes:

> Just as visually impaired people can expand the range of perceptible properties to which they are sensitive by reworking their body schema to incorporate a cane, Dreyfus's teenagers and air-traffic controllers acquire new systems of bodily and affective habits that afford direct experiential contact with threats and opportunities that can only be revealed via the medium of the technology they are using.[46]

45. McGarrah Sharp and Morris, "Virtual Empathy."

46. Ward, "What's Lacking," 14.

Ward suggests that computers and technology act as a sort of blind person's cane. Therefore, just as the cane allows the user to detect danger, so the computer or smartphone could be a gateway to detecting real challenges that trigger emotional engagement leading to the growth of things like skills and virtues. After positing this foundational argument, he goes on to write:

> Given that [the Merleau-Pontian View] (henceforth MPV) allows that affective salience can be perceived by learners in the absence of embodied interactions, online teaching must attempt to compensate for its limits by leaning harder on the ways in which bodily and affective habits *can* be shaped by online resources. And it must do so in a way informed by careful reflection both on the affective structure of understanding in the relevant domain, and on the existing portfolio of bodily and affective habits that learners bring to the table. Dreyfus is right that MPV affords a useful diagnostic framework for understanding what might be lacking in online learning. But this is cause for optimism—MPV sheds light not on the impossibility of online learning, but on what is required for it to reach its full potential.[47]

Ward concludes that, while Dreyfus is correct in pointing out the limits of online teaching for developing skill, educators are just getting started in leveraging learning management systems for teaching. If teachers "lean harder" into the ways technology can shape bodily and affective habits then there is hope for embodied skills, such as virtues, to be learned online to the point of expertise. The only significant gap in Ward's argument is the assumption that the technological medium itself is neutral and not already working to shape the learner toward its own ends, or at least the ends of the program and software designers. As argued in chapter two, technology has a way of shaping those that use it.

Research into the Internet's usefulness with respect to virtue development appears clear. As described above, the intellectual or *Wissenschaft* virtues, developed through dialectical and dialogical exchanges, are being nurtured online. Learners are engaged in discussions and accessing digital resources to advance knowledge and understanding. However, evidence showing the development of practical wisdom virtues via Web-based programs, ones that shape the character of the person, is lacking. Not only is Internet education deficient in creating the environment where habits,

47. Ward, "What's Lacking," 20.

emotions, and relationships intersect in a way that leads to wisdom, it appears to be a context where certain vices emerge.

Learning Vices Online

Technological Consumption: A Loss of Human Autonomy

Some researchers see the turn toward online education as a shift toward a pedagogy of consumerism, an endeavour that turns educational institutions into big businesses. Whereas the goal of big business is profit, educational institutions are aimed in a different direction. Schools teach individuals to think and act critically and wisely in the world. As Paul Chau claims, some schools are starting to look more like businesses and that mindset is at odds with critical thinking. Chau contends:

> When institutions start to function more like corporations and change from being in the business of education into being in the education business, higher education will no longer be the grounds for where students can be educated to critically think and question what exist [sic] in society and learn to be citizens.[48]

As part of that shift toward a big business approach, some schools have started experimenting with purchasing courses developed elsewhere. Researchers like Edward Hamilton and Andrew Feenberg point to prepackaged Internet courses as problematic:

> Reduced to information, education seemingly no longer requires its traditional social mediations—the physical classroom, the university as an institution, or the professional teacher. It can be organized like a process of industrial production of commodified goods consumed by isolated learners. It is also easy to imagine who might find such a redefinition of education attractive. It is a short step from a pedagogical model of information delivery to an industrial model of information production, and a commercial model of information marketing and consumption. The transformation of education into a product promises a new revenue stream for economically beleaguered universities. In economic terms this product resembles CDs or software, the marginal cost of which declines rapidly with the number of units produced. A popular "brand," such as MIT, might become a sort of educational Britney Spears, milking "platinum" courseware for big

48. Chau, "Online Higher Education," 181.

profits. The university finally has a "business model." University administrators eager to cut costs can find common ground here with commercial interests seeking access to the multibillion dollar education market.[49]

Hamilton and Feenberg's concerns are less pertinent to schools with in-house professors developing engaging and lively online courses. However, even highly interactive courses using platforms like Zoom, Microsoft Teams, or Google Classroom, are still designed by corporations. Those businesses have values and behind the platform, Charles Ess notes, big business interests are in play. Those businesses may couch their vision in altruistic terms, promoting education and freedom, but at the end of the day they are still motivated to produce consumers. The goal of enrolling more people and institutions, who will spend time using their tools, is good for business. This shift has concerning consequences for the development of intellectual and character virtues. Ess writes:

> As "users" of these technologies spend more and more of their time as consumers of technology, their use of the Internet and the Web may be more and more shaped by the practices of con-sumption—including their being extensively manipulated by the companies and corporations that seek to market their goods and services to users as customers. However much individuals may 'choose' to participate in these technologies as consumers, the first point is that the more we learn how to be consumers pursu-ing our self-interest vis-à-vis the seemingly limitless offerings of the Web and the Net, the less we learn how to be critical students and teachers engaged in the sorts of dialogues that help shape our self-understanding and awareness of the larger world, develop the skills of engaging with one another in real-world contexts and foster our effective engagement in the world for the sake of greater justice, freedom, and peace.[50]

According to Ess, the very act of consuming Web technologies for the pur-pose of learning makes students less able to engage in tangible and practical service in the world. Carr addresses this erosion of the concept of human-ity, from embodied and socially engaged beings in the world to an image that gets absorbed into online media. He writes:

---

49. Hamilton and Feenberg, "The Technical Codes," 231–32.

50. Ess, "Liberal Arts," 126.

When the Net absorbs a medium, it re-creates that medium in its own image. It not only dissolves the medium's physical form; it injects the medium's content with hyperlinks, breaks up the content into searchable chunks, and surrounds the content with the content of all the other media it has absorbed. All these changes in the form of the content also change the way we use, experience, and even understand the content.[51]

This concept, of how the understanding of humanity is changed through the use of machines and technology, is stated by Lewis Mumford in his 1934 book, *Technics and Civilization*:

The brute fact of the matter is that our civilization is now weighted in favor of the use of mechanical instruments, because the opportunities for commercial production and for the exercise of power lie there: while all the direct human reaction or the personal arts which require a minimum of mechanical paraphernalia are treated as negligible. The habit of producing good whether they are needed or not, of utilizing inventions whether they are useful or not, of utilizing inventions whether they are useful or not, of applying power whether it is effective or not pervades almost every department of our present civilization. The result is that while areas of the personality have been slighted: the telic, rather than the merely adaptive, spheres of conduct exist on sufferance. This pervasive instrumentalism places a handicap upon vital reactions which cannot be closely tied to the machine, and it magnifies the importance of physical goods as symbols—even as it tends to characterize their absence as a sign of stupidity and failure. And to the extent that this materialism is purposeless, it becomes final: the means are presently converted into an end. If material goods need any other justification, they have it in the fact that the effort to consume them keeps the machines running.[52]

As more time and focus is spent using technology to learn online, there is a risk that the act of using and consuming technology erodes the sense of embodied humanity and character values. As Mumford suggests, the very act of using machines may become humanity's ultimate goal. The consumption of technology may become an end in itself.

51. Carr, *The Shallows*, 90.

52. Mumford, *Technics and Civilization*, 274.

Distraction: A Loss of Contemplation, Compassion, and Empathy

Distraction may have upsides, such as alleviating boredom, but it also undermines one of the most important aspects of pastoral ministry—focused time for reflection and prayer.[53] Contemplation allows the minister to remain centered, grounded, and creative in congregational ministry, especially during anxious times. Unfortunately, technology and Internet applications do not appear to promote contemplation and imagination. For example, after researching the effects of technology on Christian school students, David I. Smith et al. conclude:

> Many digital media are structured to assist skim reading and swift location of data. Religious reading practices, in contrast, focus on depth of understanding and spiritual formation and are therefore associated with practices of reading slowly, repeatedly, communally, reverentially. Such reading is also associated with some basic Christian virtues, including patience, humility, and charity. These entail avoiding hasty judgments. The efficiency of scanning and searching for information and moving on as soon as we have located what we need can be valuable when we need to maximize the information at our fingertips. These strategies associated with such reading can, however, nurture superficiality and premature conclusions. They are also less well suited to the pursuit of personal transformation and deep engagement that belong to spiritually nourishing reading.[54]

According to David I. Smith et al. digital media do not promote deep and reflective reading, the sort of contemplation that leads to foundational Christian virtues. Picking up on this theme, Nicole Speer has found that brain scans show what Smith is indicating. Deep reading, the kind that happens when someone is immersed in a novel, is linked to imagination as readers become immersed in the story. Nicholas Carr recounts Speer's findings:

> In one fascinating study, conducted at Washington University's Dynamic Cognition Laboratory and published in the journal of *Psychological Science* in 2009, researchers used brain scans to examine what happens inside people's heads as they read fiction. They found that "readers mentally simulated each new situation encountered in a narrative. Details about actions and sensation are captured from the text and integrated with personal knowledge

53. For an excellent book focused on this theme see Peterson, *The Contemplative Pastor*.
54. Smith et al., *Digital Life Together*, 234–35.

from past experiences." The brain regions that are active often "mirror those involved when people perform, imagine, or observe similar real-world activities." Deep reading, says the study's lead researcher, Nicole Speer, "is by no means a passive exercise." The reader becomes the book.[55]

While this research does not indicate that reading fiction online is problematic, the majority of learning via the Web is not based in fiction novels. The world of online education is mediated not by fiction but by learning platforms that offer hyperlinks to reading materials, videos, and chat rooms. As will become clear in what follows, online culture promotes distraction, not deep thinking and reflection. Rather than promoting imagination through fiction reading, Carr suggests ambiguity and contemplation are aspects of humanity that need solutions. Google sees Internet user brains more like outdated computers that need to be fixed:

> In Google's world, which is the world we enter when we go online, there's little place for the pensive stillness of deep reading or the fuzzy indirection of contemplation. Ambiguity is not an opening for insight but a bug to be fixed. The human brain is just an outdated computer that needs a faster processor and a bigger hard drive—and better algorithms to steer the course of its thought.[56]

The Web is not a place that nurtures contemplation or stillness. It is, rather, distracting. In addition to learning how to navigate course materials on the school's online platform, students are also competing with the lure of social media and other diversions that vie for their attention. The temptation to shift between course materials, Web-based lectures, or even live discussions on Zoom and social media updates can be difficult to resist. The research of Joseph Firth et al., referenced in chapter 2, note the physical and psychological responses of the human body when switching between Web programs and computer windows:

> Yeykelis et al measured participants' media multi-tasking between different types of online media content while using just one device (personal laptops), and found that switches occurred as frequently as every 19 seconds, with 75% of all on-screen content being viewed for less than one minute. Measures of skin conductance during the study found that arousal increased in the seconds leading up to media switching, reaching a high point at the moment

---

55. Carr, *The Shallows*, 74.
56. Carr, *The Shallows*, 173.

of the switch, followed by a decline afterward. Again, this suggests that the proclivity for alternating between different computer windows, opening new hyperlinks, and performing new searches could be driven by the readily available nature of the informational rewards, which are potentially awaiting in the unattended media stream. Supporting this, the study also found that, whereas switching from work-related content to entertainment was associated with increased arousal in anticipation of the switch, there was no anticipatory arousal spike associated with entertainment to work-content switches.[57]

Firth et al. report that switching from work to entertainment correlates with increased arousal, but there is no such spike when switching from entertainment to work. This appears to indicate that learners' bodies are naturally inclined to pursue entertainment because of its arousal rewards, rather than shifting back toward work and the requirement to focus in order to get to places of depth, insight, and creativity that accompany contemplation and imagination. The Web appears to reward the human body with higher levels of arousal from distracting switches. Switching, the associated arousal levels of that behavior, and a loss of depth and creativity are not the only problems with Internet interruptions. Online distractions also lead to the loss of other pastoral virtues, namely empathy and compassion. Nicholas Carr writes:

> The more distracted we become, the less able we are to experience the subtlest, most distinctively human forms of empathy, compassion, and other emotions. . . . It would be rash to jump to the conclusion that the Internet is undermining our moral sense. It would not be rash to suggest that as the Net reroutes our vital paths and diminishes our capacity for contemplation, it is altering the depth of our emotions as well as our thoughts.[58]

If what Carr is saying is true, that online distractions impede the development of compassion and empathy, the acquisition of character virtues online appears to be next to impossible. Why? Because, as shown in the previous chapter with reference to Hubert Dreyfus' work and this chapter with David James' writing, healthy emotional engagement such as a concern for others, is essential in the formation of expert skill.

57. Firth et al., "Online Brain," 121.

58. Carr, The Shallows, 221.

Character Virtues: On the Job Training

When it comes to nurturing character virtues, context is important. That is why digitally based education is a challenging world in which to form character. Not only are students working against the vices of technology, they also do not have teacher experts and embodied peers in their context to help them observe and enact wisdom. Bob Gidney writes the following about the "art" of learning a profession:

> But professional practice is not simply a matter of applying academic knowledge, or the "science" of a craft, to practical problems: it comprehends more than the mechanical, or even the informed and intelligent, application of academic disciplines to occupational tasks. Indeed, the knowledge embedded in most professional work is grounded only partially in "knowledge about"; it is equally grounded in the "art" of practice—the ability to make judgements, mobilize intuitions, deploy rhetoric, weigh alternatives about what will or will not work in any given circumstance—abilities that are largely acquired and honed through practice.[59]

Gidney's research into early models of apprenticeship reveal an aspect of paideia virtue in historical contexts that cannot currently be replicated via online learning applications. By simply "hanging around" a job site, apprentices pick up not only skills for their trade but character values as well. Gidney writes:

> Work sites, it is perhaps worth adding, are more than just places where skills are learned. By simply being on site, "hanging around" so to speak, one acquires attitudes and values through listening to and watching professionals at work and play. Nor is this merely contingent. Virtually without exception, the literature on apprenticeship stresses the "hidden curriculum" of values and norms that apprentices are expected to absorb and demonstrate.[60]

This concept of picking up values and norms through observing others who are more skilled is described by Charles Ess. Citing a study looking at the differences between online and place-based students, Ess expresses the importance of embodied teaching when learning rules and concepts in specific situations:

---

59. Gidney, "Madame How," 16.
60. Gidney, "Madame How," 17–18.

Parker and Gemino (2001) found that students in a virtual seminar scored higher on the conceptual section of the final exam than place-based students. At the same time, however, students taking the virtual seminar scored significantly lower on the technique section of the final exam than place-based students. This finding is immediately consistent with Dreyfus' argument that learning how to apply rules and concepts in the specific situations we encounter as embodied beings requires teaching and learning in embodied, real-world contexts.[61]

Tara Brabazon, in a nod to Marshall McLuhan, addresses the medium of delivery when learning. Like Gidney's implicit curriculum, embedded in the delivery of the learning content, and Ess' emphasis on embodied teaching in real-world contexts, Barbazon submits that the form of delivery is formative:

> Actually, some of the best modes of teaching do not begin with the presentation of information. The error of Internet-mediated teaching is the premise that education can be reduced to questions of content. Actually, we probably learn as much through the form of delivery as the content.[62]

Barbazon's pedagogy aligns with that of physics professor, Arthur Zajonc. Zajonc co-authored *The Heart of Higher Education* with Parker Palmer. In the book he describes the need to embrace more than analytic methods of learning. He believes contemplative inquiry will lead to an epistemology of love. Given the Internet's implicit curriculum of distraction rather than contemplation, it is challenging to envision how Zajonc's pedagogy could be enacted online. He describes contemplative inquiry this way:

> I view the practice of *contemplative inquiry* as an essential modality of study complementary to the dominant analytic methods now practiced in every field. I see contemplative inquiry as the expression of an *epistemology of love* that is the true heart of higher education. *Epistemology* means "theory of knowledge," or how we know what we know. At first, love seems to have little to do with knowledge and our understanding of how it works, but if we set aside romantic love for the moment, is it not true that we come to know best that which we love most?[63]

61. Ess, "Liberal Arts," 130.

62. Brabazon, "Won't Get Googled," 162.

63. Palmer and Zajonc, *The Heart of Higher Education*, 94.

Zajonc goes on to describe the seven stages of an epistemology of love: respect, gentleness, intimacy, vulnerability, participation, transformation, and ultimately, imaginative insight.[64] Most of the terms are relational and compatible with an embodied, paideia education, yet the stages appear incompatible with the consumption and distraction offered by technology. Zajonc's epistemology of love is compatible with Freire's pedagogy, referenced in chapter 2, particularly as it relates to the generative theme. Zajonc's epistemology of love can emerge from the learner's praxis becoming the focal point of learning. With teachers and students separated from one another's praxis online, how might a shared praxis of character formation, rooted in an embodied environment, take place? If Web-based education is the exclusive program of formation, it cannot. Students learning practical wisdom are dependent on seasoned teachers to teach and embody virtue. Charles Ess writes, "if mastery, expertise, and practical wisdom are to be acquired by students as *embodied beings*, they will require teachers who *incarnate* the skills and wisdom that mark the highest levels of human accomplishment."[65]

To answer the question posed at the beginning of this chapter, "Can the Internet be used to form student character in the image of Jesus Christ?" the research appears to say no. However, just because electronically mediated classes are not the right context to teach practical wisdom does not mean that the embodied classroom is. The classroom comes with fewer trappings than the Web but it too lacks important aspects that are helpful in the formation of character. The ideal context is in everyday life, where pastoral work happens. This is why, in addition to academic courses, theological schools require practicums for programs of ministerial formation. Field education units, internships, and Clinical Psychospiritual Education units all make up parts of programs geared toward preparing pastors for ministry. How these practical and embodied aspects of education offset the deficiencies of online learning will be the focus of the next chapter.

---

64. Palmer and Zajonc, *The Heart of Higher Education*, 94–96.
65. Ess, "Liberal Arts," 131.

5

Theological Field Education for Online Students

How Valuable Are These Supervised Contexts for Charcter Formation?

I ARGUED IN THE previous chapter that online theological education promotes intellectual virtues, referred to as *Wissenschaft* virtues, but falls short of promoting a culture of character formation, where paideia virtues flourish. I concluded that chapter acknowledging that neither the Internet, nor the classroom, are ideal contexts for character formation. Embodied relationships are necessary. Pastoral programs rely on theological field education placements to prepare ministerial students in practical ways. One aspect of their preparation is the formation of character virtues. This chapter explores the value of field and clinical placements for establishing a culture of character formation that is lacking online. I will highlight research showing the role practicums play in pastoral formation programs, especially when those programs are online. As will be seen, theological field education assignments, such as congregational ministry internships and Supervised Psychospiritual Education (SPE) units, are essential parts of pastoral training programs. I will suggest that these placements, in churches, hospitals, and other contexts where students can be directly supervised, offer the potential for learning pastoral virtues found in paideia education. As students learn online, sometimes at great distances from seminaries, their field placements allow them to develop professional ministry skills as well as character virtues, with a seasoned guide by their side. I will begin by providing an overview of the history, models, and purposes of field and clinical placements for pastoral ministry students. Then, I will review two types of field education placements, Supervised Psychospiritual Education (SPE) directed by the Canadian Association for Spiritual Care (CASC/ACSS) and seminary-directed field education. I will examine their effectiveness for the growth of virtue and pastoral formation. I will also identify the challenges of each type of placement for online ministerial students. Arising from the challenges, I will argue that neither of the current types of field education placements does a good job of preparing pastors for congregational ministry. Therefore, I will conclude with a brief look at an emerging ministry model that integrates the possibility of online coursework with a strong focus on field-based learning that offers elements of paideia education.

INTRODUCTION TO FIELD EDUCATION

According to the Association of Theological Schools Standards of Accreditation, students enrolled in the Master of Divinity degree are required to complete field placements. Standard 4.4 of the Commission on Accrediting's *2020 Standards of Accreditation* states:

> The Master of Divinity degree requires supervised practical experiences (e.g., practicum or internship) in areas related to the student's vocational calling in order to achieve the learning outcomes of the degree program. These experiences are in settings that are appropriately chosen, well suited to the experience needed, and of sufficient duration. These experiences are also supervised by those who are appropriately qualified, professionally developed, and regularly evaluated.[1]

The terms "field education," "internship," and "practicum" will be used interchangeably throughout this chapter; these are defined according to the ATS standards.

---

1. The Association of Theological Schools, *Standards of Accreditation*, 92.

Theological Field Education and Online Students

With the movement toward online theological education, outlined in chapter 1, and the pandemic-fueled rush that necessitated an even hastier shift to e-learning, I assumed that theological schools would have also turned their attention to strengthening investment and research in practical field placements. This would ensure MDiv students had strong embodied field education experiences to complement their online education. While nothing about theological educators increasing a focus on field education during the pandemic surfaced in my research, I found pre-pandemic references to the heightened importance of two themes in theological education: formation and technology. In an article exploring trends in theological education, ATS executive director, Frank M. Yamada, writes about the two themes in the *Wabash Center Journal on Teaching* stating, ". . . the use of technology, particularly in distance education, and the ongoing need to rethink student formation illustrate well the conversations around emerging educational practices."[2] Yamada admits that while formation is important, each school and tradition will have to figure out what "formation" means for them:

> . . . the theme of formation is emerging in many forms and contexts, across the theological spectrum, and among all of the ecclesial families. With the fragmenting and de-centralization of religious institutions, the need to emphasize the multiple dimensions of religious formation generally and vocational formation specifically has become critical to the work of theological schools.[3]

In ATS's peer group final report, something Yamada's *Wabash Center Journal on Teaching* article references extensively, the report's section on online theological education states:

> Because the schools represent a fairly broad spectrum on the theological map . . . the group explored developing a definition [of formation] that is appropriate across the diversity, but recognized that this might not be possible. Members do agree, however, that theological education is inherently formational and that schools must have a working definition within their own contexts and be able to demonstrate that appropriate formation is taking place

2. Yamada, "Living and Teaching," 28.
3. Yamada, "Living and Teaching," 30.

through their programs, including formation that gives attention to cultural differences among students.[4]

Both Yamada and the ATS report indicate the growing importance of formation in theological schools, but the ability to define what that means is elusive. In the previous chapter, I argued that embodied relationships are crucial for pastoral formation, especially as it relates to character virtues. Online theological education provides a framework for this through field education experiences. However, there is very little written in the ATS report to address this. The peer group tasked with writing about "Formation in Online Contexts" referred to the value of formation in "students' home contexts" but made no reference to the role of formalized field education programs:

> If the campus is not the site for theological study, schools may draw upon resources for education and formation in the students' home contexts such as congregations, local mentors and spiritual directors, families, and other resources. Online technology actually aids access to and interaction with these local contexts. Formation for these "rooted learners" must make the best possible use of home contexts and recognize that the capabilities of contexts vary depending on the health of congregations, availability of qualified persons and resources, and complexities that develop when the primary ministry context for formation may be, at the same time, the place where the student provides religious leadership. Institutions with online programs need to give attention to how the role of the institution changes in this educational model. The school is no longer the primary provider of student experiences, but rather an orchestrator of the resources in which the students are embedded.[5]

The authors recognize challenges facing theological schools trying to "make the best possible use of [students'] home contexts." Online student formation takes place primarily away from the seminary campus and requires creative field-based mentorship and assessment. Therefore, it seems odd that nothing about field placements was referenced in this section of the report. There was reference to field education in the section entitled

---

4. The Association of Theological Schools, *Educational Models and Practices Peer Group Final Reports*, 9.

5. The Association of Theological Schools, *Educational Models and Practices Peer Group Final Reports*, 10.

"Residential Theological Education Peer Group Final Report," where the authors note the following:

> There was discussion about differences in field education experiences of students at residential programs compared to those in online programs. Online programs require partnerships with local churches but the scale of some programs could make it hard to make sure all is happening as it should. Residential programs may be positioned to offer more oversight and accountability, as well as the opportunity to interact with other field education students. It also may be that there is more potential for exposure to different types of settings than is true for online programs.[6]

It is difficult to draw conclusions from the peer groups about the ATS report and field education. One aspect appears clear and will become even more pronounced by the end of this chapter: even with the turn toward online learning, the role of the mentor/supervisor is paramount. However, standards for training and oversight of supervisor/mentors and the quality of supervisor-student relationships vary significantly.

A Brief History of Field Education

Based on the Standards of Accreditation, the concept of a practicum is now entrenched in the MDiv degree. However, practical, field-based experience has not always been a required part of seminary education. The movement to train clergy in practical ministry outside the seminary started in the 1920's with Anton Boisen and Dr. Richard Cabot.[7] In the 1950's, at the time of writing *The Advancement of Theological Education*, Niebuhr, Williams, and Gustafson described a growing sense of importance for helping students gain practical ministry experience, since an organized and systemic approach was only beginning to develop:

> The requirement that academic work in classroom and library be accompanied by active participation in church work has been increasingly accepted during the past twenty years. A majority of the schools now require their students to do "field work" on weekends during the school year, during the summer months, and

---

6. The Association of Theological Schools, *Educational Models and Practices Peer Group Final Reports*, 176–77.

7. For a detailed overview of Boisen and Cabot's influence on theological field education, see my section on "Background and Context of CPE."

occasionally during an "internship" year. . . . This whole movement . . . during the last twenty or thirty years has been so rapid that
its organization and direction remain somewhat in arrear [sic].[8]

In the 1950's a "field work" requirement was only just beginning to take root
in schools. As Niebuhr et al., reveal, field education was not well integrated
into the theological curriculum nor was it properly supervised. In 1966,
things started to change. Pastoral theology professor Charles Feilding, from
Trinity College, Toronto, published an ATS commissioned study putting
his finger on the need for a stronger link between the field and the seminary. His concern was for ministerial training to be seen as "professional
education." He argued for the integration of formalized field education into
pastoral formation programs stating, "For field education there must be a
'field' where some educational agency can plan and control the educational
continuum. This is far from easy to achieve, but nothing short of this can be
taken seriously as professional education."[9] It was after the study's publica-
tion that schools began more formalized field education placements, "that
included theological reflection on the practice of ministry with supervisor-
mentors and peers."[10]

MODELS OF FIELD EDUCATION

Today's field education placements provide ministerial students with practical experiences in churches, hospitals, and diverse contexts using a handful of models. The diversity of models is due to many factors but the broad
definition of field placements in the ATS Accreditation Standards is likely
one explanation. Richard J. Leyda of Talbot School of Theology has performed a systematic review of the various field education programs in order to categorize and define them. While he includes additional placement
types beyond those listed below, the core of seminary practicum programs
can be gathered into the following classifications:

1. *Integrated or Concurrent Model:* Students take academic courses while
   engaged in field education. This could be a one semester, single credit
   unit, or—in the case of a three-year MDiv degree—six semesters in
   the same placement.

8. Niebuhr et al., *The Advancement of Theological Education*, 22.
9. Feilding, "Education for Ministry," 233.
10. Floding, *Engage*, 6.

2. *Intensive Model:* Students generally have no academic coursework in addition to that required by the field placement. This is a full-time commitment that usually lasts for two months or less.

3. *Immersion or Extended Model:* Like the intensive model, students take time off from academic course work in order to focus on the field placement full-time. The difference is that this model is as short as one semester but is often up to one year in duration.[11]

These models reveal that field-based education varies greatly in terms of how requirements for practical ministry fit into a student's academic program. Practicum lengths, as well as their integration or lack of integration with coursework, are not standardized.

THE PURPOSES OF THEOLOGICAL FIELD EDUCATION

While there may be other approaches to the purpose of theological field education, I have chosen to focus on two. The first focuses on practising the theory, taught mainly through coursework in a pastoral context to gain professional skills. The second is a focus that moves beyond developing professional skills, toward a need to help students make meaning out of their experiences. I will call the first a vocational focus and the second a meaning-making focus.

A Vocational Purpose: Developing Professional Skills

Having spent several years on a research project looking at clergy education in North America, Charles R. Foster et al., concluded in their book *Educating Clergy* that field education programs act as a "bridge" between the classroom and "service to various publics":

> Field education programs are generally designed as a bridge between seminary and the congregation or other sites of clergy practice. Their purposes originate in the mission of seminaries—a mission shared by other professional schools—to educate leaders for service to various publics. The mission requires that seminaries link, in some fashion, teaching in the classroom and communal ethos with teaching in the field or sites of clergy practice.[12]

11. Leyda, "Models of Ministry," 25–29.

12. Foster et al., *Educating Clergy,* 296.

The field education context becomes a place where classroom learning gets practised by student ministers. This vocational focus also appears to be the approach of Talbot School of Theology's Dave Keehn when he writes:

> Modeled after historic apprenticeship practices, field education integrates classroom content with real-world problem solving and job competencies. It is the "placement with an organization primarily to gain work experience, learn about the nature of that work, acquire skill and knowledge in doing that work, and acquire contacts that can assist in getting a job done and building a career."[13]

Catholic educators, Eric Grabowsky and Janie M. Harden Fritz, also highlight the internship as a primary means of preparing students for a workplace profession. They write:

> An internship can be defined as an experiential learning activity providing a bridge between academic education and the world of the professions (Sgroi & Ryniker, 2002). Derived from principles of cooperative education initiated early in the 20th century (Sovilla, 1998), internships are offered by universities in response to calls by employers for greater job preparedness on the part of students (Elkins, 2002). Internship programs have been touted as a means to provide students with an opportunity to develop skills tied to job contexts (Gabris & Mitchell, 1989).[14]

A Meaning-Making Purpose: Supervised Theological Reflection

Grabowsky and Fritz nod to the vocational focus but also demonstrate the need to go beyond vocational training that focuses on technique to enable students to reflect on their experience:

> Grounding the internship within the notion *of praxis* permits connection to the notion of practical wisdom (Aristotle, 1954) as a core aspect of higher education (Churchill, 1997), which articulates a concern for action that moves beyond technique (Barrett, 1978). The metaphor of engineering opens the idea of practical wisdom, showing a need to understand a complete picture of the unique location in which one is situated in order to take constructive action (Arnett, 1999). When internships are embedded within

13. Donovan and Garrett, *Internship for Dummies*, Keehn, "Leveraging Internships," 55.

14. Grabowsky and Harden Fritz, "The Internship," 437.

a humanities framework, students engage [in] reflection nourished by a philosophical background, providing a rich educational experience drawn from what might otherwise become thin unreflective practices and answering concerns of academics who fear "the transformation of liberal arts institutions into 'trade schools'" (Corbett & Kendall, 1999, p. 75).[15]

According to Grabowsky and Fritz, this reflection on their unique situational experiences allows students to gain practical wisdom (a major focus of chapter 4), enabling them not only to learn the skills of the trade but also to become reflective practitioners with virtuous character. This shift toward reflection is a central element of what I am calling a meaning-making focus. Meaning-making field education approaches student experiences using a more holistic focus on self-awareness and the "so what?" questions arising from practices which, upon reflection, lead to future meaningful actions. This process is accomplished through the practice of theological reflection. Former director of field education at the University of Notre Dame, Regina Coll, offers a succinct yet profound definition of theological reflection. She states, "The search for meaning, when done in the light of faith, is theological reflection."[16] Leading students into the search for meaning in the light of faith is the job of a field education supervisor. Coll states:

> Formal theological reflection is what *constitutes* ministerial supervision. Acquiring skills, growing as a person, developing a ministerial identity, good in themselves, might merely lead to activism. Containing crises is not the essence of ministry; faith connections need to be made. After we have given the cup of water, visited the sick, and buried the dead, with more or less pastoral expertise, we are left with the question, "So what?" How does it fit in with the scheme of things? In the words of a traditional spirituality, "What does this have to do with eternity?"[17]

Coll sees vocational skill development as secondary to a critical engagement with the "So what?" questions that surface in ministry praxis. She believes it is the responsibility of the person giving oversight to the seminary student that has an obligation to ensure theological reflection happens. For Coll, the absence of theological reflection means that supervisors have not done their job.

---

15. Grabowsky and Harden Fritz, "The Internship," 438.

16. Coll, *Supervision of Ministry*, 91.

17. Coll, *Supervision of Ministry*, 91–92.

No matter what the subject, the important thing is to help the seminarian to make faith connections, to search for meaning, to ask "So what?" How does faith in Jesus and his message affect each situation? Theological reflection *constitutes* supervision, it is not an extra added attraction that may be ignored. It is the very heart of the supervisory relationship.[18]

Jim L. Wilson, professor of leadership formation at Gateway Seminary, and Earl Waggoner, Dean and Professor at Colorado Christian University, describe theological reflection as a process of reflection leading to action. They see formation beginning as someone identifies how their beliefs, thinking, and feelings influence their behaviors:

> Theological reflection is . . . *identifying* how our beliefs, thoughts, and feelings influence our actions, *aligning* them to our best understanding of God's truth, and *exploring* possibilities for future ministry responses. This definition of theological reflection follows the "action—reflection—action" theological reflection approach. In this approach, reflection occurs during a pause from activity to learn from the past and prepare for the future. It follows the rhythm established in the opening pages of Scripture.[19]

For Wilson and Waggoner, being formed is based on more than action. The process of reflecting allows the student to think about their actions; rumination is at the core of theological reflection. For them, action does not lead to theological knowledge; the process of reflecting on action leading to new action comprises the process of theological reflection:

> While we do not view action as a primary source of theological knowledge ("theology-in-action" approach), we do affirm that doing something is the final and necessary step for an effective theological reflection process.[20]

Field education allows students to develop ministerial skills while also creating space for asking "so what?" questions about practices. It provides a way to learn a vocation while also reflecting theologically on the vocational actions.

18. Coll, *Supervision of Ministry*, 109.

19. Wilson and Waggoner, *A Guide to Theological Reflection*, 23.

20. Wilson and Waggoner, *A Guide to Theological Reflection*, 35.

TWO TYPES OF FIELD EDUCATION: CLINICAL PASTORAL AND SEMINARY DIRECTED

This chapter, I will focus on two specific field education programs that can fit within all three of Leyda's models and provide opportunity to focus on vocational and meaning-making purposes. The first is a highly organized practicum that has standards and a certification process recognized throughout North America. In Canada, this program is administered and directed through the Canadian Association for Spiritual Care (CASC/ACSS), which offers students field-based education. The second, less structured, highly variant, and more flexible type of field education, can be described as directed primarily through the seminary in conjunction with a local church.

Supervised Psychospiritual Education (SPE)

One of the best examples of a formalized field education experience is Supervised Psychospiritual Education (SPE), offered across Canada by CASC/ACSS. CASC/ACSS defines itself and its educational mission as follows:

> A national multi-faith organization, committed to the professional education, Certification and support of people involved in spiritual care, psycho-spiritual therapy, education and research. We provide educational programs for interested persons who are preparing to become professional providers of spiritual care and psycho-spiritual therapy in a variety of institutional and community settings such as health care, corrections, education and private practice. We also educate those who are preparing for ordained/commissioned religious leadership to have competence in providing spiritual care to their faith communities.[21]

CASC/ACSS offers Supervised Psychospiritual Education (SPE), which includes Clinical Psychospiritual Education (CPE) focusing on pastoral care, and Psychospiritual Therapy Education (PTE) focusing on pastoral counselling.

> Supervised Psychospiritual Education (SPE) is an experience-based approach to learning ministry, which combines pastoral care with qualified supervision and group reflection. The program

21. "Canadian Association for Spiritual Care/Association Canadienne De Soins Spirituels."

is open to clergy, theology students and lay persons with theology training. It aims to assist persons in achieving their full potential for ministry. Programs are offered at facilities throughout Canada, including general and psychiatric hospitals, correctional centres and a variety of other locations. Each centre is connected to a theological college. Supervisor-Educators are Certified by the Canadian Association for Spiritual Care/ Association canadienne de soins spirituels (CASC/ACSS).[22]

The term SPE will be preferred throughout this chapter since it is the umbrella term for both Clinical Psychospiritual Education (CPE) and Psychospiritual Therapy Education (PTE). The American Association does not use "SPE," so there will be times when Clinical Pastoral Education (CPE) is used. To understand more about the role of SPE in theological education, a brief history of the program's origins and growth follows.

Background and Context of SPE

According to Homer L. Jernigan, Professor Emeritus of Pastoral Care and Counseling at Boston University School of Theology, Clinical Pastoral Education began close to 100 years ago when a chaplain invited a group of theological students to a Massachusetts hospital. Jernigan writes, "Anton T. Boisen is given credit for conducting the first program of Clinical Pastoral Education at Worcester State Hospital in Massachusetts in the summer of 1925."[23] As a chaplain at that hospital, Boisen welcomed students into a clinical training program. He learned about case studies from a medical doctor named Richard Cabot at Harvard and he "became interested in developing case studies highlighting the relations of certain kinds of religious experience to mental illness."[24] Boisen himself had experienced "brief psychotic episodes" and became intrigued.[25] "He thought that theological students had much to learn from mental patients, and he saw the mental hospital as a kind of 'laboratory' in which students could learn from 'the living human document.'"[26]

---

22. "Education."
23. Jernigan, "Clinical Pastoral Education," 379.
24. Jernigan, "Clinical Pastoral Education," 379.
25. Jernigan, "Clinical Pastoral Education," 379.
26. Jernigan, "Clinical Pastoral Education," 380.

Dr. Richard Cabot, Boisen's case study mentor, viewed things differently. "Cabot's views of mental illness differed markedly from Boisen's. He believed in the organic nature of mental illness and felt that theological students had nothing to learn from patients in mental hospitals."[27] He believed patients needed pastoral care and support and his vision involved physicians and ministers working together in hospital settings to heal the sick. While Boisen and Cabot disagreed as to the purpose of theological field education, they stood together believing clinical training "should be a regular part of theological education, just as supervised experience in the clinic had become a regular and required part of medical education."[28]

It did not take long for news of clinical hospital training for theological students in Massachusetts to spread. This led to the establishment of two associations to oversee clinical training for ministry:

> Many seminaries received this new clinically oriented education with great favor, and demand for the services spread. These culminated in the formation of two associations. The Council for Clinical Training of Theological Students, formed in 1930, focused their educational sites in state hospitals and prisons. Many saw this training as the best entry for the slowly emerging profession of chaplaincy. The Institute for Pastoral Care, formed in 1944, focused its training in general hospitals. Many saw this as the best entry for parish clergy.[29]

Whereas these two associations started out with different foci, they ended up coming together under the banner of the Association for Clinical Pastoral Education (ACPE):

> Many years of discussions between the Council and the Institute, and related training organizations established by the Lutherans and Southern Baptists, were required before the Clinical Pastoral Education movement could be unified under the Association for Clinical Pastoral Education (ACPE) in 1967.[30]

In Canada, two years before the ACPE merger in the United States, Professor Charles Feilding was interested in what was happening with Clinical

27. Jernigan, "Clinical Pastoral Education," 381.
28. Jernigan, "Clinical Pastoral Education," 381.
29. Ivy, "Significant Change," 151.
30. Jernigan, "Clinical Pastoral Education," 383.

Pastoral Education. Rodney Stokoe describes how the program became established in Canada:

> Charles Feilding, then Dean of Trinity College, Toronto, led or supported a number of national consultations which led to the founding in 1965 of the Canadian Council for Supervised Pastoral Education. The adjective *supervised* was chosen not to reject *clinical*, or to be different from the Americans, but to provide a description covering a wider variety of training methodologies.[31]

According to the CASC/ACSS website, SPE students moving toward ordination in a congregational setting would normally take one basic SPE unit consisting of 400 hours: 200 hours of supervised practical ministry plus 200 hours of peer and group supervision, didactics, case study presentations, and other structured learning activities. For those interested in becoming Certified Spiritual Care Practitioners, a requirement for most healthcare chaplaincy roles in Canada, a total of four units representing thousands of hours of SPE is required.[32]

This robust program offers not only ample time to practise the necessary vocational skills for spiritual care, but also offers the essential element that Coll notes above, supervised theological reflection. The mixture of practising vocational skills and reflecting on various situational encounters alongside a supervisor and peers appears to offer the paideia culture crucial for character formation. The following section will look at how SPE, with its focus on developing spiritual care competencies in students, might provide a way to develop character virtues.

SPE and Character Formation

Canadian SPE educator Simon Lasair suggests that professional spiritual care competencies[33] flow from the identity of the spiritual care provider. He recommends that a model be developed to prioritize "measuring students' personal and professional integration":

31. Stokoe, "Clinical Pastoral Education."

32. "Education FAQs: What Is CPE?"

33. According to the CASC/ACSS, "Competencies are those attributes and capacities necessary to care well. . . . We understand competencies as those personal and professional qualities, assets or skills with which Spiritual Care and Counselling Specialists meet the standards of practice in a wide variety of care giving settings." In "Competencies for Spiritual Care."

Whatever assessment model is used in CPE or PCE, measuring students' personal and professional integration needs to be understood as a central priority. . . . It is true that professionals must gain proficiency with their various professional competencies. However, the competencies ought to be viewed as expressions of the professional's integrated personal and professional identity. Measuring the professional's movement toward integration within their training thus has a greater priority in the training of students than the acquisition of specific competencies.[34]

In his article, Lasair suggests that a spiritually healthy practitioner, one with an integrated personal and professional identity, possesses the following six traits: Awareness, Openness, Wisdom, Freedom, Contentment, and Flourishing. His article details these virtues as being developed primarily through CPE's and PCE's (now known as PTE) current model of action-reflection.[35]

A decade before Lasair's article, SPE educator Gordon Hilsman argued for something similar, the assessment of virtues in SPE students and supervisors:

. . . paying attention to one another's virtues is a professional responsibility of clinical practitioners, especially as those classical characteristics of personal behavior affect attitudes toward the standards of the practitioner's primary professional organization.[36]

He suggests that SPE has an important role to play in the development of the following character virtues in students: humility, prudence, wisdom, counsel, benignity (i.e., simple goodness), fortitude, and love.[37] To the question of how to assess inner virtues, Hilsman has this to say:

Until Freud, the Christian virtues, along with the seven deadly sins, comprised the primary framework for assessing spiritual behavior in the Western world. Because of their partially observable quality and decisive starkness, they can still stand legitimately with frameworks such as the Myers-Briggs Personality Inventory, classic psychopathology, and the Enneagram as tools for evaluating behavior. Most people take umbrage at negative feedback on such traits as wisdom, love, and fortitude. When, however, the

34. Lasair, "What's the Point," 29.

35. Lasair, "What's the Point."

36. Hilsman, "Tandem Roles," 46.

37. Hilsman, "Tandem Role," 49–54.

practitioner requests assessments of virtue, the assessments can provide unique perspectives on how that professional relates to colleagues and measures up to a professional association's mission and standards.[38]

A couple of years after Hilsman's article, SPE educator Logan Jones focused on what he perceived to be a neglected subject in SPE educational theories, "attention to the disposition and character of the adult educator."[39] Jones suggested that the content of what should be learned by students is actually secondary to the character of the supervisor/educator. He writes:

> What most of us remember from our supervisors is not their theories or skill sets or how they planned a unit of CPE but rather we remember who they were to us. We tell different stories of our encounters, stories of challenge, of humor, and maybe even of anger, maybe even of their weirdness. "Could you believe it when Supervisor X did . . . ?" We remember how we were listened to, encouraged, and pressed to do the hard interior work required by this process. It is their dispositions and character that make a difference in our lives, not their theories.[40]

Revealed in the assertions above from SPE educators is a missing focus on assessing and evaluating character virtues in program supervisors and students. This does not mean that individual supervisors neglect this facet of formation. After all, Jones draws on his experience with supervisors who "pressed [their students] to do the hard interior work." However, it appears that CASC/ACSS does not possess a current standard addressing the virtues noted above. Therefore, while the virtues may be modeled and nurtured by some supervisors, there is no requirement for educators or students to embody these.

Theological Field Education and Character Formation

While SPE is one example of a well-developed and extensive field education placement, many students enter directly into congregational or other settings to be supervised by those in the field. These placements are directed through the seminary and generally supervised by practitioners doing

---

38. Hilsman, "Tandem Roles," 54.
39. Jones, "I Walk," 161.
40. Jones, "I Walk," 163.

ministerial work in that context or by someone appointed to act as mentor to the student but may not be working in the same parish.[41] As noted earlier in this chapter, the ATS standard referring to field placements states, "These experiences are in settings that are appropriately chosen, well suited to the experience needed, and of sufficient duration. These experiences are also supervised by those who are appropriately qualified, professionally developed, and regularly evaluated."[42] In order to determine how character virtues are learned in field settings, it is important to determine how field settings are chosen and by whom, since students in online programs of pastoral formation may be far removed from the seminary. In what follows, I will suggest there is no clear way to determine how or whether character virtues are being nurtured in field placements, as the standards for field education experiences and supervision of supervisors vary significantly from school to school. What appears clear is that two educational factors play large roles in character formation: the quality of community and the quality of supervision.

The Quality of Community in Field Education

In the previous chapter I argued that embodied relationships are essential for the formation and ongoing development of character virtues. As noted earlier in this chapter, theological schools are dependent on students' home contexts to provide the sort of community formation that may have happened previously in residential education. For web-based students, field education becomes a paideia education where they become encultured by the life of a congregation or clinical setting. Whereas SPE is a program with a cohort of students working under a supervisor, a non-SPE field education student may be the only seminary student in their congregational setting. That could mean they do not benefit from the peer-to-peer formation that happens when students interact in close proximity. On the upside, while other seminary students may not be around, the field education placement offers the online student potential for community built into their home congregation in the absence of a traditional residential theological school community. That community, according to Marvin Oxenham, "is the educational programme." He writes:

41. For an example of a supervised field education placement where the primary supervisor maintained phone contact due to distance, see Singer, "Supervisory Practice."

42. The Association of Theological Schools, *Standards of Accreditation*.

> The academy should not only have an educational programme, it should be one. The main shaping force on students in the academy is the community, and you need to work hard on shaping and safeguarding the community according to virtue.[43]

The health of the community representing the field education placement is crucial. As cited earlier in this chapter in the ATS' *Educational Models and Practices Peer Group Final Report*, some seminary students serve as pastors and church leaders while fulfilling their field education requirements. In certain contexts, the student may be *the* parish pastor. They are responsible to "shape and safeguard the community" while being educated by that community. There are obvious challenges with this sort of arrangement. The historic norm for field education students was to be nurtured in a community with a seasoned leader/supervisor, rather than to function as the community leader/nurturer while learning the vocation and making meaning along the way. In the historical context, students were given incremental responsibility and the supervisor was charged with looking after the whole community.[44] As noted earlier in the ATS report, there are references to needing to ensure healthy home contexts for students. However, the ability for seminaries to assess the wellbeing of those contexts is unclear.

The Quality of Supervision in Field Education

According to the ATS standards, online MDiv students are required to have practical placements with supervisors who are "appropriately qualified, professionally developed, and regularly evaluated." Returning to CASC/ACSS's model, SPE supervisors have clearly defined educational and vocational standards of supervision upon which they are assessed. However, the same cannot be said for seminary-directed theological field education supervisors. As will be seen below, students in non-SPE field placements are likely supervised by practitioners who have not been assessed to determine their capacity to supervise ministry students, including their ability to maintain self-differentiation (the subject of chapter 3), or the quality of

43. Oxenham, *Character and Virtue*, 303.

44. In reference to apprenticeships historically, Gidney writes, "Though it takes many different forms, it normally incorporates, successively, observation of work techniques, routines, and environments; on-site instruction from a senior practitioner; hands-on experience; and learning to apply academic knowledge to a practical situation; learning to make the inferences and "educated guesses" that constitute the crucial but indeterminate aspects of professional knowledge." In Gidney, "Madame How," 21.

their character (the subject of chapter 4). Therefore, they may not be helpful or suitable mentors for clergy students. Marvin Oxenham addresses the role of teachers of character in shaping the lives of students. He suggests that teachers:

> . . . represent the single most powerful tool that we have to impact a student's character. . . . Teachers of character and virtue education must, in fact, not only be able practitioners of character education but, first and foremost, they must be women and men of virtue themselves. They will be the models from whom the next generation will learn, and they should never forget that who they are and how they conduct themselves, will shape those in their care. Although we've seen that virtue and character are desirable for many professions, the stakes are particularly high for teachers in theological education because the practices for which they are training students are inseparably bound to issues of character.[45]

Just as the teacher plays a central role in student character formation, the role of the supervisor in theological field placements is paramount. Robert K. Nace, a pioneer in the development of Parish Clinical Pastoral Education writes, "It may be reasonably assumed that life experience learning in the parish provides the seminary student with a substantive 'model' of the profession."[46] In the book, *Welcome to Theological Field Education*, Charlene Jin Lee goes even further than Nace. In an insightful chapter she states the importance of not only being a model *for* ministry but living a life *of* ministry.

> A supervisor of a ministerial intern must be understood more by her person than by her functions. It is impossible to separate the roles of a minister from who the minister is. Likewise, it is impossible to lead others in discerning a vocation in ministry without having contemplated and continuing to contemplate one's own sense of call. There is, then, very little distance between a teacher and a student, between a supervisor and an intern, and between one's responsibilities as a supervisor and one's responsibilities as a minister. A supervising pastor supervises by the very act of ministering. He does not put on the supervisory hat when he sits with an intern for weekly meetings or when he observes an intern making her first pastoral care visit or preaching her first sermon. The supervisory role is not fulfilled when a supervisor completes evaluation forms or explains to the intern the life of a particular

45. Oxenham, *Character and Virtue*, 304.
46. Nace, "The Teaching Parish," 327.

congregation and the pastoral duties in it. Rather, active supervision takes place when a supervising pastor engages in ministry: when she leads worship, meditates on Scripture, prays for congregants, moderates meetings, celebrates communion, teaches young people, visits the sick, greets worshipers, comforts the mourning, expresses appreciation for the office staff, and keeps sabbath. All of these ministry acts are vital parts of supervision. Supervision is more than modeling, however; it is living. How the supervising pastor lives offers substantive glimpses for an intern who is seeking not only to know the how-to of ministry but more so to understand life in ministry.[47]

An article in the 2020 edition of *Reflective Practice* also highlights the importance of the field supervisor. Summarizing the results of a 2019 survey conducted to find out "about specific experiences of supportive supervision and intentional mentoring,"[48] these confirm the importance of the mentor:

> The relationship between supervisor/mentor and student is key to the overall ministerial formation process of theological field education. In both qualitative and quantitative answers, key words such as mentoring, listening, guiding, discussing, responsiveness, wisdom, compassion, prayerfulness, availability, and modeling of leadership appeared throughout.[49]

CHALLENGES OF SPE AND FIELD EDUCATION FOR MINISTERIAL EDUCATION

Challenges of SPE

SPE May Be Functioning at a Distance from Theological Education

SPE programs provide excellent practical education in spiritual care for theological students. However, CASC/ACSS's influence on and relationship to theological education is not apparent. In ATS's 196 page "Educational Models and Practices Peer Group Final Reports," there were no references to CASC/ACSS or the American CPE program.[50] This is one indicator that

---

47. Lee, "The Art of Supervision," 21.

48. Floding et al., "Excellence in Supervision: Listening to our Students," 195.

49. Floding et al., "Excellence in Supervision: Listening to Our Students," 202.

50. The Association of Theological Schools, *Educational Models and Practices Peer Group Final Reports.*

SPE programs function on the periphery of theological education. Jernigan, writing from an American context, offers another indicator. His article
details nine ACPE developments that have influenced the growing distance
between CPE and theological education. Four are highlighted here:

- The decision in 1950 to relate the CPE movement to the Association
  of Seminary Professors in the Practical Field over the years has meant
  increasing association of CPE with "field education" in the seminaries rather than with the more content-oriented disciplines and with
  theological education as a whole.

- The continuing effort to contribute to theological education by the
  clinical training of individual students rather than by working closely
  with theological schools or with theological education as a "system."

- The increasing split between theory and practice in the fields of
  Pastoral (Practical) Theology and Pastoral Care as seminary faculty
  members and others who are interested in the development of theory
  and research have focused on participation in organizations such as
  The Society for Pastoral Theology and the International Academy of
  Practical Theology rather than ACPE.

- The increasing focus on training chaplains, supervisors, and lay leaders and the decreasing numbers of units of training of theological
  students in ACPE.[51]

Jernigan's article raises a number of issues, some of which are uniquely
American: first, CPE has become associated with field education rather
than more academic seminary courses and programs. Since field education
itself is on the margins of the seminary, as shown above, this has meant that
CPE also finds itself on the theological education margins. Second, CPE's
development as an exceptional training program for spiritual care practitioners has focused on training individual students rather working with
theological education to develop a whole system approach to educating
spiritual care practitioners. Third, some Practical and Pastoral theologians
have chosen to focus their attention on contributing to associations not
affiliated with ACPE or CASC/ACSS, thereby widening the gap between
theological school researchers and CPE/SPE educators in the field. Fourth,
an increasing number of chaplaincy students are taking CPE units of training, which could draw focus away from congregational ministry training.

51. Jernigan, "Clinical Pastoral Education," 389.

The Canadian context varies from Jernigan's American focus. In Canada, CASC/ACSS supervisors often hold adjunct professor status at the universities and seminaries where the students are receiving academic credit.[52] Some Supervisor-Educators are also full-time professors in theological schools. Examples in Toronto are Pam McCarroll and Nazila Isgandarova at Emmanuel College, Angela Schmidt at Knox College, and Desmond Buhagar at Regis College; Kristine Lund, Peter VanKatwyk and Thomas St. James O'Connor are at Martin Luther University in Waterloo.[53] CASC/ACSS's link between the placement and the theological school is stronger than Jernigan's article indicates, particularly in Ontario. The ties between theological schools and pastoral education programs are less clear outside of Ontario and may vary from province to province.[54] Further research on the link between SPE and theological education in the pan-Canadian context is needed.

The Professionalization of SPE

In Spring 2001 an article entitled, "A White Paper. Professional Chaplaincy: Its Role and Importance in Healthcare" was published in *The Journal of Pastoral Care* by the five largest healthcare chaplaincy organizations in North American. The article marked an important step toward the professionalization of healthcare chaplaincy in the midst of what the article called "the turmoil of healthcare reform."[55] This movement toward professionalization presents two issues for students with a primary focus on congregational ministry: SPE's turn toward interfaith/multifaith spiritual care means a diminished focus on the Christian Story and SPE's growing orientation toward training students for chaplaincy rather than congregational ministry.

52. According to Dr. Pamela McCarroll, CASC/ACSS Certified Supervisor-Educator, "in the Greater Toronto Area (GTA) all CASC/ACSS Supervisor-Educators are adjunct faculty at one of the theological faculties." E-mail, March 28, 2021.

53. I am grateful for Dr. Pamela McCarroll and Dr. Thomas St. James O'Connor for pointing out the strong ties between Canadian Supervisor-Educators and clinical settings and students.

54. For an interesting description of Alberta's evolving relationship between theological schools, CASC/ACSS, and the provincial government see Pranke and Margaret Clark, "Out of the Ashes."

55. VandeCreek and Burton, "A White Paper," 92.

SPE is Disconnected from Christian Story and Vision

SPE started out as clinically oriented field education for theological students preparing for pastoral work in congregations or chaplaincy settings. In the early years, the training institutions were supported by Christian denominations.[56] Today, SPE offers multi-faith spiritual care training. That means supervisors, regardless of their own religious affiliation, ensure the training is open to general spiritual practices and not geared to only one faith.

Earlier in this chapter, I cited Regina Coll's perspective of field education supervision. She writes, "Formal theological reflection is what *constitutes* ministerial supervision." For Coll, theological reflection links the "why?" of ministerial praxis with the Christian story. Religious Educator Thomas Groome holds the same perspective on the role of the educator to guide students to reflect on the Christian Story and Vision. He believes reflection on the Christian Story is a central facet of the process of theological reflection that leads to Christian praxis. He writes:

> The educator's activity in [making accessible Christian Story and Vision] is essentially a hermeneutical one; she or he interprets and explains the aspects of Christian community Story/Vision as appropriate to the generative theme(s) or symbol(s) of the occasion and in dialogue with the stories/visions of participants. Procedurally, the educator's task is to discern both what to make accessible from the Story/Vision and how to make it accessible to participants. Each existential situation requires particular responses to these questions—what and how—in ways that we cannot anticipate here for all occasions and contexts.[57]

According to Coll and Groome, the educator/supervisor's task is to lead students in reflection on the Christian Story. This is an important step in the process of theological field education.

With the increasing focus on interfaith chaplaincy in CASC/ACSS, there is no guarantee supervisor educators hold a Christian perspective and therefore may not practise nor offer theological reflection based on the Christian Story. Students may be encouraged to reflect theologically on their experiences from their traditions, but the supervisor/educator will not necessarily, as Coll and Groome promote, lead students in a Christocentric reflection on events. Theological reflection is important for online

---

56. Jernigan, "Clinical Pastoral Education," 383.

57. Groome, *Sharing Faith*, 223.

clergy students enrolled in field-based ministry experience. A supervisor who leads students in theological reflection on the Christian Story is an important part of ministerial supervision.

SPE's Orientation toward Chaplaincy

It appears that both the Canadian and American associations continue to train theological students to be spiritual care providers to serve in congregational or institutional settings. In his 2019 article, Steven Ivy writes:

> ACPE has continued to bridge the historic dynamic tension between education for ministry and education for professional recognition. About 50% of its training units annually are single units, mostly for those in preparation for congregational leadership, while about 50% are residency units, mostly for those seeking chaplaincy vocations.[58]

According to Ivy, CPE continues to balance training both clergy and chaplains. Yet, the training is predominantly oriented toward a chaplaincy model of ministry. CASC/ACSS has established training centres across Canada; a review of these on the CASC/ACSS website shows the majority of them are located in hospitals.[59] This indicates that the majority of supervisors are working as spiritual care supervisor/educators in hospital settings. The paideia education those centres offer, by virtue of their setting and culture, is an apprenticeship into hospital chaplaincy. While this has great value for clergy when providing care to those in hospital, the impact on clerical formation in a parish setting is unclear. Jernigan raises this issue when he states, "Long-term studies are needed that can provide evidence of the extent to which Level I CPE programs influence the actual practice of ministry in local congregations."[60] The SPE practical education of pastors under the supervision of hospital spiritual care providers means that pastors are operating like chaplains, at least that is the trend the editor of *Reflective Practice* journal, Scott Sullender, has also noticed. He sees the growing influence of chaplaincy so much so that it is starting to shape congregational ministry, writing that,

---

58. Ivy, "Significant Change," 151.

59. "Education Centres."

60. Jernigan, "Clinical Pastoral Education," 391.

Several respected leaders of chaplaincy-related organizations have recently suggested that chaplaincy is becoming the predominant model of ministry in the twenty-first century. A bold statement, without a doubt! They cite as evidence the steady growth of jobs in chaplaincy in contrast to the steady decline of jobs in congregations and denominationally funded work. They note that chaplaincy positions often pay better and have better benefits and more regular hours than most congregational ministries, thus attracting more newly minted clergy. Moreover, many bivocational religious leaders these days combine part-time work serving a congregation with part-time work as a chaplain. In such cases, inevitably the dominant model that guides what they do *in both settings* is that of the chaplain. I wonder how many religious leaders of local congregations operate essentially as a chaplain, not primarily as a pastor, preacher, teacher, or even administrator. Chaplaincy as a model of ministry is becoming so widespread that caregiving is synonymous with ministry. And where do religious leaders get this model? How has it become so widely embraced? Is it possible that CPE, which has been with us now for some eighty years, has shaped a whole generation of clergypersons to think, operate, and function like chaplains, regardless of their ministry context?[61]

While it is difficult to draw conclusions from Sullender's musings near the end of the citation, his reflections on the growing role of chaplain training and its impact on congregational settings echo Jernigan's.

Challenges of Field Education

The Quality of Field Education Supervision

The importance of quality supervision and mentorship is essential to character formation and self-differentiation in congregational settings. However, research shows troubling problems with the quantity of time and the quality of supervision in field education placements. Matthew Floding et al., found inconsistencies in student reporting on the amount of time they spent with their supervisors and the quality of opportunities they were given:

> Relationship was experienced as central to excellent placement experiences, but the quantitative answers revealed that only half of the students met weekly with their supervisors/mentors. Although respect for supervisors/mentors was abundantly clear, both sets

61. Sullender, "New Forms," 7.

of data included some students who did not think they were being given meaningful ministry tasks that were supportive of their particular formation process.[62]

These results show inconsistencies in the quality of opportunities and supervision students receive in their placements. Additionally, it appears that supervisors are not held to common standards, something that is out of step with the ATS Standards for field education as noted above. Floding et al., offer this assessment of the data:

> These data underscore areas for particular emphasis in recruiting, training, and assessing excellent supervisors/mentors and placement sites. Specifically, recruiting should emphasize the affective and empathetic attributes of excellent supervisors/mentors that are reflected in our data. Training and assessment should also incorporate structural frameworks and expectations for both one-on-one meetings and individual student learning goals and opportunities. Based on the training already being offered by the authors, we expect improvement in placement site supervision will be motivated through assessment, utilization of tools that measure student experience on these dimensions, and results that are shared with current and future supervisors/mentors for clarity in supervisor/mentor expectations and continued excellence in practice.[63]

Students are not the only group to report challenges in the theological field education supervisory role. In a separate survey, the Association of Theological Field Education (ATFE) schools were asked questions about their own experiences dealing with field-based supervisors. Their responses revealed concerns related to a shortfall of commitment to mentoring students as well as difficulty getting supervisors adequately trained for the role. The survey, conducted by the Catholic Theological Union's director of field education Christina Zaker et al., solicited information from theological school field education coordinators about obstacles or frustrations they encountered when working with field supervisors.

> Participants were invited to name the obstacles or frustrations they experienced in organizing training for site supervisors/mentors. This question had the most open-ended responses, with thirty-one comments from the forty-eight respondents (65 percent). The bulk of the frustrations fell under two broad categories:

62. Floding et al., "Excellence in Supervision: Listening to Our Students," 202–3.
63. Floding et al., "Excellence in Supervision: Listening to Our Students," 202–3.

lack of time (twenty respondents) and lack of commitment (ten respondents). In the area of lack of time, thirteen of the twenty respondents noted that their supervisors/mentors had the desire to participate in training but that it was hard finding a time or format that worked. On the other hand, seven comments noted that they struggled with supervisors/mentors who had no desire to make the time to participate. Thus, a lack of commitment was partially manifested in a lack of time. In the specific comments related to lack of commitment, responses were evenly split between frustrations with sites that were only looking for "free labor" and site supervisors/mentors who were not committed to the collaborative teaching aspect of supervision. One example of a response in this category is as follows: "The on-sites model their supervision as they experienced it in seminary decades ago. Adult education principles are not on the radar."[64]

This reveals a shortage of clearly defined parameters and training for field education supervisors. When field education coordinators were asked about training that their school provided supervisors, the survey showed a broad range of options depending on the school:

> a high percentage of survey respondents relied upon manuals or handbooks (87 percent) and physical orientation (on campus) (71 percent) as primary means for training, followed by approximately half of the programs utilizing online resources and printed resources. Site supervisor reflection times (22 percent), reflection options (20 percent), and retreats (6 percent) were also employed.[65]

While there are likely some training methodologies that are immersive, such as retreats (noted by 6 percent of respondents), most methods of training lack a paideia-oriented character formation experience for supervisors, a concept that is at the heart of theological field education. Additionally, there does not appear to be a way to assess whether supervisors possess the sort of character virtues that are important for a student minister to learn.

The results from both the student surveys and the ATFE school surveys reveal the near impossibility of determining whether character virtues are being nurtured in field placements, such as the ones reported in the survey. The authors of the survey admit they are offering training for site

---

64. Zaker et al., "Excellence in Supervision: Training Site Supervisors/Mentors," 179.

65. Zaker et al., "Excellence in Supervision: Training Site Supervisors/Mentors," 175–76.

supervisors, but the follow-through will be dependent on individual theological schools and their ability to recruit, train, and assess site supervisors who will, in turn, be able to mentor and assess students working with them.

The Vast Disparities Between Theological Field Education Requirements

Generally speaking, theological schools align their MDiv programs with denominational standards for pastoral education. If denominations held similar standards, that would not be a problem. However, the standards for practical ministry experience in pastoral training programs vary greatly. For example, Anglican students enrolled in the MDiv program at Wycliffe College are expected to complete three field placements, two credits spread over one year each and one credit that is full-time for a summer.[66] In contrast, a Presbyterian Church in Canada student enrolled in the MDiv program at Knox College is expected to complete one field education placement, equal to two course credits or 10 hours per week for 24 weeks. They are also expected to complete a course "Practicum in Mission (inc. Cuba trip)," which appears to be a mission trip equal to one course credit.[67] A Roman Catholic student enrolled in the MDiv at Regis College is required to take one unit of theological field education as a placement consisting of 250 hours of supervised ministry and one unit of theological reflection as part of an integration seminar.[68] These three schools not only reveal differences in the amount of time students spend in their placements, their handbooks also point to differences in how programs are administered. Regis has a 36-page Theological Field Education Handbook for students and supervisors outlining the finer points of the program. Wycliffe, on the other hand, had no references to a handbook of theological field education on their website and their online basic degree handbook contained no references to theological field education. This small sample of theological field education programs from three Toronto School of Theology institutions show the vast disparities in practical training of clergy among Christian denominations and their associated theological schools. As Web based learning grows these disparities may allow institutions to see what other schools are doing

---

66. Wycliffe College, "Master of Divinity (MDiv)."

67. Knox College, "Program Tracker MDiv (PCC)."

68. Regis College, "Master of Divinity (MDiv)."

and loosen the requirements for practical ministry placements, thereby lessening the focus on character formation.

Field Education on the Margins of the Theological Seminary

Before Charles Feilding's mid-twentieth century "Education for Ministry" article in *Theological Education*, it appears field education was not a formal part of theological curricula. Since his article was published, as noted earlier in this chapter, field education has been added. However, there is reason to believe the addition of field education into ministerial education programs is an "add on" to academic coursework rather than becoming integral to ministerial training methodology. McMaster Divinity College professors Steven Studebaker and Lee Beach highlight this reality and call for changes to the teaching, writing, and conception of field education:

> field education . . . lingers on the margins of the academy. The theological curriculum often treats field education as a second-class citizen. Of course, no Christian school would say that. But look at how they count field education for credit in the curriculum; it does not count like course work and thesis writing. Field education should be integrated with the more academic side of the theological curriculum and not only run parallel to it. Placing field education and embedded ministry formation experience at the center of the theological curriculum also calls for theological scholars to consider ways to implement experiential learning components into their teaching and, at times, into their writing. The scholar's role is to help students cultivate the art of converting their ongoing learning into practice. Techniques that can facilitate integrated learning include the use of case-based learning experiences throughout the curriculum, field trips, and directed reflection on bridging personal experience with theoretical knowledge. The benefit of making these adaptations is that theological educators, along with their scholarship, will reach and equip emerging leaders.[69]

Bruce P. Powers, former academic dean and professor of Christian Education, refers to field education credits as being part of the informal curricula in theological schools. He sees a disconnect between learning through formal coursework and learning through other means, such as field placements:

---

69. Studebaker and Beach, "Friend or Foe," 53–54.

In many schools, the faculty manages the formal curriculum and student personnel officers manage the informal. We don't usually say that, however, because the faculty is responsible for the curriculum. But, without learning outcomes that include the formal and informal elements of curriculum, formation will continue to be disconnected for many students.[70]

While some schools' field education departments are directed by non-academics, as noted by Powers, others have professors directing departments. The professors, if also teaching and researching, can be overcommitted and overextended. This concern surfaced in the survey of ATFE school field education staff. Zaker et al., describe one person's experience of being left alone to struggle under the load of teaching and managing a department with thin resources:

> Concern about the value institutions place on theological education was also noted. One respondent indicated, "We really have only one ministry professor (myself) teaching a full load, mentoring our new students in spiritual formation, and also running the supervised ministry program." After serving as director and full-time faculty member for twenty-five years, a respondent's faculty position was discontinued. This respondent encouraged the group to share with seminary leadership the importance of theological field education, specifically the value of the field education director serving as a regular faculty member. As noted regarding site visits, budget cuts and time constraints also impact field educators' sense of the value their institutions place on field education. Accrediting bodies such as the Association of Theological Schools play an important role in naming field education as critical to a ministerial degree.[71]

If field education is an undervalued aspect of theological education, as it appears to be, then online students may not get the sort of modeling, mentoring, and assessment that would come as part of a well-integrated program. If schools shifting their ministerial education programs online are depending on field education to bolster the sort of in-person and on-site learning found in residential models, the research seems to indicate that the structures to train and assess clergy supervisors for those sorts of robust field education experiences are inadequate.

70. Mercier, "Balancing Formation," 307.

71. Zaker et al., "Excellence in Supervision: Training Site Supervisors/Mentors," 181.

Given these findings, field-based education, offering online students embodied experiences to learn how to function as a pastor, may not be as fruitful as once hoped. Returning to an article quoted extensively in the early parts of this book, "(Not) Being there" by Miller and Scharen, the authors write:

> There is no question that better integration between classes and the "real world" happens more quickly and more organically if students remain in their context. [Online Distance Education] has made this possible. Instead of dislocating students, who must come to the professor and classroom, the professor and classmates connect to their immediate work and ministry lives.[72]

The idea that online students have opportunities to stay connected to their faith communities and learn in the "real world" leaves many questions about the quality of community measured by the strength of their relationships in the supervision they may receive or lack thereof. There are important educational questions, such as: Is the supervisor trained and qualified? Is the context appropriate for supervision? Are the pattens of differentiation between the pastor and congregation healthy or unhealthy? What student learning outcomes are in place to address vocational as well as character formation? And who is monitoring the student's progress toward those outcomes? These questions require further exploration.

COMPETENCY-BASED THEOLOGICAL EDUCATION

Given the challenges of training and assessing field education supervisors for seminaries and the lack of clear vision for training pastors for congregational ministry in CASC/ACSS, I am providing an example of an emerging theological education model that integrates embodied mentoring with online courses.[73] An intriguing model of pastoral education that has recently garnered the attention of ATS is Competency-Based Theological Education (CBTE). The origins of CBTE can be traced back to a non-theological counterpart of educators, the Competency-Based Education Network (C-BEN).

72. Miller and Scharen, "(Not) Being There," 23.

73. CASC/ACSS functions using a competency based educational framework. CASC/ACSS's four key competency domains of Professional Identity, Knowledge, Professional Ethical Conduct, and Professional Skills do not include a direct requirement for the development of character virtues. A document outlining CASC/ACSS competencies is available here: https://spiritualcare.ca/explore-spiritual-care/cascacss_competencies/

Representing over 30 colleges and universities in the United States, C-BEN defines competency-based education as follows:

> Competency-based education combines an intentional and transparent approach to curricular design with an academic model in which the time it takes to demonstrate competencies varies and the expectations about learning are held constant. Students acquire and demonstrate their knowledge and skills by engaging in learning exercises, activities and experiences that align with clearly defined programmatic outcomes. Students receive proactive guidance and support from faculty and staff. Learners earn credentials by demonstrating mastery through multiple forms of assessment, often at a personalized pace.[74]

In an article focused on the emerging influence of CBTE in seminaries, senior editor of *Faith Today* magazine, Karen Stiller, describes some of the practical ways this new model is influencing pastoral education. She highlights some competencies expected to be exhibited by MDiv students at Grace Theological Seminary before graduating:

> Some examples of competencies required in theological education, borrowed from the 18 competencies in the "Deploy" MDiv program at Grace Theological Seminary in Indiana, include: "Thinking Critically in Ministry," "Research and Writing," "Practicing Biblical Hermeneutics," "Utilizing Biblical Languages," "Embracing Cultural Diversity," and "Initiating Transformational Change." Achieving mastery of each competency can be a multiyear process. The validity of assessment (that is, determining whether a student has actually achieved mastery of a competency) is of profound importance. In most CBTE programs, a team of mentors determines whether a student has mastered a competency. For example, at Grace, a student's "ministry mentor," "formation mentor," and "faculty instructor" must agree when a student has mastered a competency. Their assessment may be based on written work, hands-on ministry in the parish setting, testing, or a combination of these.[75]

The "team of mentors" approach to working with students at Grace Theological Seminary is a departure from traditional MDiv degree programs. These may provide faculty mentors and a field supervisor, but the mentors and supervisor would not be expected to work together throughout the

---

74. "What Is Competency-Based Education."
75. Stiller, "Enthusiasts," 6.

student's program to assess their development of competencies and readiness for pastoral ministry.

ATS has cautiously approved CBTE degree programs based on courses and credits while categorizing programs not based on these as experimental and in need of approval. This excerpt is from an ATS statement, released in January 2020 and effective as of July 2020:

> CBTE programs are fairly new to theological schools but have drawn increasing interest among the ATS membership. As part of the Educational Models and Practices Project, a group of ten ATS schools met for several years to explore this approach to ministerial education. Findings from that peer group inform these guidelines. Two of the first ATS schools to implement CBTE programs were Northwest Seminary in Canada in 2013 and Sioux Falls Seminary in the US in 2014. Since Northwest's *Immerse* program is not based on courses or credits, it required approval as an experiment by the ATS Board of Commissioners. That approval was granted in 2014 for five years, which was changed in 2019 to ongoing approval as an exception. Since Sioux Falls' *Kairos* MDiv program is based on courses and credits, it did not require special approval. However, when they expanded that CBTE program to include all of their graduate programs (MDiv, MA and DMin) and eliminated the campus residency requirement, the school received approval by the Board in 2019 to offer all those CBTE programs as exceptions to residency. In 2017, the Board granted approval for Grace Theological Seminary to offer its CBTE MDiv and MA programs as a five-year experiment. Their *Deploy* programs are not course or credit based and were the first ATS "direct assessment" CBTE programs granted approval by the USDE to be eligible for Title IV aid.[76]

ATS recognizes the growing influence of CBTE within educational circles and has started to offer support for schools looking to experiment with this model.

> The continuing interest in CBTE among ATS schools has led to the initiation of annual CBTE conferences, which are subsidized in part through ATS. The first was hosted in 2018 by Northwest Baptist Seminary and drew more than 100 participants, over half from ATS schools. The second in 2019 was hosted by the

---

76. "Guidelines on Competency-Based."

Competency-Based Education Network at their annual conference, which draws hundreds of persons interested in CBE (and now CBTE).[77]

CBTE is only starting to work its way into ATS-accredited theological schools. It offers opportunities for students to lean into more practical aspects of pastoral education and could offer embodied educational opportunities with a mentor while also taking courses online. The value of this sort of program is that there are longer term relationships established and expectations for the student to show certain competencies, going beyond the academic dialogue and dialectics of *Wissenschaft* toward nurturing a culture where character virtues take centre stage.

Susanna Singer, retired professor of ministry development at Church Divinity School of the Pacific, describes some of the elements of her experience as a supervisor/mentor of a ministerial student. While her experience is not CBTE, the strong focus on ministry practice and multi-pronged mentorship shows the value of this sort of focus. She writes about her experience supervising a student pastor from a distance. The student, an old friend Christopher Wallace, was "a long-time Episcopalian, unusually well-read and theologically informed." Christopher had a robust network of support including a number of supervisors. Singer writes:

> Christopher had several supervisors: a retired priest with temporary charge of his congregation discussed practical issues arising from their shared ministry there; online courses allowing Christopher to discuss academic issues with instructors; practical training in pastoral ministry with a local chaplain provided another arena for reflection and supervision; and regular email exchanges with me which were intended to integrate his program of formation and study. Several unusual elements in Christopher's situation— his high level of church experience, his strong motivation for self-directed study, and his superior writing skills—were advantages as we began.[78]

Christopher notes that the most valuable aspect of his distance education "was the flexibility of the program, its integration of academics and ministry practice, and focused supervision from several sources."[79]

---

77. "Guidelines on Competency-Based."

78. Singer, "Supervisory Practice," 129–30.

79. Singer, "Supervisory Practice," 131.

Embodied relationships are essential for the formation of virtuous character. For students enrolled in online programs of pastoral formation, the field education placement provides immersion in a paideia community with a supervisor/mentor who provides a ministerial example. Given the peripheral role of field education in theological schools, including the weak ties between seminaries and field placements on the one hand and the lack of clarity about how well SPE prepares pastors for pastoral ministry on the other, the opportunity to develop character virtues appears unclear.

Conclusion

ONLINE THEOLOGICAL EDUCATION CONTINUES to evolve as schools adjust to the changing needs of students, faculty, and society. In what follows I return to my guiding questions to provide answers based on my research; I explain the significance of my answers for theological education; I address limitations in my research; and I propose directions for possible future research.

ANSWERING MY RESEARCH QUESTIONS

Online Theological Education and Pastoral Formation: Examining the Effects

The first guiding question from my introduction is, "What effect do shifts toward online courses have on those enrolled in programs of pastoral formation?" My research shows online courses affect students in both positive and negative ways.

Technology Shapes Student Learning

POSITIVE SHAPING—STRENGTHS OF ONLINE LEARNING

In chapter 1 I described ways in which technology provides reasons for optimism for pastoral formation programs. According to Linda Cannell, two benefits of online learning are the opportunities for adult professionals to enroll in courses and increased global access to education.[1] Garrison,

---

1. Cannell, "Review," 6.

Anderson, and Archer's Community of Inquiry model of online education provides a three-fold method of engaging students, teachers, and curriculum in ways that appear to enhance matters of sourcing material and generating solutions.[2] Internet learning provides ways for time to become flexible, resources to become quickly and easily accessible, and teachers to use a variety of learning formats.[3] E-learning that depends on text-based interaction between students and teachers also allows for more critical and thoughtful engagement with ideas.[4] Additionally, the text-based interactivity provided by online forums offers a context where introverts, extroverts, and according to Anita Louisa Cloete, "marginalised voices could be heard."[5] For those preparing for pastoral ministry, online education allows students to remain in their home contexts, something a growing number of theological educators see as "more effective" for ministerial training.[6]

Negative shaping: Deficiencies of Online Learning

In chapter 1 I also focused on the challenges of e-learning. Martha McCormick cites concerns about the Internet being used to "colonize" diverse cultures while O'Sullivan and Palaskas reference ways the Web has been used by some groups to "strengthen their control over others."[7] I referenced a variety of issues with MOOCs, such as poor engagement among students and high rates of drop out.[8] There are also broad challenges related to Web-based learning, including the social isolation students feel, malfunctioning systems and signal strength, and the need for students to be much more self-directed.[9] There are concerns on the faculty side of online education, which do not directly affect students but may have indirect effects on student learning: faculty abilities to access good training and instructional design as well as questions about the quality of faculty mentorship of online students.[10] Edwin Chr. van Driel also cites concerns about lost

2. Garrison et al., "Critical Inquiry," 93.

3. Anderson, "Teaching," 344.

4. Garrison, *E-Learning in the 21st Century*, 16.

5. Cloete, "Technology and Education," 5.

6. Miller and Scharen, "(Not) Being There," 23.

7. McCormick, "Webmastered," O'Sullivan, and Palaskas, "The Political Economy."

8. Pike and Gore, "The Challenges," 154.

9. Kibby, "Hybrid Teaching," 87.

10. Tanner, "Online Learning at ATS Schools: Part 2," and van Driel, "Online

opportunities for online pastoral students to learn about diversity ". . . in the relationships that are being formed in the communal life on campus."[11] These deficiencies all play a role in how online education affects pastoral student learning. They address some of the educational matters of Web-based education but there are deeper ways that technology affects student learning. I tackled these ways in chapter 2.

Technology's Formative Nature

In chapter 2 I examined the effects of technology on human "being." Viewing technology as a non-neutral agent, I looked at technology through a technological determinist framework.[12] Drawing from the research of Joseph Weizenbaum, I showed how computer usage can induce strong emotional responses in humans, including feelings of intimacy.[13] This insight provided the foundation for my research, focusing on the role of computers and technology in affecting emotional systems, student capacity to learn self-differentiation, and aspects of emotional fusion with devices. Furthermore, the findings of Weizenbaum and Brent Waters reveal how machines and technology limit the kinds of questions that can be asked and the ways data are organized, thereby narrowing the field of learning.[14] I explored this ordering of the human-machine relationship by reviewing the work of Martin Heidegger and his juxtaposition of technology's "revealing" versus the "revealing" of *poiēsus*.[15] Technology "challenges-forth" in a way that distorts, while *poiēsus* "brings-forth," allowing what is already there to bloom. As humans interact with technology, as is the case with Web-based education, what is "revealed" is an unnatural and distorted formation of human "being." Weizenbaum and Postman also show how technology reduces and even eliminates the need for human judgements, potentially limiting the development of human skill.[16] This insight is particularly important in the latter half of chapter 3, dealing with the role of embodied mentorship in learning self-differentiation, and all of chapter 4, focused

Theological Education."

11. van Driel, "Online Theological Education," 77.

12. Kanuka, "Understanding E-Learning.

13. Weizenbaum, *Computer Power and Human Reason*, 7.

14. Waters, *From Human to Posthuman*, 127.

15. Heidegger, *The Question Concerning Technology*.

16. Postman, *Technopoly*, 101.

on virtue acquisition as a form of skill development. The modern obsession with data and their effects, such as diminishing the value of humanities[17] and drawing attention away from "moral and spiritual sensibilities,"[18] shows how technology affects student learning *and* institutions of higher education.[19]

Marshall McLuhan offers perspective on how media shape humans. McLuhan's description of the way media obscure certain aspects of reality demonstrates how directing human attention toward the image, what he called "figure," allowed for other things to go unnoticed, what he called "ground."[20] McLuhan's insights applied to online education show how course contents function as "figure," whereas the Internet platform functions unnoticed as the "ground." The software and applications used to deliver course contents are rarely considered yet are formational in and of themselves. Additionally, the student context can be considered the "ground." Therefore, using an online platform means the context or "ground" of the students and teachers gets missed in favour of the disembodied content of the lesson. These issues become problematic when human embodiment and the fundamental doctrine of the incarnation are subtly devalued by new modes of education, such as online learning.[21]

Near the end of chapter 2, I suggest technology negatively affects social well-being. The research of Robert Kraut et al., reveals that Internet usage leads to family members "feeling isolated and depressed" and experience overall "declines in family communication."[22] Horwood and Anglim's study found that, like the emotional attachments to Weizenbaum's computer, students could be described as emotionally attached to their smartphones, thus contributing to technostress,[23] while Leonard Reinecke et al., found everyday Internet use plays a pivotal role in "procrastination and its psychological effects."[24]

The use of technology, particularly the Internet, has also been shown to negatively affect the brain. In chapter 2 I cited research from Joseph Firth

---

17. See Tilley, "Opposing the Virtual World."

18. Kroeker, "Technology as Principality," 172–73.

19. Friedman, *A Failure of Nerve*, 130.

20. Gordon, *McLuhan*, 129.

21. Gay, *Modern Technology*.

22. Kraut et al., "Internet Paradox."

23. Horwood and Anglim, "Problematic Smartphone Usage."

24. Reinecke et al., "Permanently Online," 873.

et al., showing smartphone "checking" behaviors associated with "information rewards."[25] These patterns contribute to distraction and to people who "perform worse in various cognitive tasks" when compared to those who do not participate in smartphone "checking."[26] Mark Ellingsen suggests that Internet distractions keep the entire brain active at the expense of concentration and memory.[27] In chapter 4 I looked more deeply at distraction and the Web, highlighting the work of David I. Smith et al., who note the design of digital media is to assist with "skim reading and swift location of data" contrasted with religious reading "associated with practices of reading slowly, repeatedly, communally, reverentially."[28] Nicholas Carr references a study by Nicole Speer showing how deep reading is linked to imagination and has similar effects on the brain as does recounting real world experiences.[29] Between the "checking" behaviors and lack of provision for deep, focused reading, Carr sees a reduction in certain healthy human responses such as "empathy, compassion, and other emotions," where Internet and technological engagement increases.[30]

Online Theological Education and Pastoral Formation: The Adequacy of Online Courses for Ordained Ministry

In addition to the question pertaining to technology and its formational qualities, my second and closely related research question addressed the MDiv Program as a whole: "Are *online* learners studying for ordained ministry being adequately prepared?" Drawing from my research, predominantly in chapters 3 through 5, my answer to this question is "no."

In chapter 2 I suggest the traditional understanding of "pastor" is that of an embodied presence of love and service who communes with God and God's people. I drew this concept from Will Willimon's interpretation of *diakonoi* as "butler" and "waiter"[31] as well as the defined role of the priest from the *Program of Priestly Formation*, where priests serve by "embodying

---

25. Firth et al., "Online Brain," 120.

26. Firth et al., "Online Brain," 121.

27. Ellingsen, "Neurobiological Data," 7.

28. Smith et al., *Digital Life Together*, 234–35.

29. Carr, *The Shallows*, 74.

30. Carr, *The Shallows*, 221.

31. Willimon, *Pastor*, 35.

[Christ's] way of life and making him visible in the midst of the flock . . . ."[32] In each of these definitions, the embodied presence of the pastor or priest is central. For those taking online courses as part of their pastoral degree, opportunities for embodied learning with others is not part of the coursework.

In chapter 3 I argued that pastors are required to learn how to self-differentiate as they enter challenging and complex congregational systems. Returning again to the work of Will Willimon, I point to his definition of Christian ministry as "countercultural."[33] Standing against a cultural movement, particularly when emotional systems are anxious, is an act of self-differentiated leadership. Ronald Richardson also describes the importance of learning self-differentiation, calling it, "*the* basic requirement for good leadership in the church."[34] I also drew from Edwin Friedman[35] and Majerus and Sandage[36] to reference the place of Differentiation of Self (DoS) in the life of religious leaders. Learning how to self-differentiate is an important aspect of pastoral education. In chapter 3, I suggested Web-based students could be living in poorly differentiated systems, whether it be their homes or churches, and online courses would serve to maintain those emotional systems in ways a residential community experience could unbalance and reorient. Additionally, online students have a greater chance of becoming "emotionally fused" with technology due to the need for them to use computers and smartphones to access the Internet for theological education classes, research, and assignments. Elieson and Rubin's research shows how online participants in their study samples had "significantly lower levels of differentiation than did the clinically depressed sample"[37] There is an urgent need for self-differentiated religious leaders, and shifting pastoral formation programs online is a troubling step backward for schools. In chapter 3 I conclude Internet education is not a helpful context for promoting self-differentiation. Citing the work of Hubert Dreyfus on the Internet and skill development, I argued the Web is not able to nurture self-differentiation in students. Embodied mentors are crucial.

32. United States, *Program of Priestly Formation*, 9.

33. Willimon, *Pastor*, 70.

34. Richardson, *Creating a Healthier Church*, 86.

35. Friedman, *Generation to Generation*.

36. Majerus and Sandage, "Differentiation of Self."

37. Elieson and Rubin, "Differentiation of Self," 135.

In chapter 4, I argued that pastoral education includes learning virtues. Virtues, according to Olli-Pekka Vainio, "express some sort of excellence."[38] Practical wisdom, knowing not only the right thing to do but being able to live it out as demanded by context, is at the heart of character virtue. The development of virtue is similar to learning a new skill. According to David James, habit, relationships, and emotion all play into the equation of developing virtue.[39] As I noted in the previous chapter, the Web is not conducive to higher levels of skill development. Instead, a culture of virtue is required, where virtues are embodied and learned like an apprenticeship where the student learns by "hanging around" the job site.[40] Online education promotes certain intellectual virtues, what I called *Wissenschaft* virtues, however the paideia character virtues, acquired through encultured embodiment, are not suited to online learning. Instead, the Web has a way of forming certain vices detrimental to a way of learning practical wisdom. These vices arise due to the lure toward consumption and the increasing influence of for-profit corporations on higher education. This influence is a concerning trend that may cause students, faculty, and administrators to cease thinking critically about technology and its uses. The little that has been written from theological educators about this very topic is evidence of this issue going largely unnoticed and speaks to McLuhan's "ground" getting lost as educators focus on using the technology rather than thinking about its uses.

Internet courses are a large part of pastoral student programs but they are not the only aspect, practicums also play a role. Those enrolled in an ATS accredited online MDiv degree program cannot complete their program without crucial, embodied, field-based learning. In chapter 5, I investigated the effectiveness of theological field education for nurturing self-differentiation and character virtues in students. I discover some potential, but as a whole there is no way to ascertain whether these programs foster character virtues or self-differentiation. The possibility exists but assessment is lacking. Furthermore, the Association of Theological Schools acknowledges the significant value of "formation" in theological education but has decided to leave the definition of that term to individual schools.[41]

38. Vainio, *Virtue*, 11.

39. James, "The Acquisition of Virtue."

40. Gidney, "Madame How."

41. The Association of Theological Schools, *Educational Models and Practices Peer Group Final Reports*, 9.

The inability or unwillingness of the ATS and individual schools to define and assess formative aspects of pastoral programs could be the primary reason theological educators are not addressing the formative elements of the Internet. The very means of course delivery may play an erosive role in nurturing self-differentiation and character virtues in pastoral education.

In chapter 5 I examined two types of field education, one administered by the Canadian Association for Spiritual Care (CASC/ACSS) and the other directed by the seminary. I found neither to focus specifically on character formation or learning self-differentiation. Furthermore, while Supervised Psychospiritual Education (SPE) provided excellent training in practical spiritual care, its focus tended to be on chaplaincy rather than pastoral ministry. While seminary directed field placements offered practical experience in congregational settings, the training and assessment of supervisors in these diverse settings varied from school to school. My conclusion about the effectiveness of these field places is that neither should be assumed to provide the sort of embodied mentorship experiences that prepare an online student to be better self-differentiated with stronger character virtues. While these may be nurtured, there is no way of assessing whether these outcomes are part of the program.

THE SIGNIFICANCE OF MY CONCLUSIONS FOR THEOLOGICAL EDUCATION

In response to my guiding research questions, I have three recommendations:

1. We need to define and assess *formation*;

2. We need to assess and redefine the role of *theological field education*;

3. We need a *contextual pedagogy* in *online* theological education.

The Need to Define and Assess "Formation"

While I understand the complexity facing the ATS as a body that oversees standards and assessment of a very large and diverse group of schools, ATS should go beyond acknowledging the importance of formation to address the *definition* of "formation." Given the formational role of technology and the increasing "emotional fusion" that is taking place between student and device, there is a need to take a stronger stand in defining these three areas and how they are being addressed by standards: technology and formation; character formation; and self-differentiated leadership formation. Even if ATS does not address these areas, I urge schools to consider addressing them in their pastoral education programs.

Technology and Formation

Technology and formation require addressing the issues with technology's formative nature, addressing the role of the Internet and device usage (e.g., smartphones) and their contribution to high rates of anxiety among online student populations, and how theological education will preserve the value of embodied mentorship. I recommend schools consider their current and future use of technology for Web based teaching and consider limits to their use in pastoral formation programs.

Character Formation

Character Formation includes acknowledging the role of embodied relationships and mentorship in skill development, particularly as it relates to character virtues in theological students. I recommend schools define character formation for students and faculty in pastoral formation programs and establish a means of assessing outcomes. Institutions should consider creating standards that describe expected virtues and, recognizing virtues are fostered like skills, create systems that support the development of those virtues. This is described by Marvin Oxenham when he states,

> . . . for character and virtue education to be alive and well in a theological school, its practices should be *clear*. Evidence of this would include specific references in mission statements, recognizable programme learning outcomes and explicit conceptual and theological frameworks that undergird character and virtue education.[42]

This may entail rethinking pastoral formation programs to bring theological field education from the edges of the program, as described by Studebaker and Beach,[43] to the core where academic courses are currently. Oxenham writes, ". . . character and virtue education should be moved from the periphery of extra-curricular activities to the centre of accredited

42. Oxenham, *Character and Virtue*, 50.
43. Studebaker and Beach, "Friend or Foe."

and certified educational delivery."[44] Competency-Based Theological Education, described at the end of chapter 5,[45] may be a helpful step in this direction, but more research is needed to assess longer term outcomes of this form of theological education.

Self-Differentiated Leadership Formation

Self-differentiated leadership formation includes recognizing the influence of Internet technology and its role, if not in fostering chronic anxiety, then in creating a context where chronically anxious students may pursue theological education.[46] Therefore, schools should be assessing and assisting online students who may be in poorly differentiated systems to find new patterns through healthy and embodied relational communities. Additionally, students in online programs of pastoral formation may be "emotionally fused" with their devices; Internet education allows for that fusion to only deepen. I recommend schools find ways to assess levels of self-differentiation for online students through deeper connections with well trained supervisors and create limits for the use of technology for students in online programs of pastoral formation.

The Need to Assess and Redefine the role of Theological Field Education

I have concerns about the role and place of theological field education, the quality of supervision and supervisor training, and the growing role of CASC/ACSS in the training of ministerial students for chaplaincy rather than congregational ministry specifically. These concerns were written about before the pandemic, which forced seminary courses to move online. If these theological field education concerns were issues when students learned in embodied classrooms, how much more have the concerns grown now that embodied education is that much more difficult? As I have argued, embodied learning is essential for the formation of character virtues and learning self-differentiation. Paideia, not *Wissenschaft*, is the best way to nurture these learning elements. Theological field education is the only

44. Oxenham, *Character and Virtue*, 51.
45. Stiller, "Enthusiasts."
46. Elieson and Rubin, "Differentiation of Self," 136.

remaining requirement of a pastoral formation program that holds the possibility of paideia. Unfortunately, I have shown there are significant deficiencies with field education. Theological field education should be assessed with consideration for how practical experience in mentorship/apprenticeship can complement online learning, without it seeming an addendum to theological curricula. Allowing field education to continue being a "second class" element in pastoral formation programs is no longer an option in an online world. Perhaps what Charles Ess proposes would be helpful:

> Especially if we can use Dreyfus' taxonomy as an accurate description of the stages and proper trajectory of liberal learning—i.e. towards the development of real-world skills, judgment, and practical wisdom—then it seems that liberal arts education would indeed benefit from the careful and appropriate use of the best possibilities of distance learning in conjunction with the best possibilities of face-to-face education. This means, roughly, that we would use appropriate and cost-effective distance learning approaches for the early stages of learning (i.e. the acquisition of rules and concepts) in conjunction with teaching and learning in face-to-face contexts to foster students' abilities to appropriately apply such knowledge in the multiple contexts we encounter day to day as embodied human beings. In particular, such face-to-face teaching and learning seems essential to achieving the highest goals of liberal learning: the cultivation of human excellence, including the pursuit of practical wisdom.[47]

Contextual Pedagogy in Online Theological Education

In 2019, two books explored the present and future state of theological education among ATS schools.[48] Valentin and Wheeler, editors of these books, portray theological schools caught between a tension of theological tradition and societal change. Sadly, neither deal directly with the rising importance of online theological education. I see this as a striking indicator schools have not grappled with the growing formative qualities of technology and the Internet with respect to human "*being.*"

One theme arising from these two books is the growing need for schools to be aware of their context, whether that be their history, affiliations,

---

47. Ess, "Liberal Arts," 131.

48. Valentín, *Looking Forward with Hope*, Wheeler, *Disruption and Hope*.

location, or demographics, etc. As described in chapter 2, technology has a way of focusing human attention on data rather than realities embedded and embodied in human contexts. There is a growing need to develop and further employ pedagogical methods in keeping with the embodied student contexts. We must ensure pastoral education is not reduced to data on the one hand, or anti-technology sentiment on the other.

THE LIMITATIONS OF MY RESEARCH

I limited the scope of research on theological education to that focused on a Christian pastoral office and role. Given the theological diversity within Christian traditions, I could have spent a whole chapter investigating the pastoral office and role. Instead, I chose to briefly address it in two chapters from a small sample of Christian denominations and thus focus on the value of embodied presence that appears common, rather than parsing out nuances and differences between various denominations.

The understanding of *Wissenschaft* and paideia in theological education has been written about in terms of the history of theological education. However, it has not been used as a lens for understanding the various perspectives of "formation" and spiritual development in online learning. In chapter 4, I used these terms to address what I saw as differences in perspectives on online "formation," and I am not aware of anyone else using these terms. More research is required to determine whether they may be helpful in defining "formation" as it relates to intellect and character online. The results of the 2015–2016 Graduating Student Questionnaire appear to show character virtues that depend on relationships with others are not readily developed online. This is only one survey and my conclusions based on this may be incorrect when compared to other surveys. Additional research is required to support more definitive claims.

In my final chapter I briefly outlined an emerging model of education, Competency-Based Theological Education. Time constraints did not allow me to explore other models beyond CBTE. This is one example of a new mode of educating, but there may be other options. Neither did I have the time or resources to focus specifically on the Canadian context of online learning and seminary directed theological field education. I would have liked to delve into this context more fully and completely. I was able to focus on CASC/ACSS and some elements that are unique to Canada, but I did not get a chance to do the same with seminary-directed theological field education. It would have been interesting to see how Canadian seminaries specifically are working out their theological field education programs.

DIRECTIONS FOR FUTURE RESEARCH

Three aspects for my future research agenda rise to the surface from this book: first, given the increasing focus on online education and education removed from embodied human community, how might apprenticeship be useful in an increasingly online educational world? I touched on these aspects, arguing for the value of embodied mentors in learning self-differentiation as well as pastoral skill development. There are additional resources for me to explore, including Donald Schön's *The Reflective Practitioner: How Professionals Think in Action* and *Educating the Reflective Practitioner*, and J. Lave & E. Wenger's, *Situated Learning: Legitimate Peripheral Participation*. I am interested in looking more closely at whether an increased focus on pastoral apprenticeship, what I have termed a "paideia education," is possible without diminishing the value of academic study via *Wissenschaft*.

Second, and closely related, I would like to see how theological field education might become more highly valued and feature more prominently in seminary pastoral education programs. There are questions related to finding and training skilled and virtuous supervisors, such as:

- How are supervisors trained and qualified for theological field education supervision?

- Is the context appropriate for the student? How is this determined and by whom?

- Are the patterns of differentiation between the pastor and congregation healthy or unhealthy? In an online learning context, who is qualified to assess this?

- What student learning outcomes are in place to address vocational as well as character formation? Who monitors the student's progress toward those outcomes, especially in cases where the student is serving as the sole minister of the congregation?

The answers to these questions should not vary much from institution to institution, although they do. In response to the wide variety of theological field education requirements, I am interested in exploring whether a Canadian association of theological field educators could be established to serve in a similar way as the CASC/ACSS, setting up competencies and standards for supervisors in congregational settings.

Third, exploring the question of how theological schools should respond critically (and not necessarily negatively) to the growing influence of technology and education, there are two aspects I would like to pursue in the future: one focuses on technology's effect on students and the other focuses on its effect on theological school administrators and faculty. In dealing with students and technology I am interested in exploring the question, what difference does embodiment make when pastoral students are coming to theological schools already with strong identities and ways they have been formed online? Students and faculty are increasingly relying on technology. How should seminaries respond? To what extent should technologies be leveraged within programs of pastoral formation? Could a countercultural posture, as in the early days of the monastic movement, be helpful? In examining the effects of technology on theological schools and faculty, I am also interested in exploring the ways technology promotes anxiety within theological administrators and faculty. The growing influence of decision-making based on data as a possible way to avert fiscal anxiety is likely having an impact on theological schools and their faculty. This area seems ready for exploration.

As I reflect on the end of this project and the beginnings of others to come, I am struck by a George Grant quote I stumbled upon while writing this conclusion. In his essay entitled "Faith and the Multiversity," Grant bemoans the scientific method of research as an act of summoning objects "before us to answer our questions." This objectifying of things leaves no room for faith and love in higher education. Grant posits:

> . . . as this paradigm of knowledge becomes increasingly all pervasive, faith as the experience that the intelligence is illuminated by love, must have less and less significance in the central work of the multiversity. Indeed, what has happened in modern society as a whole is that knowledge *qua* knowledge is detached from love *qua* love.[49]

Faith, love, and knowledge of God *should* be at the very heart of theological education, but are they? As technology evolves and pastoral education program administrators, faculty, and students attempt to keep pace with change—pursuing "objects" and data that *appear* valuable—there is a risk of losing touch with the very Being, the God who is Love, who defines

49. Grant et al., "Faith and the Multiversity," 392–93.

human "being." After all, the First Epistle of John states, "God is love" not "God is the object of love."[50] Grant's description of the tension between academic knowledge and faith in education reminds me of David Kelsey's explanation of early paideia, before *Wissenschaft* became the dominant educational model. Cited in chapter 1, Kelsey describes the nucleus of paideia as a conversion of the soul in community: "Insightful knowledge of the Good requires a conversion, a turning around of the soul from preoccupation with appearances to focus on reality, on the Good . . . Education as paideia is inherently communal and not solitary."[51] In a world where students and educators are growing more and more isolated while seated in front of screens summoning objects and images, "before us to answer our questions," it might be time to consider a different model of pastoral formation. That model would focus on developing a lived pedagogy where knowledge of God is nurtured in educators and students through faith, love, and embodied community as the nexus and heart of pastoral education. This may well be the focus of my next project.

50. This can be found in 1 John 4:8 and 4:16.
51. Kelsey, *Between Athens and Berlin*, 9.

Bibliography

Anderson, Terry. "Teaching in an Online Learning Context." In *The Theory and Practice of Online Learning*. Edited by Terry Anderson. Edmonton, ON: AU Press, 2008.

Aristotle. *Aristotle: Introductory Readings*. Translated by Terence Irwin and Gail Fine. Indianapolis, Indiana: Hackett, 1996.

Athanassoulis, Nafsika. "Acquiring Aristotelian Virtue." In *The Oxford Handbook of Virtue*. Edited by Nancy E. Snow. New York, NY: Oxford University Press, 2018.

Bain, Andrew M. "Theological Education in Early Christianity: The Contribution of Late Antiquity." In *Theological Education: Foundations, Practices, and Future Directions*. Edited by Andrew M. Bain and Ian Hussey. Eugene, OR: Wipf & Stock, 2018.

Bainton, Roland H. *Yale and the Ministry: A History of Education for the Christian Ministry at Yale from the Founding in 1701*. New York, NY: Harper & Brothers, 1957.

Bergen, Lori, Tom Brimes, and Deborah Potter. "How Attention Partitions Itself During Simultaneous Message Presentations." *Human Communication Research* 31.1 (2005) 311–36.

Blomberg, Doug. *Wisdom and Curriculum: Christian Schooling after Postmodernity*. Sioux Center, IA: Dordt, 2007.

Blossom, Jay. "Piecing Together the Accreditation Quilt: A Conversation with Daniel O. Aleshire." *In Trust* (2013). https://www.intrust.org/Magazine/Issues/New-Year-2013/Piecing-together-the-accreditation-quilt.

Bonhoeffer, Dietrich. *Life Together: The Classic Exploration of Christian Community*. Translated by John W. Doberstein. New York: HarperCollins, 1954.

———. *The Cost of Discipleship*. New York: Touchstone, 1995.

Bowen, Murray. *Family Therapy in Clinical Practice*. New York: J. Arson, 1978.

Brabazon, Tara. "Won't Get Googled Again: Searching for an Education." In *Brave New Classrooms: Democratic Education & the Internet*, edited by Joe Lockard and Mark Pegrum, 153–68. New York: Peter Lang, 2007.

Brown, Eliza Smith, and Chris Meinzer. "New Data Reveal Stable Enrollment but Shifting Trends at ATS Member Schools." *Colloquy Online* (March 2017).

"Canadian Association for Spiritual Care/Association Canadienne De Soins Spirituels." Canadian Association for Spiritual Care/Association canadienne de soins spirituels. 2021. https://spiritualcare.ca.

Bibliography

Cannell, Linda. *Theological Education Matters: Leadership Education for the Church.* Charleston, SC: Booksurge, 2008.

———. "A Review of Literature on Distance Education." *Theological Education* 36.1 (1999) 1–72.

Carr, Nicholas. *The Glass Cage: Automation and Us.* New York: Norton, 2014.

———. *The Shallows: What the Internet Is Doing to Our Brains.* New York: Norton, 2010.

———. *Utopia Is Creepy and Other Provocations.* New York: Norton, 2016.

Carter, Nick. "A House Built on Sand? A Blunt Look at the Assumptions of Theological Education." In *Looking Forward with Hope: Reflections on the Present State and Future of Theological Education.* Edited by Benjamín Valentín. Eugene, OR: Cascade, 2019.

Chau, Paule. "Online Higher Education Commodity." *Journal of Computing in Higher Education* 22.3 (2010) 177–91.

Cloete, Anita Louisa. "Technology and Education: Challenges and Opportunities." *Hervormde teologiese studies* 73.3 (2017) 1–7. https://dx.doi.org/10.4102/hts.v73i4.4589.

Coll, Regina. *Supervision of Ministry Students.* Collegeville, MN: Liturgical, 1992.

"Competencies for Spiritual Care and Counselling Specialist." Canadian Association for Spiritual Care/Association canadienne de soins spirituels. 2011. http://www.spiritualcare.ca/flow/uploads/docs/Competencies.doc.

Coupland, Douglas. *Mashall McLuhan: You Know Nothing of My Work!* New York: NY: Atlas, 2010.

Dahlberg, Lincoln. "Internet Research Tracings: Towards Non-Reductionist Methodology." *Journal of Computer-Mediated Communication* 9.3 (2004). https://dx.doi.org/https://doi-org.myaccess.library.utoronto.ca/10.1111/j.1083–6101.2004.tb00289.x.

DeCesare, Susan D. "Anxiety and Depression: Self Differentiation as a Unique Predictor." PhD diss., Marywood University, 2008.

Donovan, Craig P., and Jim Garrett. *Internship for Dummies.* New York, NY: Hungry Minds, 2001.

Dreyfus, Hubert L. *On the Internet.* 2nd ed. New York: Routledge, 2009.

D'Costa, Gavin. "Is Missiology an Academic Discipline?" In *Christianity and Education: Shaping Christian Thinking in Context,* edited by David Emmanuel Singh and Bernard C. Farr, 211–24. Eugene, OR: Wipf & Stock, 2011.

"Education." Canadian Association for Spiritual Care/Association canadienne de soins spirituels. 2021. https://spiritualcare.ca/education_home/.

"Education Centres." Canadian Association for Spiritual Care/Association canadienne de soins spirituels 2021. https://spiritualcare.ca/education_home/education-centres/.

"Education FAQs: What Is CPE?" Canadian Association for Spiritual Care/Association canadienne de soins spirituels. 2021. https://spiritualcare.ca/education_home/esc-faqs/.

Elieson, Melisa V., and Linda J. Rubin. "Differentiation of Self and Major Depressive Disorders: A Test of Bowen Theory among Clinical, Traditional, and Internet Groups." *Family Therapy* 28.3 (2001) 125–42.

Ellingsen, Mark. "Neurobiological Data on What Online Education Could Be Doing to Our Spirituality and Our Brains: Some Augustinian/Niebuhrian Reflections." *Theological Education* 52. 2 (2019) 1–11.

Erikson, Erik H. *Identity and the Life Cycle.* New York: Norton, 1994.

Ess, Charles. "Liberal Arts and Distance Education: Can Socratic Virtue (*Aretē*) and Confucius' Exemplary Person (*Junzi*) Be Taught Online?" *Arts and Humanities in Higher Education* 2.2 (2003) 117–37. https://dx.doi.org/10.1177/147402220300200 2002.

Esselman, Thomas. "The Pedagogy of the Online Wisdom Community: Forming Church Ministers in a Digital Age." *Teaching Theology & Religion* 7.3 (2004) 159–70.

Farley, Edward. *Theologia: The Fragmentation and Unity of Theological Education.* Philadelphia: Fortress, 1983.

Feilding, Charles R. "Education for Ministry." *Theological Education* 3.1 (1966) 1–252.

Firth, Joseph, John Torous, Brendon Stubbs, Josh A. Firth, Genevieve Z. Steiner, Lee Smith, Mario Alvarez-Jimenez, John Gleeson, Davy Vancampfort, Christopher J. Armitage, and Jerome Sarris. "The "Online Brain": How the Internet May Be Changing Our Cognition." *World Psychiatry: Official Journal of the World Psychiatric Association (WPA)* 18.2 (2019) 119–29. https://dx.doi.org/10.1002/wps.20617.

Floding, Matthew. *Engage: A Theological Field Education Toolkit.* Lanham, MD: Rowman & Littlefield, 2017.

Floding, Matthew, Bonnie Abadie, Kristina Lizardy-Hajbi, and Caroline McCall. "Excellence in Supervision: Listening to Our Students." *Reflective Practice: Formation and Supervision in Ministry* 40 (2020) 194–205.

Foster, Charles R., Lisa E. Dahill, Lawrence A. Golemon, and Barbara Wang Tolentino. *Educating Clergy: Teaching Practices and Pastoral Imagination.* San Francisco: Jossey-Bass, 2006.

Foster, Richard. *Celebration of Discipline: The Path to Spiritual Growth.* Third ed. New York: HarperCollins, 1998.

Fowler, James. *Stages of Faith: The Psychology of Human Development and the Quest for Meaning.* San Francisco: HarperCollins, 1995.

Freire, Paulo. *Pedagogy of the Oppressed.* Translated by Myra Bergman Ramos. New York, New York: Continuum, 2007.

Friedman, Edwin H. *A Failure of Nerve: Leadership in the Age of the Quick Fix.* Edited by Margaret M. Treadwell and Edward W. Beal. New York: Seabury, 2007.

———. *Generation to Generation: Family Process in Church and Synagogue.* Paperback 2011, Reprint. New York: Guilford, 1985.

Gadotti, Moacir. "Freire's Intellectual and Political Journey." In *The Wiley Handbook of Paulo Freire*, edited by Carlos Alberto Torres, 33–50. Hoboken, NJ: Wiley, 2019.

Gallagher, Sean, and Jason Palmer. "The Pandemic Pushed Universities Online. The Change Was Long Overdue." Harvard Business Review. 2020. https://hbr.org/2020/09/the-pandemic-pushed-universities-online-the-change-was-long-overdue.

Garrison, D. Randy. *E-Learning in the 21st Century: A Framework for Research and Practice.* 2nd ed. New York: Routledge, 2011.

Garrison, D. Randy, Terry Anderson, and Walter Archer. "Critical Inquiry in a Text-Based Environment: Computer Conferencing in Higher Education." *The Internet and Higher Education* 2.2–3 (2000) 87–105.

Gay, Craig M. *Modern Technology and the Human Future: A Christian Appraisal.* Downer's Grove, IL: IVP Academic, 2018.

Gerlock, Jennifer A. "Sense of Community Online: Self-Regulated Learning and Avoiding the Drama Triangle." MA thesis, University of Lethbridge, 2012.

Gidney, Bob. ""Madame How" and "Lady Why": Learning to Practice in Historical Perspective." In *Learning to Practise: Professional Education in Historical and*

Bibliography

Contemporary Perspective, edited by Ruby Heap, Wyn Millar, and Elizabeth M. Smyth, 13–42. Ottawa: University of Ottawa Press, 2005.

Gin, Deborah H. C., G. Brooke Lester, and Barbara Blodgett. "Forum on Seminary Teaching and Formation Online." *Teaching Theology & Religion* 22.1 (2019) 73–87.

González, Justo L. *The History of Theological Education*. Nashville: Abingdon, 2015.

Gordon, W. Terrence. *McLuhan: A Guide for the Perplexed*. New York: Continuum, 2010.

Grabowsky, Eric, and Janie M. Harden Fritz. "The Internship: Bridge between Marketplace and Liberal Arts Education in the Catholic Tradition." *Catholic Education: A Journal of Inquiry and Practice* 10.4 (2007) 436–48.

Grant, George Parkin, Arthur Davis, and Henry Roper. "Faith and the Multiversity (1978)." In *Collected Works of George Grant: Volume 4, 1970–1988*, edited by Arthur Davis and Henry Roper. Toronto: University of Toronto Press, 2005.

Groome, Thomas H. *Sharing Faith: A Comprehensive Approach to Religious Education & Pastoral Ministry*. New York, NY: HarperCollins, 1991.

"Guidelines on Competency-Based Theological Education (CBTE)." The Association of Theological Schools. 2020. https://www.ats.edu/files/galleries/guidelines-for-cbte-programs_(15_April_2020).pdf.

Hamilton, Edward, and Andrew Feenberg. "The Technical Codes of Online Education." In *Brave New Classrooms: Democratic Education & the Internet*, edited by Joe Lockard and Mark Pegrum, 225–50. New York: Peter Lang, 2007.

Harrison, Mike. "What Do the Theologically Educated Look Like?" *Dialog* 53.4 (2014) 345–55. https://dx.doi.org/10.1111/dial.12138.

Hawkins, Thomas H. "From the 3Rs to the 3Ws: Continuing Education in a Digital Age." *Quarterly Review* 24.2 (2004) 168–80.

Heidegger, Martin. *The Question Concerning Technology and Other Essays*. Translated by William Lovitt. New York: Harper & Row, 1977.

Hembrooke, Helene, and Geri Gay. "The Laptop and the Lecture: The Effects of Multitasking in Learning Environments." *Journal of Computing in Higher Education* 15.1 (2003) 46–64.

Hess, Mary E. *Engaging Technology in Theological Education: All That We Can't Leave Behind*. Lanham, MD: Rowman & Littlefield, 2005.

Hilsman, Gordon J. "Tandem Roles of Written Standards and Personal Virtue in Appraising Professional Practice." *Reflective Practice: Formation and Supervision in Ministry* 30 (2010) 46–58.

Hockridge, Diane. "What's the Problem?: Spiritual Formation in Distance and Online Theological Education." *Journal of Christian Education* 54.1 (2011) 25–38.

Horwood, Sharon, and Jeromy Anglim. "Problematic Smartphone Usage and Subjective and Psychological Well-Being." *Computers in Human Behavior* 97 (2019) 44–50. https://dx.doi.org/https://doi.org/10.1016/j.chb.2019.02.028.

Hutchins, Robert M. *The University of Utopia*. Chicago: University of Chicago Press, 1964.

Ivy, Steven S. "Significant Change in the North American Spiritual Care Education and Psychotherapy Movement." *Journal of Pastoral Care & Counseling* 73.3 (2019) 150–52. https://dx.doi.org/10.1177/1542305019867863.

James, David N. "The Acquisition of Virtue." *The Personalist Forum* 2.2 (1986) 101–21.

Jernigan, Homer L. "Clinical Pastoral Education: Reflections on the Past and Future of a Movement." *The Journal of Pastoral Care & Counseling* 56.4 (2002) 377–92.

Jiang, Manyu. "The Reason Zoom Calls Drain Your Energy." 2020. https://www.bbc.com/worklife/article/20200421-why-zoom-video-chats-are-so-exhausting.

Bibliography

Jin Lee, Charlene. "The Art of Supervision and Formation." In *Welcome to Theological Field Education!*, edited by Matthew Floding, chapter 2. Lanham, MD: Rowman & Littlefield, 2011.

Jones, Logan C. "I Walk through Life Oddly: Dispositions, Character, and Identity in Clinical Pastoral Education." *Reflective Practice: Formation and Supervision in Ministry* 32 (2012) 159–70.

Kanuka, Heather. "Understanding E-Learning Technologies-in-Practice through Philosophies-in-Practice." In *The Theory and Practice of Online Learning*, edited by Terry Anderson, 91–120. Edmonton, Alberta: AU Press, 2008.

Keehn, Dave. "Leveraging Internships: A Comparison of Ministry Internship Programs as Realistic Job Previews to Prepare for Vocational Ministry." *The Journal of Youth Ministry* 14.1 (2015) 54–77.

Kelsey, David H. *Between Athens and Berlin: The Theological Education Debate*. Grand Rapids: Eerdmans, 1993.

———. "Spiritual Machines, Personal Bodies, and God: Theological Education and Theological Anthropology." *Teaching Theology & Religion* 5.1 (2002) 2–9.

Kerr, Michael E., and Murray Bowen. *Family Evaluation: An Approach Based on Bowen Theory*. 1st ed. New York: Norton, 1988.

Kibby, Marjorie D. "Hybrid Teaching and Learning: Pedagogy Versus Pragmatism." In *Brave New Classrooms: Democratic Education & the Internet*, edited by Joe Lockard and Mark Pegrum, 87–104. New York: Peter Lang, 2007.

Knox College. "Program Tracker MDiv (PCC)." https://knox.utoronto.ca/wp-content/uploads/2021/07/MDiv-Program-Tracker_210720.pdf.

Kraut, Robert, Michael Patterson, Vicki Lundmark, Sara Kiesler, Tridas Mukopadhyay, and William Scherlis. "Internet Paradox : A Social Technology That Reduces Social Involvement and Psychological Well-Being?" *American Psychologist* 53.9 (1998) 1017–31.

Kroeker, Travis. "Technology as Principality: The Elimination of Incarnation." *Pro Ecclesia* 24.2 (2015) 162–77.

Lasair, Simon. "What's the Point of Clinical Pastoral Education and Pastoral Counselling Education? Political, Developmental, and Professional Considerations." *Journal of Pastoral Care & Counseling* 74.1 (2020) 22–32. https://dx.doi.org/10.1177/1542305019897563.

Leclercq O.S.B., Jean. *The Love of Learning and the Desire for God: A Study of Monastic Culture*. Translated by Catharine Misrahi. 3rd ed. New York: Fordham University Press, 1982.

Leyda, Richard J. "Models of Ministry Internship for Colleges and Seminaries." *Christian Education Journal* 6.1 (2009) 24–37. https://dx.doi.org/10.1177/073989130900600104.

Lownds, Peter. "Wake up and Dream!: A Polyphonic Contextualization of Paulo Freire." In *The Wiley Handbook of Paulo Freire*, edited by Carlos Alberto Torres, 83–88. Hoboken, NJ: Wiley, 2019.

Majerus, Brian D., and Steven J. Sandage. "Differentiation of Self and Christian Spiritual Maturity: Social Science and Theological Integration." *Journal of Psychology and Theology* 38.1 (2010) 41–51.

McCormick, Martha Henn. "Webmastered: Postcolonialism and the Internet." In *Brave New Classrooms: Democratic Education & the Internet*, edited by Joe Lockard and Mark Pegrum, 75–86. New York, NY: Peter Lang, 2007.

Bibliography

McGarrah Sharp, Melinda, and Mary Ann Morris. "Virtual Empathy? Anxieties and Connections Teaching and Learning Pastoral Care Online." *Teaching Theology & Religion* 17.3 (2014) 247–63.

McGoldrick, Monica, Randy Gerson, and Sueli Petry. *Genograms: Assessment and Intervention.* 3rd ed. New York: W. W. Norton, 2008.

McLuhan, Marshall, and Quentin Fiore. *The Medium Is the Massage.* Toronto: Random House, 1967.

Mercer, Ronald L., Jr., and Mark Simpson. "What Would Kant Tweet?: The Utilization of Online Technology in Courses Involving Formation, Meaning, and Value." *Theological Education* 49.2 (2015) 1–18.

Mercier, Ronald A. "Balancing Formation and Academic Learning." In *C(H)AOS Theory: Reflections of Chief Academic Officers in Theological Education,* edited by Kathleen D. Billman and Bruce C. Birch, 319–31. Grand Rapids: Eerdmans, 2011.

Miller, Glenn T. "A Community of Conversation: A Retrospective of the Associaltion of Theological Schools and Ninety Years of North American Theological Education." (2008).

Miller, Sharon L., and Christian Scharen. "(Not) Being There." *Auburn Studies* 23 (2017) 1–49.

Miller-McLemore, Bonnie J. "Practical Theology and Pedagogy: Emobdying Theological Know-How." In *For Life Abundant: Practical Theology, Theological Education, and Christian Ministry,* edited by Dorothy C. Bass and Craig Dykstra, 170–94. Grand Rapids: Eerdmans, 2008.

Mumford, Lewis. *Technics and Civilization.* New York: Harcourt Brace, 1934.

Nace, Robert K. "The Teaching Parish and the Supervising Pastor." *Theological Education* (Summer 1975): 319–28.

Nichols, Mark. "The Formational Experiences of on-Campus and Theological Distance Education Students." *Journal of Adult Theological Education* 13, no. 1 (2016): 18–32. https://dx.doi.org/10.1080/17407141.2016.1158495.

Niebuhr, H. Richard. *The Purpose of the Church and Its Ministry: Reflections on the Aims of Theological Education.* New York: Harper & Brothers, 1956.

Niebuhr, H. Richard, Daniel Day Williams, and James M. Gustafson. *The Advancement of Theological Education.* New York, NY: Harper & Brothers, 1957.

Oxenham, Marvin. *Character and Virtue in Theological Education: An Academic Epistolary Novel.* Carlisle, UK: Langham, 2019.

O'Sullivan, Mary Low, and Tom Palaskas. "The Political Economy of the "New" Discourse of Higher Education." In *Brave New Classrooms: Democratic Education & the Internet,* edited by Joe Lockard and Mark Pegrum, 35–54. New York: Peter Lang, 2007.

Palmer, Parker J. *To Know as We Are Known: Education as a Spiritual Journey.* Paperback ed. San Francisco: HarperCollins, 1993.

Palmer, Parker J., and Arthur Zajonc. *The Heart of Higher Education: A Call to Renewal.* San Francisco: Josey-Bass, 2010.

Peterson, Eugene H. *The Contemplative Pastor: Returning to the Art of Spiritual Direction.* Grand Rapids: Eerdmans, 1993.

———. *Working the Angles: The Shape of Pastoral Intergrity.* Grand Rapids: Eerdmans, 1987.

Pike, Graham, and Hannah Gore. "The Challenges of Massive Open Online Courses (MOOCs)." In *Creativity and Critique in Online Learning: Exploring and Examining*

Innovations in Online Pedagogy, edited by Jacqueline Baxter, George Callaghan, and Jean McAvoy, 149–68. New York: Palgrave Macmillan, 2018.

Postman, Neil. *Amusing Ourselves to Death*. New York, New York: Penguin, 1985.

———. *Technopoly: The Surrender of Culture to Technology*. 1st Vintage Books ed. New York: NY: Vintage, 1993.

Powers, Bruce P. "Developing a Curriculum for Academic, Spiritual, and Vocational Formation." In *C(H)AOS Theory: Reflections of Chief Academic Officers in Theological Education*, edited by Kathleen D. Billman and Bruce C. Birch, chapter 12. Grand Rapids, MI: Eerdmans, 2011.

Pranke, Darlene, and Margaret Clark. "Out of the Ashes: The Alberta Consortium for Supervised Pastoral Education Program." *Journal of Pastoral Care & Counseling* 74, no. 4 (2020): 241–49. https://dx.doi.org/http://dx.doi.org/10.1177/1542305020951756.

Regis College. "Master of Divinity (M.Div.)." Accessed 6 April, 2021. https://regiscollege.ca/academics/mdiv/.

Reinecke, Leonard, Adrian Meier, Stefan Aufenanger, Manfred E. Beutel, Michael Dreier, Oliver Quiring, Birgit Stark, Klaus Wölfling, and Kai W. Müller. "Permanently Online and Permanently Procrastinating? The Mediating Role of Internet Use for the Effects of Trait Procrastination on Psychological Health and Well-Being." *New Media & Society* 20, no. 3 (2018): 862–80. https://dx.doi.org/https://doi.org/10.1177/1461444816675437.

Richardson, Ronald W. *Becoming a Healthier Pastor: Family Systems Theory and the Pastor's Own Family*. Minneapolis, MN: Augsburg Fortress, 2005.

———. *Creating a Healthier Church: Family Systems Theory, Leadership, and Congregational Life*. Minneapolis, MN: Augsburg Fortress, 1996.

Roberts, Jennifer J. "Online Learning as a Form of Distance Education: Linking Formation Learning in Theology to the Theories of Distance Education." *HTS Teologiese Studies/ Theological Studies* 75, no. 1 (2019): 1–9. https://dx.doi.org/https://doi.org/10.4102/hts.v75i1.5345.

Rockwell, Steven C., and Loy A. Singleton. "The Effect of the Modality of Presentation of Streaming Multimedia on Information Acquisition." *Media Psychology* 9 (2007): 179–91.

Romer, Daniel, Zhanna Bagdasarov, and Eian More. "Older Versus Newer Media and the Well-Being of United States Youth: Results from a National Longitudinal Panel." *Journal of Adolescent Health* 52.5 (2013) 613–19.

Scharen, Christian. "Learning Ministry over Time: Embodying Practical Wisdom." In *For Life Abundant: Practical Theology, Theological Education, and Christian Ministry*, edited by Dorothy C. Bass and Craig Dykstra, 265–89. Grand Rapids: Eerdmans, 2008.

Singer, Susanna. "Supervisory Practice in a Distance-Learning Program of Formation for Ministry." *Reflective Practice: Formation and Supervision in Ministry* 31 (2011).

Smith, Annie Kathleen. "The Cell and the Self: Exploring the Relationship between Cell Phone Involvement and Differentiation of Self." PhD diss., George Washington University, 2017.

Smith Brown, Eliza. "Accessible, Effective: How Online Theological Education Is Shifting the Formation Model." *Colloquy Online* (October 2016).

Smith, David I., Kara Sevensma, Marjorie Terpstra, and McMullen. Steven. *Digital Life Together: The Challenge of Technology for Christian Schools*. Grand Rapids: Eerdmans, 2020.

Bibliography

Smith, James K. A. *Desiring the Kingdom: Worship, Worldview, and Cultural Formation.* Grand Rapids: Baker Academic, 2009.

Steinke, Peter L. *Uproar: Calm Leadership in Anxious Times.* Lanham, MD: Rowman & Littlefield, 2019.

Stichter, Matt. *The Skillfulness of Virtue: Improving Our Moral and Epistemic Lives.* Cambridge: Cambridge University Press, 2018.

Stiller, Karen. "Enthusiasts, Skeptics, and Cautious Explorers: A Snapshot of the Seminary Community's Differing Viewpoints on Competency-Based Theological Education." *In Trust* 2019. https://www.intrust.org/Magazine/Issues/New-Year-2019.

Stokoe, Rodney J. R. "Clinical Pastoral Education." *The Nova Scotia Medical Bulletin.* 1974. https://spiritualcare.ca/flow/uploads/docs/cpehistory_stokoe.pdf.

Stuart-Buttle, Ros. *Virtual Theology, Faith and Adult Education: An Interruptive Pedagogy.* Newcastle upon Tyne: Cambridge Scholars, 2013.

Studebaker, Steven, and Lee Beach. "Friend or Foe? The Role of the Scholar in Emerging Christianity." *Theological Education* 48.2 (2014) 43–56.

Sullender, Scott. "New Forms and Models of Ministry: Editor's Introduction." *Reflective Practice: Formation and Supervision in Ministry* 40 (2020) 6–11.

Tanner, Tom. "Online Learning at ATS Schools: Part 1—Looking Back at Our Past." *Colloquy Online* (March 2017).

———. "Online Learning at ATS Schools: Part 2—Looking around at Our Present." *Colloquy Online* (March 2017).

Tenner, Edward. *The Efficiency Paradox: What Big Data Can't Do.* New York: Knopf, 2018.

The Association of Theological Schools. "About ATS." Accessed March 23, 2020. https://www.ats.edu/about.

———. *Educational Models and Practices Peer Group Final Reports.* 2018. https://www.ats.edu/files/galleries/peer-group-final-report-book.pdf.

———. *Educational Standards.* 2012. https://www.ats.edu/uploads/accrediting/documents/second-public-draft-of-standards-with-annotations%20%2810%20Feb%202020%29.pdf.

———. *Standards of Accreditation.* 2020. https:/www.ats.edu/uploads/accrediting/documents/standards-of-accreditation.pdf.

Thompson, Ross A. "A Perspective from Developmental Psychology." In *Cultivating Virtue: Perspectives from Philosophy, Theology, and Psychology*, edited by Nancy E. Snow, 279–306. New York: Oxford University Press, 2014.

Tilley, Robert. "Opposing the Virtual World of Late-Capitalism: A Biblical Theology of Education." In *Teaching Theology in a Technological Age*, edited by Yvette Debergue and James R. Harrison, 65–85. Newcastle upon Tyne, UK: Cambridge Scholars, 2015.

Titelman, Peter. "The Concept of Differentiation of Self in Bowen Theory." In *Differentiation of Self: Bowen Family Systems Theory Perspectives*, edited by Peter Titelman, 3–64. New York: Routledge, 2014.

———. *Triangles: Bowen Family Systems Theory Perspectives.* New York: Routledge, 2008.

Torres, Carlos Alberto. *Diálogo Com Paulo Freire.* São Paulo, Brazil: Edições Loyola, 1979.

Tracy, David W. "Can Virtue Be Taught: Education, Character and the Soul." *Theological Education* 24.1 (1988) 33–52.

Turkle, Sherry. *Alone Together: Why We Expect More from Technology and Less from Each Other.* 3rd ed. New York: Basic, 2017.

United States Conference of Catholic Bishops. *Program of Priestly Formation.* 5th ed. Washington, DC: United States Conference of Catholic Bishops, 2006.

Bibliography

Vainio, Olli-Pekka. *Virtue: An Introduction to Theory and Practice*. Eugene, OR: Cascade, 2016.

Valentín, Benjamín, ed., *Looking Forward with Hope: Reflections on the Present State and Future of Theological Education*. Eugene, OR: Cascade, 2019.

Vallor, Shannon. "Virtue Ethics, Technology, and Human Flourishing." In *Technology and the Virtues: A Philosophical Guide to a Future Worth Wanting*, 17–34. New York: Oxford University Press, 2016.

van Driel, Edwin Chr. "Online Theological Education: Three Undertheorized Issues." *Theological Education* 50.1 (2015) 69–79.

VandeCreek, Larry, and Laurel Burton. "A White Paper. Professional Chaplaincy: Its Role and Importance in Healthcare." *The Journal of Pastoral Care* 55.1 (2001) 81–97.

Ward, Dave. "What's Lacking in Online Learning? Dreyfus, Merleau-Ponty and Bodily Affective Understanding." *Journal of Philosophy of Education* 52.3 (2018) 1–23.

Waters, Brent. *From Human to Posthuman: Christian Theology and Technology in a Postmodern World*. Burlington, VT: Ashgate, 2006.

Weizenbaum, Joseph. *Computer Power and Human Reason*. San Francisco: Freeman, 1976.

Westfall, William. "Some Practical Acquaintance with Parochial Duties." In *Learning to Practise: Professional Education in Historical and Contemporary Perspective*, edited by Elizabeth M. Smyth, Wyn Millar, and Ruby Heap, 43–68. Ottawa: University of Ottawa Press, 2005.

"What Is Competency-Based Education?" Competency-Based Education Network. 2021. https://www.cbenetwork.org/competency-based-education/.

Wheeler, Barbara G., ed. *Disruption and Hope: Religious Traditions and the Future of Theological Education*. Waco: Baylor University Press, 2019.

Willard, Dallas. *The Great Omission: Reclaiming Jesus's Essential Teachings on Discipleship*. New York: HarperCollins, 2006.

Willimon, William H. *Pastor: The Theology and Practice of Ordained Ministry*. Nashville: Abingdon, 2002.

Wilson, Jim L., and Earl Waggoner. *A Guide to Theological Reflection: A Fresh Approach for Practical Ministry Courses and Theological Field Education*. Grand Rapids: Zondervan Academic, 2020.

Wycliffe College. "Master of Divinity (MDiv)." https://www.wycliffecollege.ca/programs-courses/academic-programs/master-divinity-mdiv.

Yamada, Frank M. "Living and Teaching When Change Is the New Normal: Trends in Theological Education and the Impact on Teaching and Learning." *The Wabash Center Journal on Teaching* 1.1 (2020) 23–36.

Young, Brad. *Meet the Rabbis: Rabbinic Thought and the Teachings of Jesus*. Peabody, MA: Hendrickson, 2007.

Yung, Hwa. "Critical Issues Facing Theological Education in Asia." In *Christianity and Education: Shaping Christian Thinking in Context*, edited by David Emmanuel Singh and Bernard C. Farr, 69–80. Eugene, OR: Wipf & Stock, 2011.

Zaker, Christina, Tanya Linn Bennett, Thomas Elliott, and Tamara Wilden. "Excellence in Supervision: Training Site Supervisors/Mentors." *Reflective Practice: Formation and Supervision in Ministry* 40 (2020) 174–83.